NIGHT'S BLACK

DOUBLE TAP

EXPANSION BOOK

DEVELOPED BY KENNETH HITE

WRITTEN BY ADAMUS
HINDMARCH
HITE
KULP
LINDKE
PALMER
PLANT
AND WIELAND

CREDITS

PUBLISHER: SIMON ROGERS

DEVELOPER AND EDITOR: KENNETH HITE

AUTHORS: JOHN ADAMUS, WILL HINDMARCH, KENNETH HITE, KEVIN KULP, CHRISTIAN LINDKE, JAMES PALMER, WILL PLANT, ROB WIELAND

ADDITIONAL MATERIAL: JOHN ADAMUS, GARETH RYDER-HANRAHAN, KENNETH HITE

GUMSHOE SYSTEM: ROBIN D. LAWS

ARTISTS: STEFANO AZZALIN, DAVID LEWIS JOHNSON, PHIL REEVES, CHRIS HÜTH

ART DIRECTION: CATHRIONA TOBIN

INDEX: JANICE SELLERS

COVER ART: ALESSANDRO ALAIA

INTERIOR DESIGN & LAYOUT: CHRIS HÜTH

©2013 Pelgrane Press Ltd. All rights reserved. Night's Black Agents is a trademark of Pelgrane Press Ltd.

CONTENTS

INTRODUCTION	6
AGENTS' COMPANION	7
ABILITIES	8

INVESTIGATIVE ABILITIES — 8

- Accounting — 8
  - Ability Focus: Money Laundering — 8
  - TFFB: Locating the Stash of Guns — 9
  - Sample Spend Benefits — 9
  - Sample Clues — 9
- Archaeology — 9
  - Ancient Vampire Artifacts — 9
  - TFFB: That's Not a Knife — 9
  - Sample Spend Benefits — 9
  - Sample Clues — 9
- Architecture — 10
  - Houses of the Dead — 10
  - TFFB: Getting Into the Castle — 10
  - Sample Spend Benefits — 11
  - Sample Clues — 11
- Art History — 11
  - TFFB: Attacking the Private Gallery Show — 11
  - Sample Spend Benefits — 11
  - Sample Clues — 11
- Astronomy — 11
  - Ability Focus: Fermi's Paradox — 11
  - TFFB: The Stars Are Right — 12
  - Sample Spend Benefits — 12
  - Sample Clues — 12
- Bullshit Detector — 12
  - Ability Focus: Common Tells — 12
  - TFFB: Flipping an Unsuspecting Mole — 12
  - Sample Spend Benefits — 12
  - Sample Clues — 12
- Bureaucracy — 12
  - TFFB: The Mile High Clubbing — 13
  - Sample Spend Benefits — 13
  - Sample Clues — 13
- Chemistry — 13
  - Ability Focus: Handling Radioactive Material — 13
  - TFFB: Montezuma's Revenge — 13
  - Sample Spend Benefits — 13
  - Sample Clues — 13
- Cop Talk — 13
  - British Police Jargon — 13
  - TFFB: Quietly Calling the Cavalry — 14
  - Sample Spend Benefits — 14
  - Sample Clues — 14
- Criminology — 14
  - Ability Focus: Vampire Murders — 14
  - TFFB: Extracting the Consigliere — 14
  - Sample Spend Benefits — 15
  - Sample Clues — 15
- Cryptography — 15
  - TFFB: Glad Handing — 15
  - Sample Spend Benefits — 15
  - Sample Clues — 15
- Diagnosis — 15
  - Ability Focus: Hematology — 15
  - TFFB: Developing Tainted Blood — 16
  - Sample Spend Benefits — 16
  - Sample Clues — 16
- Data Recovery — 16
  - TFFB: The Forgotten Safety Deposit Box — 16
  - Sample Spend Benefits — 16
  - Sample Clues — 16
- Electronic Surveillance — 17
  - Ability Focus: Cloning a Mobile Phone — 17
  - TFFB: Intercepting the Courier — 17
  - Sample Spend Benefits — 17
  - Sample Clues — 17
- Flattery — 17
  - TFFB: Borrowing High-Performance Cars — 17
  - Sample Spend Benefits — 18
  - Sample Clues — 18
- Flirting — 18
  - TFFB: Route Ambush — 18
  - Sample Spend Benefits — 18
  - Sample Clues — 18
- Forensic Pathology — 18
  - Ability Focus: Time of Death — 18
  - TFFB: Protecting Your Neck — 19
  - Sample Spend Benefits — 19
  - Sample Clues — 19
- Forgery — 19
  - Ability Focus: Identity Document Forgery — 19
  - TFFB: Stocking Up on Semtex — 19
  - Sample Spend Benefits — 19
  - Sample Clues — 19
- High Society — 19
  - The Most Expensive Hotels in Europe — 19
  - TFFB: The Birthday Party Extraction — 20
  - Sample Spend Benefits — 20
  - Sample Clues — 20
- History — 20
  - Ability Focus: Usual Suspects — 20
  - TFFB: Tracking a Feeding Vampire — 21
  - Sample Spend Benefits — 21
  - Sample Clues — 21
- Human Terrain — 21
  - TFFB: Finding the Archbishop — 21
  - Sample Spend Benefits — 22
  - Sample Clues — 22
- Interrogation — 22
  - Conducting A Police Interview — 22
  - TFFB: Stopping the Train Bombing — 22
  - Sample Spend Benefits — 22
  - Sample Clues — 23
- Intimidation — 23
  - TFFB: Shock and Awe — 23
  - Sample Spend Benefits — 23
  - Sample Clues — 23
- Law — 23
  - Ability Focus: European Firearms Laws — 23
  - TFFB: Moving a Firearms Cache — 24
  - Sample Spend Benefits — 24
  - Sample Clues — 24
- Military Science — 24
  - Ability Focus: Special Operations Forces — 24
  - TFFB: Raid the Abandoned Military Base — 25
  - Sample Spend Benefits — 25
  - Sample Clues — 25
- Negotiation — 25
  - TFFB: Scratching Their Back — 26
  - Sample Spend Benefits — 26
  - Sample Clues — 26
- Notice — 26
  - TFFB: Fight With Your Eyes Open — 26
  - Sample Spend Benefits — 26
  - Sample Clues — 26
- Occult Studies — 26
  - Ability Focus: Leading A Séance — 26
  - TFFB: Surprising Satanists — 27
  - Sample Spend Benefits — 27
  - Sample Clues — 27
- Outdoor Survival — 28
  - TFFB: Set Traps Around the Remote Safe House — 28
  - Sample Spend Benefits — 28
  - Sample Clues — 28

NIGHT'S BLACK AGENTS – DOUBLE TAP

Pharmacy	28
Ability Focus: The 10 Biggest Street Drugs	28
TFFB: Party Like It's 1999	29
Sample Spend Benefits	30
Sample Clues	30
Photography	30
TFFB: Now Give Me Suspicious	30
Sample Spend Benefits	30
Sample Clues	30
Reassurance	30
Ability Focus: Ten Steps of a Classic Grift	30
TFFB: Getting Inside	
the Executive Boardroom	31
Sample Spend Benefits	31
Sample Clues	31
Research	31
Ability Focus: Secret Archives	31
TFFB: It's Too Dark to Read	31
Sample Spend Benefits	31
Sample Clues	31
Streetwise	32
A Glossary of Criminal Slang	32
TFFB: The Bump and Run	32
Sample Spend Benefits	32
Sample Clues	32
Tradecraft	33
A Glossary of Espionage Jargon	33
TFFB: Slipping the Noose	33
Sample Spend Benefits	33
Sample Clues	33
Traffic Analysis	34
Ability Focus: Dumpster Diving	34
TFFB: Killing the Kraken	34
Sample Spend Benefits	34
Sample Clues	34
Urban Survival	34
Ability Focus: The Bug-Out Bag	34
TFFB: Safe House Raid	35
Sample Spend Benefits	35
Sample Clues	35
Vampirology	35
Ability Focus: The Vampire Subculture	35
TFFB: The Remington Allergist	36
Sample Spend Benefits	36
Sample Clues	36

GENERAL ABILITIES   36

Athletics	38
Ability Focus: Parkour	38
Investigative Sample Clues	38
New Cherries	38
Conceal	38
Ability Focus: Stash Spots	38
Investigative Sample Clues	39
New Cherry	39
Digital Intrusion	39
Investigative Sample Clues	39
New Cherries	39
Disguise	39
Investigative Sample Clues	40
New Cherries	40
Driving	40
Ability Focus:	
Aggressive Driving Maneuvers	40
Investigative Sample Clues	40
New Cherry	40
Explosive Devices	40
Ability Focus: Plastic Explosives	40
Investigative Sample Clues	41
New Cherry	41
Filch	41
Ability Focus: Pickpocket Teams	41
New Cherry	41
Gambling	42
Ability Focus: European	
Casino Table Games	42
Investigative Sample Clues	42
New Cherries	42
Hand-to-Hand	42
Ability Focus:	
Martial Arts Mixer	42
Investigative Sample Clues	43
New Cherry	43
Infiltration	43
New Cherries	43
Mechanics	44
Investigative Sample Clues	44
New Cherries	44
Medic	44
New Cherry	45
Piloting	45
Ability Focus:	
Surviving A Plane Crash	45
Investigative Sample Clues	45
New Cherry	45
Preparedness	45
New Cherries	45
Sense Trouble	45
Ability Focus:	
The Cooper Color Code	45
New Cherry	46
Shooting	46
Investigative Sample Clues	46
Shrink	47
New Cherries	47
Surveillance	47
New Cherries	47
Weapons	47
Ability Focus: Knife Grips	47
New Cherry	48

TRICKS OF THE TRADE   49

NEW THRILLER MANEUVERS   49
Non-Combat Maneuvers	49
Alibi	49
Blending Agent	50
Calculated Risk	50
Card Up The Sleeve	50
Danger Zone	50
Digital Judo	50
For Your Eyes Only	50
Grease Monkey	51
Like Smoke	51
m4d sk1llz	51
Quick Change	51
Run and Hide	51
Safety's On	51
Signature Wheels	52
Verbal Trauma Unit	52
Watching the Watchers	53
Combat Maneuvers	53
Mark and Strike	53
One-Two Punch	53
Perfect Drop	53
Thrown Clear by the Blast	53

ACHIEVEMENT REFRESHES   54
Achievements	54
Ad Hoc Achievements	56

ADAPTIVE TRADECRAFT   56
Determine when the Car Leaves	56
Suggested Benefits	56
Fake an Injury	57
Suggested Benefits	57
Conceal Liquids on your Person	57
Suggested Benefits	57
Monitor a Negotiation	57
Suggested Benefits	57
Make a Convenient Wall Safe	57
Suggested Benefits	57
Pwn a Webcam	57
Suggested Benefits	57
See in Darkness Quickly	57
Suggested Benefits	58
Get in Without a Ticket	58
Suggested Benefits	58
Write in Invisible Ink	58
Suggested Benefits	58
Communicate Despite Monitoring	58
Suggested Benefits	58
Hide Documents	58
Suggested Benefits	58
Build a Bulletproof Briefcase	59
Suggested Benefits	59
Pretend to Drink	59
Suggested Benefits	59
Take Fingerprints in the Field	59
Suggested Benefits	59

STANDARD OPERATING PROCEDURES   60
The Cartagena Rules	60

Commander's Intent	60	
You're Already Prepared	60	
Nobody Does It Better	60	
Choose the Most Awesome Alternative	60	
Get the Lay of the Land	60	
Hack the Exposition	61	
Wheat from Chaff	61	
Ask About Red Herrings	61	
Follow the Clear Lead	61	
Never Turtle Up	61	
Phone a Friend	61	
Support Other Players	62	
What's the Worst that Can Happen?	62	
Retreat is an Option	62	
There Are Different Kinds of Pressure	62	

MATERIEL — 63

MORE GEAR — 63
- The Q Rule — 63
- Communications — 63
- Disguise — 64
- Explosive Devices — 64
- Infiltration — 66
  - Car Hacking — 67
- Mechanics — 67
  - 3D Printers — 67
- Surveillance — 68
- Vehicles — 68
  - Vehicle-Based Equipment — 69

FIREARMS — 72
- Users and Missions — 72
- Gun Cherries — 74
- Accessories and Ammunition — 75
  - Special Ammunition — 76
  - Grenade Launchers — 76

THRILLER CONTESTS & MANHUNTS — 78

DIGITAL INTRUSION — 78
- Speed and Maneuver — 78
- The Lead — 79
  - Thriller Contest Results — 79
- Thrilling Elements — 79
- Special Thriller Hacking Rules — 80
  - Investigative Ability Uses — 80
  - Swerve — 80
  - Digital Judo — 81
  - Sudden Escape — 81

INFILTRATION — 81
- The Lead — 81
  - Thriller Contest Results — 82
- Thrilling Elements — 82
- Special Thriller Sneaking Rules — 83
  - Investigative Ability Uses — 83
  - A Note About Disguises — 83
  - Watching the Watchers — 83
  - Swerve — 83
  - Attacking Guards — 83
  - Run and Hide — 84
  - Sudden Escape — 84

SURVEILLANCE — 84
- Speed and Maneuver — 84
- The Lead — 85
  - Thriller Contest Results — 85
- Thrilling Elements — 85
  - Surveillance Raises — 86
- Special Thriller Trailing Rules — 86
  - Investigative Ability Uses — 86
  - Attacking Watchers — 86
  - Other General Abilities — 86
  - Swerve — 86
  - Sudden Escape — 87

MANHUNTS — 87
- Hot Lead — 87
  - Starting Hot Lead — 87
  - Changing Hot Lead — 87
  - Earning Hot Lead — 88
  - Multiple Hot Leads — 88
- Putting Out The Net — 88
- Gambits — 89
- Roosting and Elimination — 90

DIRECTOR'S COMPANION — 91

ELEMENTS — 92

CAMEOS — 92

ESTABLISHING SHOTS — 98

MONSTERS — 106
- Bloodworking — 106
- Curse — 106
- Chupa — 106
- Ekimmu — 107
- Homunculus — 108
- Penanggalan — 109

NOSFERATU — 110

STORIES — 112

PULLING THEM APART — 112
- Mechanisms of Faction — 112
  - Frayed, Stressed, and Broken — 112
  - The Suitors and the Beloved — 113
- The Suspyramid — 114
  - Tier One: Intrigue — 114
  - Tier Two: Strife — 114
  - Tier Three: Paranoia — 115
  - Tier Four: Vengeance — 115
  - Tier Five: Slaughter — 116
  - Tier Six: Collapse — 116

SOLITARY HEROES — 116

VARIANT ERAS — 117
- Victorian Era — 117
  - Investigative Ability Changes — 118
  - Social Class — 118
  - General Ability Changes — 118
- World War II — 119
- Cold War — 119
  - Investigative Ability Changes — 119
  - General Ability Changes — 119

ADDENDA — 121
- Cherry Summary Sheet — 122
- New Thriller Combat Options — 124
- Suspyramid Diagram — 125
- Vampire Powers Summary Sheet — 126

INDEX — 129

INTRODUCTION

With all the Conspiracies, the intrigue, the danger, it's hard to know what exactly is and isn't on your side. When every shadow from the back alleys of Bucharest to the back benches of the parliament could hide an inhuman enemy, it's hard to tell what solid ground you can stand on. What can you depend on? Can you make a difference? Trust no one and nothing except the silver bullets in your Glock. To make a difference, aim true.

Even then, sometimes that first shot isn't a killer. Sometimes you need a double tap.

Burned once, and trying to avoid the firefight, the resourceful, well-connected, well-informed agent is the one who lives to die another day, while the unsure, the weak, and the ill-equipped find themselves on the wrong side of something with fangs. They run for the sunlight and if they're lucky they can take a brief moment to die warm and human. A worse fate may be in store for the agent who isn't smart enough to die …

The **Night's Black Agents** corebook (**NBA**) presented a lot of information to help agents uncover and succeed against Conspiracies of all sizes, against all manner of twisted machinations. And while there's plenty of ammunition there, sometimes you need more. More gear. More abilities. More options. All that is in here.

You may have heard this project leaked back when it was called the "Agent's Companion," a name that went by the boards for two reasons. First, we've added some material to the outline for the use of Directors as well: inspirational NPCs, more vampiric monsters, and some notes about running one-on-one single-player games, just for starters. Thus it's not an "Agent's Companion" per se any more.

The second reason is we wanted a general name for this type of book, a name that could potentially span the Pelgrane lines: a book that you'd come to expect for any Pelgrane game, a book of extras and twists, not needed for core game play but informative and inspiring nonetheless. That's why the full name of this book is **Double Tap: The Night's Black Agents Expansion Book.** An expansion book gives you more room to play in, expanding possibilities and illustrating potentialities we didn't have room for in the core book, new mechanics that the core book sparked in other designers (like Will Plant's Achievements, or James Palmer's internal conflict Suspyramid algorithm, both of which are here) plus ideas that the first rush of players and playtesters have requested.

So consider this the next level, a higher pay grade and higher-than-double-0 clearance. It's time to take the fight to the Conspiracy.

This time, it's not just a headshot. Better go for the double tap.

AGENTS' COMPANION

You've been in the foxholes. You've been in deep cover. You've seen the fight up close and personal, earning more than a fair share of wounds and scars along the way. This portion of the book will help you empower and develop agents able to stand against any opposition, providing them tools, tricks, and know-how so that in any situation, the agent comes out alive.

ABILITIES

This section expands on the coverage of abilities in the ***Night's Black Agents*** corebook. Every ability is addressed, with a few exceptions. Some abilities receive detailed treatment in the corebook already, while others cover such a very broad field that providing useful information at random is unlikely. Health and Stability are sui generis pools the other abilities preserve or, if things go south, endanger.

INVESTIGATIVE ABILITIES

Each entry lists a few important aspects of the ability as used in thriller fiction and sometimes in real-world espionage. Some specific details of some abilities receive close-up treatment as Ability Foci; some entries also include characteristic equipment associated with the ability. For each ability, we provide one example Tactical Fact-Finding Bonus (TFFB) (***NBA***, pp. 108-109), three sample benefits from a spend (***NBA***, p. 46), and three vampiric traces or clues the Director can use or the agents can seek out in the course of an operation.

Pools gained as the result of a spend last either for the remainder of the scene or the remainder of the operation, at the Director's discretion.

Where applicable, glyphs indicate the vampire type most likely to have left such a clue.

ACCOUNTING

Accounting is, famously, how they got Capone. And, pace Deep Throat, it's how they got Nixon: "Follow the money." Less famously, it's how the federal authorities in many countries track organized criminal conspiracies and terror groups. Illegal activity costs money and (usually) makes money. That money leaves footprints, and sometimes it leaves fingerprints, even if vampires leave neither.

ABILITY FOCUS: MONEY LAUNDERING

PLACEMENT: The money earned from illegitimate activities is placed in a legitimate institution. Large cash deposits in banks are common at this stage, which makes it the riskiest part. Either the bank must be fooled into thinking the money is legit, or the bank must be willing to deal with criminals. Both approaches have their faults.

LAYERING: Moving the money from institution to institution. This includes wire transfers, dummy withdrawals and anything that can be done to make the account seem real, as well as make the money harder to track. Hard assets are often purchased at this stage like houses, luxury vehicles, and art.

INTEGRATION: The money is withdrawn looking like it was part of a legal transaction. The yacht is sold, materials are purchased for a legitimate business or money is invested in the stock market. Often, the legitimate business gets a larger than normal cut of the money for their silence.

ADDITIONAL LAUNDERING TECHNIQUES

BLACK MARKET CURRENCY EXCHANGES: Trading one stockpile of blood money for another is a grand criminal tradition. The facilitator of such an exchange can be anyone from a fellow shadow organization to a rich individual looking to dodge taxes on their income.

SMURFING DEPOSITS: Many legitimate banks work under laws that red flag transactions over a certain amount. In the U.S., for example, transactions over $10,000 are reported to the government. Smurfing breaks down large cash deposits into smaller, manageable amounts that don't trigger these alarms.

OVERSEAS ACCOUNTS: An oldie but a goodie. Bouncing money through countries with powerful secrecy laws allows for anonymous withdrawals and deposits. It also makes following the money nearly impossible. Popular offshore destinations include the Bahamas, Bahrain, the Cayman Islands, Hong Kong, Turkish Cyprus, and Singapore.

UNDERGROUND BANKS: Certain banks in the Middle East and Asia went paperless thousands of years ago. They use something of an honor system to monitor transactions as well as being older than most of the governments they operate in. The *hawala* system of Pakistan and *fie chen* Chinese system provide a heady mix of ancient conspiracy and personal banking.

LEGITIMATE BUSINESS: There are always struggling business people looking for cash infusions to build a better life for themselves. Often the line between legitimate investment and front company is razor thin. Construction, waste management, and entertainment venues are all popular choices thanks to the many off-book expenses that occur, as well as the fact that they can "lose money" but manage to stay in business.

SHELL COMPANIES: A company that exists in name only solely for the purpose of layering money: e.g., LaunderCo purchases an office building and then turns around and sells it without ever moving one bit of furniture inside. Popular shell companies include investment funds, service providers, and anything that can move money with a minimum of physical assets or employees.

TACTICAL FACT-FINDING BENEFIT: LOCATING THE STASH OF GUNS

Accounting tracks down the payments to the warehouse. The team can choose to either destroy the guns (Explosive Devices, Difficulty 3) or move them (Piloting/Driving, Difficulty 5). If the agents destroyed the guns, all the thugs have Shooting reduced by 3 due to a lack of ammo and confidence in whatever weapons they scrounge up. If the agents stole the guns, they get a team pool in Shooting equal to 4 times the margin of success on their Piloting or Driving roll (minimum 4).

SAMPLE SPEND BENEFITS

- You can siphon a little from the shell company's slush fund for your own devices. Gain 2 points for your next Network spend to acquire gear on the black market.
- You've used the same money launderer as the bratva. You don't have to spend time acquiring a contact, but try to be careful in your inquiries so as not to disrupt your friend's business. Or, burn your friend to pull the bratva into the open.
- The money spent on medical expenses is almost as good as busting into the doctor's office for a look at the file. Gain a 2-point Diagnosis pool to figure out the ailments the mark suffers from.

SAMPLE CLUES

- ⊕ The amount of money being donated to St. Florian's Church should have the priests wearing handmade Italian shoes, but the receipts show the money is going to security for the crypt.
- 👽 The ship's cargo manifest doesn't match up with the surveillance photos. The object under the tarp looked like a craft of unknown origin, not five tons of iron ore.
- Why are the payments to Dr. Bergmann's office continuing even though the treatments stopped two years ago?

ARCHAEOLOGY

Archaeology and espionage have been blood brothers since the days when T.E. Lawrence and Max von Oppenheim dueled in the fading Ottoman Empire to uncover lost cities and map Turkish military positions. In this century, archaeologists still go to remote backwaters with expensive sensor gear and satellite phones: are they digging up Ubar, or stirring up rebels?

ANCIENT VAMPIRE ARTIFACTS

Espionage tales often center around the acquisition of an item. Nuclear launch codes, a missing scientist or a computer virus all serve the purpose of putting the heroes in danger and setting them against memorable bad guys. Some items are older than others.

These artifacts add a dash of pulp archaeologist flair to your game, which isn't too surprising. The old pulps that inspired the man in the fedora contained plenty of spy tales.

PANDORA'S BOX: This is the box that supposedly released monsters upon the world when opened. The box could be what transforms humans into vampires, or pieces of the box could detect when a vampire is present. It could also be a crashed alien menagerie ship from thousands of years ago.

THE FOURTH NAIL: Most versions of this story claim that Jesus was meant to be crucified with four nails instead of three. Somehow the fourth nail went missing thanks to a Gypsy and Jesus gave special dispensation to them for easing his suffering. This could mean anything from knowing ancient lore on how to deal with vampires to keeping ancient weapons hidden in their wagons that are brutally effective against the undead.

THE GRAIL: The cup that Christ used at the Last Supper is soaked in so much blood mythology that it could work as anything from an ancient alien cure for vampirism to the ultimate purification vessel for infected mutant blood. The Grail as a living, human bloodline vessel has also come into vogue recently -- what if the agents learn the Grail is one of their own?

TACTICAL FACT-FINDING BENEFIT: THAT'S NOT A KNIFE

Archaeology identifies the Dagger of Freyr as the one the blood cult needs. Once inside the storage facility, the agents can switch the dagger in the crate out for a dummy (Conceal, Difficulty 4) or lift it off one of the restoration workers (Filch, Difficulty 5). Without the right component, the Rite of Sanguine Empowerment doesn't work. The cult, still waiting for its leader to assume the title of vampire lord, is surprised for two rounds if the team attacks during the ceremony.

SAMPLE SPEND BENEFITS

- Identifying the true nature of St. Stephen's fingerbone bolstered the padre's spirits. Gain a 3-point Shrink pool to keep him in good mental shape long enough to finish the exorcism.
- There's one place she could sell the statue: Marrakesh. If you tip off Yusuf, he can delay her long enough for your team to hop a redeye and get it back.
- Don Julio is a collector of nudes and ancient pornographic art. Gain a 2-point Negotiation pool with him thanks to the pieces your connections can provide.

SAMPLE CLUES

- 👽 Dr. Whitman's published work is little more than "ancient astronaut" drivel. This unpublished manuscript, however, makes some connections between certain digs that disturb you.
- ☣ Explanations for the curse of King Tut's Tomb included bacterial agents sealed inside the tomb. What if Professor Grimaldi unleashed a similar effect on her excavation team?
- The chamber below the office block is a Roman mithraeum. Spaces like these were used to initiate members

into the cult of Mithras with a meal. Though you don't recall ones with restraints on the benches.
- The museum bought some of the pieces for pennies on the dollar. Nichols must have been on the move and just wanted enough money to go on the run.

ARCHITECTURE

When you studied it in the military, you may have called it "civil engineering," or just "engineering."

HOUSES OF THE DEAD

CRYPT: A stone chamber beneath the main altar of a church. Relics, sarcophagi, and important members of the church are often buried in crypts. Crypts are features in churches built before the 11th century, after which point relics could be displayed on the main floor of the church. After that time, most cathedrals built burial vaults for major patrons.

MEGALITHIC TOMB: Above ground burial spaces built with large stones covered with dirt or smaller stones. Many of these tombs also feature ritual spaces and evidence that ceremonies took place before the bodies were put inside the tomb.

CATACOMB: Tunnels beneath ancient cities built for religious burial practices. Originally referred to the Roman catacombs (primarily Christian) located under roads leading to the capital city, since it was illegal to bury the dead inside the city. The term was expanded to other tunnel systems in 1836 such as the ones built beneath Paris.

MAUSOLEUM: A free-standing building erected to hold human remains. Often built as testaments to the power and wealth of the dead resting within. They may be as simple as the ones found in a cemetery or as ostentatious as the Taj Majal, which was built for Mumtaz Mahal, the Shah Jehan's third wife. She died giving birth to their 14th child.

OSSUARY: A collection of skeletal remains. Remains are buried elsewhere temporarily and then moved to the ossuary once only the bones remain. Some feature carefully stacked bones. Others compact the remains into smaller containers to make room for fresh dead.

TACTICAL FACT-FINDING BENEFIT: GETTING INTO THE CASTLE

Architecture allows you to map an efficient route into the dungeons. Taking the tour during the day allows the team to check out blind spots in the video coverage (Surveillance, Difficulty 4). Coming back at night when you can extract the artifact, those blind spots let you get in and out quicker. Gain a team pool of 8 points that can be used for Infiltration (to get into the castle) or Conceal (to stash the artifact onsite for later retrieval).

SAMPLE SPEND BENEFITS

- Pre-fab housing like this all has the same weaknesses. Gain a 3-point Infiltration pool while sneaking around.
- The Contessa loves your suggestions for her mansion's decor. Gain a 2-point High Society pool to represent how long you stay in her favor.
- You've done work for the firm that built Kammerer's corporate HQ. The construction shortcuts and code violations can be had for a few pints at the pub.

SAMPLE CLUES

- 👁 The skulls in the thirteenth row of the ossuary all have pointed incisors that don't look filed.
- This air shaft is designed so that it never gets any direct sunlight – an unusual feature in an apartment block.
- 👽 ⊛ The arrangement of the stones in the forecourt of this megalithic tomb reminds you of the logo you saw on the truck parked outside your safe house.

ART HISTORY

Everybody knows the greats of the past, from Sandro Botticelli to Francis Bacon. But who are the gallery set talking about now? Drop these names at happenings, openings, or auctions.

ABEL ABDESSEMED: Conceptual artist, film, sculpture, painted objects. His repeated use of videotaped cruelty to animals as a motif has sparked controversy and riots.

OLAFUR ELIASSON: Immersive environments using light and color, water sculpture, optical illusions, monotone painting, modern Dada installations.

TRACEY EMIN: Installations, monoprints, paintings, neon sculpture, fabric work. Collected by Elton John and other celebrity glitterati.

LLYN FOULKES: Surrealist painting, iconography, music, tableaux incorporating found objects and photographs.

RASHID JOHNSON: Photography, music, spoken word, video, sculpture. His work often combines African-American history and culture with alchemy, divination, astrology, and other occult sciences.

EDWARD RUSCHA: Word paintings, murals, art books, art with food. A founding father of Pop Art.

JIM SHAW: Ink on canvas, paintings, dream drawings, punk rock. Has curated controversial shows of art found at amateur sales and thrift shops.

LUC TUYMANS: Paints imagistic versions in oil of photographs, movie and TV stills, and other quasi-historical works. "Sickness should appear in the way a painting is made."

JEFF WALL: Meticulously posed and composed photographic transparencies creating the illusion of spontaneity, photographs commenting on paintings and literary works. Blends multiple digital images into a single work.

TACTICAL FACT-FINDING BENEFIT: ATTACKING THE PRIVATE GALLERY SHOW

Art History identifies which paintings are worth stealing. Walking the floor (Surveillance, Difficulty 4) or hacking the security feed (Digital Intrusion, Difficulty 5) locates them in the gallery. The agents plan a daring attack that triggers multiple alarms on purpose as they keep close to valuable paintings. The chaos (and desire to not damage priceless artwork) increases agent Hit Thresholds by 1.

SAMPLE SPEND BENEFITS

- You get a flashback to remember where you saw this sculpture for the first time, and meeting the beautiful woman who watched you look at it. You suddenly remember that she left no reflection in the glass.
- His Lordship was very happy that you prevented him from purchasing the forgery. His influence gains you a 2-point High Society pool while in the United Kingdom.
- You met Bishop Latrava at a Vatican Museum charity function. If he doesn't surface on the rumor of an uncatalogued Modigliani, you'll eat your hat.

SAMPLE CLUES

- It's definitely a forgery. But telling Mel the forger who did this has been alive for two hundred years will get you laughed out of Venice.
- 👽 The orange sun above the landscape doesn't come from a faded pigment. In light of the vessel you discovered two nights ago, you realize now that it represents the craft's star of origin.
- ⊛ You thought the rumors of Monnink's use of blood as media were ridiculous. That was before you saw Blood Countess' rich, deep reds. Standing in the vault's silence, you swear you hear a heartbeat.

ASTRONOMY

ABILITY FOCUS: FERMI'S PARADOX

In 1950, physicist Enrico Fermi wondered why, if there is intelligent life in the universe, we haven't seen any evidence. In 1975, Michael Hart explored this question more deeply in writing.

The logical progression of Fermi's Question, aka the Great Silence:

- Our sun is relatively young in a galactic sense. There should be billions of stars that are older.
- If there are billions of stars like ours, there should be billions of worlds that can develop life like Earth.
- If those Earth-like planets develop life like us, some of them should have developed interstellar travel by now.
- A galaxy the size of our own should be colonized within tens of millions of years
- The short version: Where is everybody?

Theories and solutions:

There aren't any civilizations there yet. Intelligent life is a rarity even in the billion to one odds of the universe. Earth is not a typical planet. It's a rare mix of the proper conditions. The rise of intelligence is a jewel we should treasure.

The clock is ticking. Intelligent races have to deal with their own civilization-ending events. Their influence is cyclical and the same technology that could take them to the stars factor into their destruction. We just haven't pushed The Button yet.

Extinction events. It happened to the dinosaurs. It probably happened to other worlds. It could still happen to us. One day, a meteor hits the planet and all our forward progress means little.

Humans can't or won't hear. White noise written off by radio telescopes and SETI officials are actually highly compressed data streams we are unable to process.

Aliens are here, but They cover it up. This is the lip of the rabbit hole that goes from astronomy to UFO conspiracy.

While this information is obviously useful for a game with alien vampires, the question can inspire solutions to any conspiracy questions, like "Why isn't everyone who gets bit turned into a vampire?" and "If the conspiracy is so powerful, why is it still in hiding?"

TACTICAL FACT-FINDING BENEFIT: THE STARS ARE RIGHT

Astronomy pinpoints the night and location of the ritual from the star chart. Scouting out the location requires either sneaking in before the ritual starts and finding a hiding spot (Surveillance, Difficulty 4) or swiping a set of robes and milling about as the cult arrives (Disguise, Difficulty 3). Go weapons free while all eyes are on the Master of the Void Drinkers, and the team gets one round of surprise for every agent in place.

SAMPLE SPEND BENEFITS

- These astrophysics seminars are such meat markets. Gain a 2-point Flirting pool with any attendee.
- Running silent at night before moonrise means they can't see you coming. Gain a 3-point Piloting pool under cover of darkness.
- You've had some interesting discussions with the professor on the MUFON forum. Let him know your handle and scullybear64 should be more than happy to discuss the missing students.

SAMPLE CLUES

- The starry sky in the painting is carefully rendered. You can use it to determine the location of the castle you need to infiltrate.
- The drops of blood were deliberately placed. It's the constellation Orion the hunter. Looks like some other vampire killers got here first.
- 👁 ⊕ The vampire's strength is somehow linked to the moon. It feeds on the full moon, and hides during the new moon.

BULLSHIT DETECTOR

ABILITY FOCUS: COMMON TELLS

BODY LANGUAGE: Eye contact is a big one. Most untrained liars will look away when they lie. Hands move to the mouth, face or throat. Physical movement becomes stiff or non-existent. The body turns away from the questioner. The liar puts an object between themselves and the interviewer, like a book or a coffee cup.

EMOTIONAL GESTURES: Lying often involves a clash of verbal intent against emotional truth. Smiles go on a little too long. Slight delays between emotional reaction and verbal answers make answers sound forced. Expressions are often limited to the mouth. Someone genuinely surprised, for example, shows it with their whole face: jaw, cheek, eye, and brow movement.

VERBAL CONTEXT: A guilty person often goes on the defensive. Liars often use distancing language. This includes euphemisms like "rubbed out," clinical terminology like "exsanguinated," or even telling an alibi in the third person, like a story. Answering questions with the interviewer's own words buys the liar time to work on a good answer. These answers may not answer the question directly. Pronouns in untrue statements are garbled or monotone, but pronouns in truthful statements are emphasized.

MICROEXPRESSIONS: A recent field of study categorizing how the face shows emotion. Microexpressions fall into seven areas: anger, disgust, fear, sadness, happiness, surprise, and contempt. These expressions cross cultural and linguistic lines. They can't show if someone is lying, but careful study can point to such conclusions. Someone unsurprised by the mention of the death of a loved one, for example, may have already known about it.

TACTICAL FACT-FINDING BENEFIT: FLIPPING AN UNSUSPECTING MOLE

Bullshit Detector shows your contact is lying to you about contact with the Crimson Patriots. Feeding the mole false information requires recognizing information the mole finds valuable (Shrink, Difficulty 5) and making sure he gets back to the opposition to deliver the story (Surveillance, Difficulty 4). The false information convinces the Crimson Patriots you are vulnerable on a certain date and time. Instead, you now have a 10-point team pool for Preparedness or Shooting on their attack, since they are playing right into your hands.

SAMPLE SPEND BENEFITS

- He's trying to convince you he's a big fish in the organization. Take a 2-point Human Terrain pool to use as you remember all the names, dates, and places he's spouting.
- Knowing how to impersonate someone means knowing how to lie like they do. Take a dedicated 3-point Disguise pool when portraying this individual.
- You've caught the executive in a lie. Perhaps her husband will be interested in talking to you now that you can tell him what she's lying about.

SAMPLE CLUES

- ⊕ 👁 Often, liars blink excessively when they tell a falsehood. This guy's not blinking. At all.
- ⊕ ⊕ The polygraph is showing abnormal readings. Questions about what happened in Nice send the cab driver's vitals into very low areas, like he's been conditioned.
- She's not serious about detonating the device.

BUREAUCRACY

EUROPEAN FIREARMS PASS: Papers that allow a person to carry one or more firearms listed between member states. Issued to hunters, target shooters, firearms dealers and specialist collectors for museums.

DUAL NATIONALITY: An EU resident lives and works in the EU. An EU citizen has a passport from one of the countries in the union. Becoming a citizen requires filing for dual citizenship. This can be done through tracing lineage, marriage, or residency.

FOREIGN INVESTOR PASSPORTS: Countries hit hard by the recent financial crisis have turned to foreign investors to help them out of their jam. Hungary has a law that offers citizenship to anyone that buys a certain amount of special government bonds. Spain is considering offering citizenship to anyone that buys a home.

SCHENGEN AREA: Twenty-six European countries passed a law in 1985 that loosened the requirement on passports when travelling between them. The European Union grandfathered this rule in upon its formation. If you hold a passport from the EU, you don't have to show it when travelling between these countries. The 26 countries in the Schengen Area were Austria, Belgium, Czech Republic, Denmark, Estonia, Finland, France, Germany, Greece, Hungary, Iceland, Italy, Latvia, Liechtenstein, Lithuania, Luxembourg, Malta, Netherlands, Norway, Poland, Portugal, Slovakia, Slovenia, Spain, Sweden, and Switzerland. The UK, Ireland, Cyprus, and Romania still require presentation of an EU passport at the border.

TACTICAL FACT-FINDING BENEFIT: THE MILE HIGH CLUBBING

Bureaucracy tells you who to drop a dime to in order to flag a passport and delay the flight's boarding. Hacking the booking computers makes sure that your team are the only passengers on the flight (Digital Intrusion, Difficulty 4) and the team makes it on board unrecognized (Disguise, Difficulty 4). When the pawn of the Conspiracy boards, the agents have the flight time to work him over. The agents get a 10-point Hand-to-Hand group pool to exact their revenge -- or to capture him and set up an Interrogation spend.

SAMPLE SPEND BENEFITS

- Your meticulousness in filling out forms makes you an expert in forging them. Gain a 2-point Forgery pool for these papers.
- You make sure the team is always restocked. Refresh your Preparedness by 3 points.

- If you tip off the border guard to the smugglers, she'll let your harmless group of tourists through.

SAMPLE CLUES

- ⊕ The girls' academic records show they all have similar nationalities and traits. Looks like His Dark Lordship has a certain taste.
- ⊕ The reassignment of church officials coincides with the failed exorcisms.
- The same customs agent was working every night a container went through. He's either very bent or very incompetent.

CHEMISTRY

ABILITY FOCUS: HANDLING RADIOACTIVE MATERIAL

First, know the intensity of the radioactive hazard. A white label denotes a Level I threat, enough to set off a Geiger counter but not pose an immediate health risk. A yellow Level II label indicates significant radioactive emission outside the packaging. A yellow Level III label applies to the most dangerous material, including fissile material.

In addition to common-sense precautions (don't eat lunch near radioactive material), utilize the three defenses: time, distance, and shielding. Plan your activities to minimize time near radioactives. Where at all possible use tongs, clamps, tweezers, or other tools to extend your distance from the material. Similarly, use a cart if possible to avoid carrying material by hand. For Level II and above, use at least two pairs of disposable gloves (replacing the outer pair frequently), as well as coats, goggles or full-face protectors, and (in the lab) fume hoods or other protective equipment.

Shielding depends on the specific type of radiation: high-Z (atomic number) materials are better against gamma radiation but can actually become irradiated by neutron radiation. A centimeter of lead halves the amount of gamma radiation received; bismuth oxide works almost as well, is much lighter, resists neutron radiation better, and can be applied as a cream to exposed skin or under gloves.

TACTICAL FACT-FINDING BENEFIT: MONTEZUMA'S REVENGE

Chemistry mixes up an odorless, tasteless compound that causes stomach cramps, fatigue, and diarrhea. Getting it into the food supply requires either dressing up like food preparation staff (Disguise, Difficulty 3) or intercepting the food before it reaches the mess hall and sprinkling the chemicals on it (Filch, Difficulty 4). The guards suffer flu-like symptoms for the next 24 hours. The team gains a 10-point team Infiltration pool as patrol routes are interrupted and guards are distracted.

SAMPLE SPEND BENEFITS

- You know how to improve the purity of the product with no impact to the cartel's bottom line. Gain a 2-point Streetwise spend when dealing with the Colombians.
- You can improvise explosives or incendiaries from the stuff in the lab. You're so good at it, in fact, that you roll two dice for the damage from the blast and use the higher result.
- You know a shortcut that can complete this test in an hour instead of waiting two days for the results to come back.

SAMPLE CLUES

- ☣ 👽 The blood sample contains enough foreign elements that the person it came from should be lying here dead right next to the victim.
- ⊕ The lipstick on the dead man's collar left an unusual chemical for cosmetics: sulfur.
- Someone cut this cocaine with an organic substance. You'd guess blood, but you don't know why human blood would be used that way.

COP TALK

BRITISH POLICE JARGON

ABH: Actual Bodily Harm.
ASP: Extensible metal baton, named for a baton manufacturer, Armament Systems and Procedures.
Banged up: Locked up in a cell.
Black rat: Traffic patrol officer.
Blag: Robbery.

Blues and Twos: The lights and (two-tone) siren on a police car, ergo, a police car.
Brains Department: CID (Criminal Investigation Division), used (often sarcastically) by Uniform Branch.
Button Mob: Uniform Branch, used by CID. Also *woodentops*.
Caution: Formal police warning, roughly equivalent to U.S. *Miranda* reading. A suspect "under caution" may have his statements given in evidence at trial.
Corres: Paperwork, correspondence.
Dancers: To run away; "He was on his dancers."
Drum: Residence; "We'll give his drum a spin."
Factory: Police station. Also *the Nick*.
Filth: Derogatory term used for police by criminals.
Going Equipped: In possession of materials used in committing a crime, i.e., possessing burglar's tools.
Grass: An informant, or to inform. Also *snout*.
IC6: Of Arabic appearance, an Arab; IC4 is Pakistani; IC1 is white European. After the Identification Codes in criminal databases.
Job, in the: Working for the police; "Her man's in the Job, as well."
Lag: Prison inmate.
NCPA: No Cause for Police Action.
Nicked: Arrested.
Nondy: Surveillance or stakeout vehicle, from "nondescript."
Panda: Non-pursuit police vehicle.
Run in: Yard for stolen or impounded vehicles.
Shout: Incident called in on the radio; "Were you at that shout in Coventry Street?"
Spin: Search.
T Call: Urgent call to police requiring immediate response.
Tooled up: Armed, used of criminals.
TWOC: Taken Without Owner's Consent; theft, usually of a car or boat. TWOCking connotes joyriding.

TACTICAL FACT-FINDING BENEFIT: QUIETLY CALLING THE CAVALRY

With judicious **Cop Talk**, you find out which CI (confidential informant) is wearing a wire tonight. Tuning your radio equipment to broadcast on that wire's frequency requires swiping a police radio (Filch, Difficulty 4) or hacking their wireless network (Digital Intrusion, Difficulty 5). If the negotiations don't go well and you need a distraction to get away, you can bring the cops "accidentally" to the scene with a few well-chosen words. Gain a 10-point team Athletics pool while escaping the meet as police cars swarm the area.

SAMPLE SPEND BENEFITS

- Sprinkling in the right lingo gets you into places when you've "left your badge on the desk." Gain a 3-point Infiltration pool to get around inside police headquarters.
- You finger the bent cop by what his fellow officers won't say about him. Now you pump him: Good cop? 2-point pool to Reassurance. Bad cop? 2-point pool to Intimidation.
- The lieutenant might not believe your story about the Red Fungus, but she knows she's unable to handle whatever is killing the working girls. As long as you promise to never come back to her city after you kill that thing, she won't arrest you.

SAMPLE CLUES

- ⊛ All the witnesses described the scene exactly the same. Word for word, like they were each given a script.
- ☻ You've been around enough Feds to recognize their cheap suits. Those two guys in black aren't wearing government issue poly blend.
- Every precinct has some poor schmuck they give the unsolvables. Look for the detective with the lowest clearance rate and he'll have any vampire murders.

CRIMINOLOGY

ABILITY FOCUS: VAMPIRE MURDERS

BÉLA KISS: Amateur astrologer and occultist who killed at least 17 women in Cinkota, Hungary from 1903 to 1914. Investigators found the bodies stuffed into metal barrels, drained of blood, with wounds on their necks. He was sighted in Budapest, but vanished during WWI.

FRITZ HAARMANN: Between 1918 and 1924, the "Butcher of Hanover" murdered over 20 young men and boys by biting through their necks, and possibly sold their flesh on the black market. Guillotined in 1925, his head is preserved at the Gottingen medical school.

PETER KÜRTEN: The "Vampire of Düsseldorf" killed at least 9 women in 1929 and drank their blood; his first victim was a girl in 1913. He was beheaded in 1931 for his crimes, which also included a number of hammer assaults.

JOHN HAIGH: The "Acid Bath Vampire" killed 9 people in London and Sussex between 1944 and 1949. He drank his victims' blood, sold their possessions and property, and dissolved their bodies in acid to avoid conviction for murder. That last precaution was in vain; Haigh was hanged in 1949.

MAGDALENA SOLIS: Former prostitute hired by cult leaders in Yerba Buena, Mexico, to impersonate the "Blood Goddess." She turned out to be a psychopath, orchestrating at least six vampiric human sacrifices in April and May of 1963. After the Federales broke up the cult, she was sentenced to life in prison.

TSUTOMU MIYAZAKI: Obsessive horror and anime fan killed, vampirized, and molested the corpses of four little girls in Tokyo in 1988-89, while persecuting their families with postcards and phone calls. He claimed a "Rat Man" told him to kill; he was hanged in 2008.

JOSHUA RUDIGER: Believing he was a 2,000 year old vampire, he attacked at least four homeless people in San Francisco, slashing their throats and drinking their blood. One woman died, and in 1998 Rudiger was sentenced to 23 years to life in prison.

TACTICAL FACT-FINDING BENEFIT: EXTRACTING THE CONSIGLIERE

Criminology identifies the advisor to the well-connected but not well-prepared Don, the consigliere who makes key decisions in a crisis. Tracking him until he's vulnerable can be done through buddying up to him at the poker table (Gambling, Difficulty 4) or the old fashioned van across the street from the club (Surveillance, Difficulty 5). Then it's just a snatch-and-grab. For 48 hours after the consigliere is taken out of the picture, the Don thrashes about aimlessly, and the agents get a 20-point pool for any General ability use against the mafia. This adds to any bonuses from the adversary map (*NBA*, p. 113).

SAMPLE SPEND BENEFITS

- You did a few years undercover work. Gain a 3-point Sense Trouble pool during the money handoff.
- You recognize the vehicle from an Interpol cable as a known smuggler's craft. Gain a 3-point Conceal pool to identify secret hatches and holding areas on it.
- They call it the Ripper Room. Scotland Yard keeps it quiet, but they have every letter, confession, and scrap from every nutcase claiming responsibility for the Whitechapel murders. You got to use it for your last true crime novel.

SAMPLE CLUES

- 😈 Meth addicts might bite someone, but drinking blood afterward doesn't fit the profile.
- 👽 You know what Interpol agents dress like, and it certainly isn't a black suit and mirrorshades.
- Gaspar let your team have these guns for a song. They might be hot or in bad shape.

CRYPTOGRAPHY

CIPHER: A cipher replaces letters with other symbols. Letters, numbers, or symbols can all be used. Substitutions range from swapping a letter with another to setting one letter to a symbol of some significance to the encrypter.

CODE: A code replaces words with other words. This can be anything from a euphemism or jargon in speech to an innocuous page to tip employees off to a dangerous situation. Hospitals page fictitious doctors to areas all the time, such as "Dr. Firestone" for a fire in the building.

"ETAOIN SRHLDCU": The most common letters in the English language according to a Google analysis of website and search data.

FREQUENCY ANALYSIS: One of the bedrocks of cryptography. The amount of times something appears in a message,

the more likely it is a common letter or word. A simple substitution cipher will usually feature the letter "e" most commonly. Once the e is discovered, the word "the" is usually close behind. That word offers context clues as well as other words using the letters of that word.

TACTICAL FACT-FINDING BENEFIT: GLAD HANDING

Cryptography deduces that the code phrase "Ulster Shield" means that personnel are forbidden to carry weapons on that operation or in that location. Scouring Conspiracy traffic for "Ulster Shield" mentions (Digital Intrusion, Difficulty 5) gives you a time and place where the Conspiracy assets on site will be unarmed. The agents get a 10-point group pool for any combat abilities, since they don't have to worry about snipers.

SAMPLE SPEND BENEFITS

- You cracked the encryption perfectly. Refresh your Forgery pool by 3 points when faking communications from the leader.
- That symbol is clearly important to them. Gain a 2-point Notice pool when looking for it in the archives.
- You'd be surprised at the people who subscribe to a Times crossword forum. Obsessive detail-oriented people, with an interest in hidden meanings. In other words, analyst central -- an impressive post or six gins up some real crowdsourcing potential.

SAMPLE CLUES

- 👽 It looks like the file is a partial translation of an Invader message. It's a good place to start decoding their language.
- ✠ Project SALIGIA takes its name from the first Latin letters of the seven deadly sins: superbia, avaritia, luxuria, invidia, gula, ira, acedia.
- 😈 "Dr. Strong" is a call for a patient to be restrained. East Ward C is probably where the victim was taken.

DATA RECOVERY

SYSTEM FAILURE: The most common reason for recovering data is an operating system failure. The easiest way around this is by hiding data in a disk partition. The partition is a chunk of drive memory that is independent from any operation system. It's a good place to hide data that's either too important to lose or be found.

UNDELETION: Data that is deleted normally does not disappear immediately. It waits in a segment of memory freed up to be overwritten as needed. Connections through the directory structure are severed, but big pieces of the data remain if one knows where to look.

HARDWARE DAMAGE: Spies are rough on computers. Bullet holes, blood, and being fought over while skiing down the Swiss Alps are generally not covered by an extended warranty. A hard disk failure can be recovered but it's usually only a one-time affair, recovering as much data as possible before sending it off to the scrap heap.

TACTICAL FACT-FINDING BENEFIT: THE FORGOTTEN SAFETY DEPOSIT BOX

Data Recovery from the trashed smart phone pulls the location of a bank with a long-lost asset, as well as plenty of pictures of the courier. Checking the bank record (Digital Intrusion, Difficulty 4) shows the box is still there with contents undisturbed. Dressing up as the courier (Disguise, Difficulty 5) allows the agents to check out the box. The item inside the box was something important to the Vampire Queen during her mortal life. Brandishing it gives the agents one round of surprise against her.

SAMPLE SPEND BENEFITS

- This paparazzo followed the lead singer of Firethorn everywhere. Lots of enlarged JPEGs later, and you have a nice collection of images of his entourage — even the ones who don't have shadows.
- You got what you needed from the laptop. You left a little surprise in the partition just in case any more "undocumented flu cases" break out. Gain a 3-point Digital Intrusion refresh after Dr. Wolscomb uses her laptop in the hospital's system.
- You can pull up a great satellite image of the whole complex, down to the tracks left in the grass by the guards. Get a 3-point Infiltration pool to break in.

SAMPLE CLUES

- ☣ You thought the blood ruined the hard drive. The blood IS the hard drive.
- ☣ You've seen a lot of weird things end up inside tower cases, but you never thought you'd see grave dirt.
- ☣ The band's demo has instructions from their Satanic masters backmasked into the seventh track.
- Fuqua should take the shot, even if the bagman drops the laptop in the canal. You're sure you can pull the code names from the drive after some time with a bank of hair dryers.

DIAGNOSIS

ABILITY FOCUS: HEMATOLOGY

HEMOCHROMATOSIS: Toxic condition brought on by too much iron, produced by drinking or transfusing blood to excess. Symptoms include cirrhosis (spidery veins, spotting on palms, red fingernail tips, rotten breath), breast growth and testicular contraction in males, chest and joint pain, and tanning of skin.

HEMOPHILIA: A hereditary disease that keeps blood from clotting or coagulating. It is more likely to be found in males. Scabs form but don't stay in place. Severe cases can bleed for days or weeks.

IDIOPATHIC THROMBOCYTOPENIC PURPURA (ITP): A lack of platelets in the blood, causing abnormal bruising or skin discoloration. Patients suffering from ITP run the risk of dying from internal bleeding upon suffering blunt trauma.

LYMPHOMA: A blood cancer caused by white blood cells acting abnormally. They live longer and multiply faster and damage internal organs in addition to the body's immune system.

LEUKEMIA: A cancer that overproduces white blood cells. Too many white blood cells weaken the other important parts of the blood.

POLYCYTHEMIA VERA: A disorder characterized by an oversupply of red blood cells. It can present as itching, angina, or in extreme cases, swollen and bluish extremities.

PORPHYRIA: A genetic condition characterized by overproduction of porphyrins, the building blocks of heme (a main component of hemoglobin). Symptoms include dark red urine, extreme photosensitivity, withdrawn gums, sensitivity to garlic and other strong odors, and aberrant hair growth, along with hallucinations, paranoia, and other mental disorders. In 1985, Canadian biochemist David Dolphin proposed porphyria as an explanation for vampire legends; his theory remains highly controversial.

TACTICAL FACT-FINDING BENEFIT: DEVELOPING TAINTED BLOOD

Studying vampire blood samples with **Diagnosis** suggests ways to counteract its strengths. Getting vampire blood requires a subtle jab with a syringe (Filch, Difficulty 4 plus Alertness Modifier) or unwilling donors (successful Weapons attack for no damage, against vampire's Hit Threshold). Once you've tainted the sample, it takes another successful attack to re-infect the vampire (Weapons with a syringe, or Shooting with a tranq gun). Exposed bloodsuckers lose 4 points from their Aberrance pool. Each successful Filch or attack roll acquires enough blood to create one dose.

SAMPLE SPEND BENEFITS

- Your license may no longer be valid, but sounding like a doctor never changes. You can get into the secure wing of the hospital.
- The bite doesn't transfer the condition. Gain a 2-point Reassurance pool while treating the policemen's wounds.
- Dr. Rogan's come a long way from breast implants in Beverly Hills. Maybe you'll ask him why a vampire needs a plastic surgeon when you show up in his foursome at the country club.

SAMPLE CLUES

- ☣ Results from a standard blood test come back meaningless; to the untrained eye, this blood sample is contaminated. You recognize that the sample is synthesizing all the blood types it consumed.
- ☣ The cruet inside the tabernacle was emptied of wine and filled with human blood. Great way to defile a church.
- The equipment stolen from the container matches up with what you'd need to turn a van into a bloodmobile.

ELECTRONIC SURVEILLANCE

ABILITY FOCUS: CLONING A MOBILE PHONE

Mobile networks have two basic structures. CDMA2000 networks identify phones by their unique number – depending on the network, this might be an Electronic Serial Number (ESN), Mobile Equipment Identifier (MEID), or Mobile Identification Number (MIN). Changing your phone's ESN, MEID, or MIN to match the target phone makes your phone a clone – capable of sending and receiving calls as if it were the target phone. Finding the target phone's identifier requires only a few minutes with that phone, or Digital Intrusion into the cellular network's computers. Some phones can be hacked into essentially broadband receivers, picking up all calls through a given CDMA2000 network relayed by the nearest cell tower. This rapidly becomes a Traffic Analysis problem.

The more common UTMS (built on the older GSM platform) depends on a specific piece of hardware in each phone, its Subscriber Identity Module (SIM) card. This card holds an integrated circuit that stores not just details of the cellular service but as many as 250 contact numbers "memorized" by the phone. Cloning a SIM card requires access to that specific SIM card and some specialized equipment (see *SIM Card Copier/Reader*, p. 68). In a Dust-mode game, cloning a SIM card usually takes hours or days; cinematic SIM card copiers take only one or two minutes. It might be possible, with Digital Intrusion into the cellular phone network database and a Cryptography spend, to decode the Ki (authentication key) of a SIM card you do not have access to – then, it's just Mechanics to build and code a duplicate SIM card.

TACTICAL FACT-FINDING BENEFIT: INTERCEPTING THE COURIER

Electronic Surveillance picks up on an exchange between an agent of the Conspiracy and another party; in between football talk, the agents get word of a shipment underway. The agents pick up on the courier by his Juventus cap (Surveillance, Difficulty 4) and plant a tracker on him (Filch, Difficulty 5). Tracking his movements over the next week fills in three more boxes on the adversary map, with the associated benefits. Any ambush of a Conspiracy asset along the courier's route adds an extra round of surprise.

SAMPLE SPEND BENEFITS

- The password to get into the the Crimson Club is "Ice skate."
- Of course you already installed cameras in the safe house. Gain a 3-point Shrink refresh when talking with a teammate.
- You've finally watched all the video you recovered from the cameras; the dead drop has to be under the acanthus tree, and the signal is a pink flyer stapled to the kiosk across the roundabout.

SAMPLE CLUES

- 👽 You thought that strange feedback was a white noise generator. It's the actual conversation going on between the Void Eaters.
- 🎬 The interference coincides with the reported times that Verhoeven's astral form visits with his minions.
- Yep, that's definitely bat sonar in the background of the board meeting.

FLATTERY

SPECIFIC PRAISE: Pay attention to your target's deeds. Point out specific accomplishments you find noteworthy. Show you were paying attention while they were talking. Use their name often.

CULTIVATE INSIDE CONNECTIONS: Express shared interests. Ask specific questions of likes. Tie stories back to previous things your target mentioned. Illustrate connections and shared experiences.

BE IMPRESSED: Point out accomplishments and express positive attitudes. Doctors want to show off their medical school. Authors want to be told of their creativity. Parents want to be told how adorable their kids are.

EMPHASIZE NON-PHYSICAL STRENGTHS: It's easy to compliment someone on their looks. Laughing at their jokes or reacting to their stories goes much farther in making a connection.

TACTICAL FACT-FINDING BENEFIT: BORROWING HIGH-PERFORMANCE CARS

Flattery shows how impressed you are with Diaz' collection of exotic autos. Let the experts pick the cars that will serve your purpose (Mechanics or Driving, Difficulty 4) so that rather than hitting the bank, you can hit the armored truck transporting the statue. Gain a 5-point team Driving pool for every point of Flattery you spent; each such pool is one more car you get to use.

SAMPLE SPEND BENEFITS

- Grimbaldi appreciates how much you enjoy the girls in his club. Gain a 2-point Streetwise pool for asking him about Naples's underworld.
- You congratulate Marion on her first gallery show since her attack. Gain a 3-point Shrink pool to help her recover.
- You let Detective Buchert make the collar and even wrote up a fake letter from Interpol praising him. The next time you're in Vienna, he'll owe you one.

SAMPLE CLUES

- ⊛ Telling Dr. Kirskov how much you loved her dissertation on pandemic management makes her happy to look at your viral spread algorithm.
- ☠ You put just enough camaraderie in your voice that the Air Force major leaves one of 17 cubes from the safe deposit box behind for you to study.
- The overworked video library technician appreciates the fact you got him lunch. You have full access to the archives while he takes fifteen for a sub and a smoke.

FLIRTING

LONGING LOOKS: Let your eyes linger on your target for just a fraction longer than they should. Long eye contact triggers the "flight or fight" reaction. Triggering reactions is what flirting is all about.

TAKE IN THE VIEW: Subtly check out as much of your target as possible. Start in non-sexual areas like the face, neck and shoulders. Subtle glances to more exciting areas can tip off a target to your intentions. If you get caught staring, laugh it off and admit you were looking where you shouldn't.

FIRST IMPRESSIONS: Picking the right venue for a first date makes a good impression. A clever or expensive date can transfer your target's impressions of the area onto you. Pick a place that confers the idea you want to get across, be it arty, hip, elegant, or sophisticated.

DRESS TO IMPRESS: Men want to look coordinated and slightly concerned with their appearance. Women want to look alluring without showing off too much. There's some truth to the idea that a first date is like a job interview.

SHARE AN EXPERIENCE: A little bit of danger goes a lot want to get hearts pumping. Skydiving or a running gun battle might be a bit much, but spending time ice skating or hitting a vampire film festival for research works. Connecting over an intense experience is an easy way to get inside someone's defenses.

SECOND THAT EMOTION: Mirror your target's reaction to stimuli. If they laugh, you laugh. If they show compassion, you show compassion. Emotional compatibility is one of the keys to physical compatibility. If you laugh at the same jokes, you're on your way to connecting.

LAUGH FIRST: It breaks the ice. Everyone thinks they have a good sense of humor. Laughing right away makes things more casual and relaxed.

SMILE: It seems like a simple technique. Smiling while the target is talking lets them know you're enjoying yourself and want to hear what they have to say. The subtler the smile, the better the reaction.

HOW DO THEY FEEL: If you're running out of things to say, let the other person lead the conversation. Ask them how they feel about a subject. Women will talk about their feelings more. Men will talk about their experiences.

TACTICAL FACT-FINDING BENEFIT: ROUTE AMBUSH

Checking out the club with **Flirting** tells you which girl the enforcer is really into. It's a lot easier to follow her (Surveillance, Difficulty 3) than it is him (Difficulty 6), and she's a lot easier to grab without too much of a struggle. A judicious call to him from her cell phone, and he's walking into a meet where you've mapped out all the angles: a team 10-point Shooting pool waits for him and his boys.

SAMPLE SPEND BENEFITS

- You can tell how much she likes you by how she laughs. Gain a 3-point Filch pool to lift anything out of her purse, or, lucky dog, her apartment.
- Hans likes a girl in a short skirt and a long jacket. Dress to impress, and gain a 2-point Bureaucracy pool when you ask him to look up bank records.
- You recognize the CIA agent sitting across from you. Maybe he'll unlock your handcuffs if you crack a joke about the night you spent in that hotel in Vienna.

SAMPLE CLUES

- ⊛ That ten would never leave with the three. When he spilled his drink on her, he doused her in pheromones.
- ⊕ The recordings of the confessions make it clear exactly at what point Father Marco lost his soul.
- While he's off calling his wife with an excuse about working late, you can rifle his office unobserved — or plant a camera to give your trap some teeth.

FORENSIC PATHOLOGY

ABILITY FOCUS: TIME OF DEATH

ALGOR MORTIS: Bodies cool after death. Corpses lose 2°C in the first hour and about 1°C per hour after that, reaching the ambient temperature in 16 hours. A body under water loses around 3°C per hour and reaches water temperature in about 5 or 6 hours. These times are wide estimates: blood loss, body type, and other factors can alter them.

LIVOR MORTIS: Gravity pulls blood downward in a corpse, discoloring the skin. These "bruises" set in from 30 minutes to 2 hours after death; moving the body later doesn't change the livor pattern. Corpses drained of blood, of course, don't show any livor.

GASTRIC ANALYSIS: A small meal digests in about an hour; a large meal takes up to 5 hours. By analyzing the amount of digested matter and its progress through the intestines, if you know the time of the victim's last meal you can estimate the time of death.

RIGOR MORTIS: Unmetabolized calcium ions in the muscles stiffen them within 2 to 4 hours of death, beginning with the muscles of the face and neck. By 12 hours, the whole body is at maximum rigor, which begins dissipating at 36 hours after death. By 60 hours, unless the temperature is extremely cold, rigor has entirely disappeared. The victim's fitness and biochemistry can alter these times, as well.

VITREOUS HUMOR TEST: The chemistry of the eyeball breaks down after death, becoming contaminated with potassium, urea, and hypoxanthine. With careful sampling (at up to 120 hours postmortem) and software analysis, these contamination curves can give a time of death accurate within 5 hours.

DECOMPOSITION: Putrefaction begins at death, becoming odoriferous within 24 hours and visible within 36. Bloating lasts about a week after that. Insects begin to infest the body in swarms after two weeks. A body left in the open can be skeletonized in 10 to 30 days. A buried body's fat and muscle tissue begins decomposing into waxy adipocere in about 3 months, completing the process in 18 months or so. Calcium eventually leaches out of bones within 50 years; older bones don't stick to moist surfaces.

TACTICAL FACT-FINDING BENEFIT: PROTECTING YOUR NECK

An analysis of the victims' **Forensic Pathology** indicates the upior's neck bite rendered the victim passive. Building combat-capable Lexan collars requires multiple prototypes (Mechanics, Difficulty 3) and rigorous field testing (Athletics, Difficulty 5 or Weapons, Difficulty 4). In a close combat, the armored collars raise the agents' Hit Threshold by 1 when facing the upiorny, who have to recalibrate their instinctive attack pattern.

SAMPLE SPEND BENEFITS

- The DNA results are back faster than normal -- it's a match.
- It gets lonely in the Munich morgue. Gain a 2-point Cop Talk pool when you talk shop with Herr Reiff.
- You once did make-up for a zombie movie. Gain a 3-point Disguise refresh to make your "death wound" look very convincing.

SAMPLE CLUES

- ⊕ The lack of blood in the pentagram carved on the victim's chest indicates it was done after she was dead. That may mean the vampire wanted to prevent others from taking her blood.
- 👽 The fingerprints weren't a match. But then, they also didn't register as fingerprints at all, due to subtle deviations in the patterns.
- ⊕ Though there were several cuts and bites on the victim, there was only mutated saliva in the bite near the femoral artery.

FORGERY

ABILITY FOCUS: IDENTITY DOCUMENT FORGERY

BIOMETRICS: The distinguishable characteristics that identify a human being. A photo, fingerprint, voiceprint, and DNA sample are all biometrics. The more secure a document, the more biometrics it uses.

SIMPLE ID: Most ID cards feature data of the individual and a photo ID. Making one of these IDs up is as simple as scanning a real document, altering it with a photo editor on a computer, printing out the fake on an inkjet printer, and then laminating the card. These work best for quick flashes or one-time uses.

COMPLEX ID: More secure facilities have IDs that use coded magnetic strips or holograms to make forging IDs difficult. Newer cards also include hidden chips or RFID tags that can be read by a transmitter.

TACTICAL FACT-FINDING BENEFIT: STOCKING UP ON SEMTEX

Forgery gets the team badges for a rail foundry in Brno that uses plastic explosives to shock-harden manganese-steel rails. Getting a stash of Semtex might involve dressing up in steelworker jumpsuits or engineer lab coats (Disguise, Difficulty 4) or re-routing a shipment in the dispatch computer (Digital Intrusion, Difficulty 5). The agents gain two full refreshes of Explosive Devices during the next operation, to reflect the plentiful supplies on hand.

SAMPLE SPEND BENEFITS

- Brentson knows it's a fake -- he asked you for two more to sell to some frenemies. You'll know who has bad ID, and Brentson will owe you one to boot.
- You must study the master if you are to replicate him. Gain a 2-point Art History spend to reflect your time when you lived and breathed Rembrandt.
- Nobody's going to question the General's papers. Gain a 3-point Disguise refresh when you hit the checkpoint.

SAMPLE CLUES

- The royal blue paint on this alleged Monet didn't exist before 1990.
- 👽 The signature on these release documents is printed by an autopen, or something similar. The letters are too flat and regular to be human-made.
- ⊕ The letter is in Aleister Crowley's hand, except it's dated five years after he died.

HIGH SOCIETY

THE MOST EXPENSIVE HOTELS IN EUROPE

RITZ-CARLTON HOTEL, MOSCOW
SUITE: Ritz-Carlton Suite ($16,400 per night)
AMENITIES: 237 square meters, rain shower and two baths with sauna
TACTICAL ADVANTAGE: Proximity to Red Square, the Kremlin, and St. Basil's Cathedral.

WESTIN EXCELSIOR, ROME
SUITE: Suite Cupola ($23,153 per night)
AMENITIES: Hand-painted ceilings, dining room seats 10
TACTICAL ADVANTAGE: Excellent angle on the Via Veneto below, private exercise room keeps agents from going soft.

CIRAGAN PALACE KEMPINSKI, ISTANBUL
SUITE: Sultan Suite ($27,704 per night)
AMENITIES: 180-degree view of the Bosphorus Strait, multiple LCD screens
TACTICAL ADVANTAGE: 24-hour butler service means backup is a phone call away.

LE RICHEMOND, GENEVA
SUITE: Royal Armleder Suite ($28,894 per night)
LOCATION: Geneva, Switzerland
AMENITIES: Three large bedrooms, marble bathroom
TACTICAL ADVANTAGE: Bulletproof windows offer sniper-free relaxation.

GRAND RESORT LAGONISSI, ATHENS

SUITE: Royal Villa ($47,645 per night)

AMENITIES: Personal butler, two large indoor pools, barbecue facilities, pianist (upon request)

TACTICAL ADVANTAGE: A private beach lets you come and go as you please.

TACTICAL FACT-FINDING BENEFIT: THE BIRTHDAY PARTY EXTRACTION

High Society gets an invitation to DeSilva's private island. The rest of the team can get in as the agent's entourage (boyfriend, bodyguard, etc.) and sabotage the fireworks (Explosive Devices, difficulty 5). When the fireworks display starts, the actual explosions distract security enough to give the agents one round of surprise for each point by which the Explosive Devices test result exceeded 4. Good timing and planning (Preparedness, Difficulty 4) has a boat ready and the doctor near the dock.

SAMPLE SPEND BENEFITS

- Regale everyone with a flashback about your time in the Monaco driving circuit before you gain a 3-point Driving pool refresh.
- The Laurent family is notorious in Paris, but their mistresses and bastards are almost as interesting if you know the dirt. Gain a 2-point History pool to track their influence.
- That fellow's tuxedo is off the rack, not Savile Row at all. Looks like we're not the only professionals here.

SAMPLE CLUES

- ⊕ The stories about the Black Mass orgies the Villanovas held on their island take on a new meaning now you know that vampires exist.
- ☉ The royal family married into itself one too many times. The vampires are related to some very twisted branches on that tree.
- Sergio never used to drink red wine.

HISTORY

One of the best things about games with immortal creatures of the night is being able to turn a famous (or infamous) figure into one so the players can interact with them.

ABILITY FOCUS: USUAL SUSPECTS

VLAD III DRACULA: Born in 1431. "Died" in 1476. Dubbed Vlad *Tepes* ("the Impaler") posthumously because of his fondness for impaling enemies and criminals on pikes. He was Voivode (Prince) of Wallachia, not Count of Transylvania, and mighty foe of the Turks. The name "Dracula" comes from his father, Vlad II Dracul, who received the name upon induction into the Hungarian Order of the Dragon in 1431. *Dracula* means "little dragon."

ELIZABETH BATHORY: The "Blood Countess" lived in Hungary from 1560-1614. Accused of collaborating with four others on the murder of 650 victims, though only convicted of 80 murders. Bricked into Cachtice Castle in 1610, she "died" four years later. The legend of her bathing in the blood of virgins to retain her youth originated in the first published account of her trial, written by a Jesuit in 1729.

LORD BYRON: The main character of the novel *The Vamypre* was named Lord Ruthven but based on the famous poet George Gordon, Lord Byron. There is some confusion over who wrote the story, as it was published under Byron's name but attributed to his doctor, John Polidori. Byron was known for his excesses: financial, romantic, and aesthetic. He died in Missolonghi, Greece, while assisting rebels against the Turks.

JACK THE RIPPER: Jack the Ripper is to conspiracy theories what Kevin Bacon is to modern American cinema. He stalked the Whitechapel district of London in 1888. The name comes from one of the letters to the press, which may have been created by reporters trying to sell newspapers. Jack has five dead prostitutes officially attributed to him, but his body count could include six more in Whitechapel and another six in Managua in 1889.

TACTICAL FACT-FINDING BENEFIT: TRACKING A FEEDING VAMPIRE

History narrows down the area where a similar clutch of killings has happened every century. Throwing a net over the area finds this century's feeding ground (Surveillance, Difficulty 25). Treat this as a continuing challenge (**NBA**, p. 50); each agent can make one test per night. Once found, the agents' Difficulties for Infiltration, Sense Trouble, and Surveillance of the site are reduced by 1 — as is the vampire's Hit Threshold against a sniper.

SAMPLE SPEND BENEFITS

- Your poetry professor at Cambridge wrote more books on Byron than you have passports — if anyone knows the name of the surgeon who bled him in Greece, it's old Wakeley.
- You read an account of an assault on this castle during the Thirty Years' War. Gain a 2-point Architecture pool to take advantages of the castle's secret passages and features.
- You've studied the Swiss Guard extensively. Gain a 3-point Disguise pool to when wearing their ceremonial dress.

SAMPLE CLUES

- ✪ Five cities. Five murders each. He's mimicking the Ripper killings on purpose, drawing a pentagram between the five cities.
- He wears the sigil ring that was supposedly buried with the Marquis 150 years ago.
- ✪ The spread of the vampire virus — Sevastopol, Istanbul, Genoa -- follows the same path as the Black Death in 1347. Perhaps some outbreaks then weren't just the disease.

HUMAN TERRAIN

Organizational culture is not just the feel of an organization. It's also how the organization hangs together when it faces hardships. It's the difference in the company culture of a web company like Google versus a traditional company like Renault. It also applies to religions, crime families, blood cults, and hospitals.

There are many elements common to large organizations. These elements overlap, often causing friction that an outsider can use to their advantage.

THE PARADIGM: The public core values of the organization. What it does, why it does it, and how it does it. A charity organization exists to collect money from wealthy patrons to distribute to individuals or organizations who need that money to survive. A church offers a safe place of worship and some feeling of spiritual succor. Exposing activities that go against the paradigm -- such as the charity putting a large amount of the funds collected up the board's nose -- destabilizes the work.

CONTROL SYSTEMS: How the organization monitors itself and makes sure it's doing what it sets out to do. This could be anything from a corporation's mission statement to the enforcers in a criminal gang making sure the street dealers aren't skimming off the top. Organizations that use positive reinforcement are vulnerable to attacks that remove the cool bennies for their members while groups that use negative reinforcement often harbor turncoats looking to start a revolution.

ORGANIZATIONAL STRUCTURES: These structures are how information flows up through the hierarchy and work flows down to the cogs. Everybody's serving somebody, be it the mailroom sorter and his supervisor or the CEO and her shareholders. Interrupting this flow makes the organization more vulnerable to outside interference. Remove the *consigliere* that knows all the passwords for the mob family accounts and they have to spend resources re-securing those assets.

POWER STRUCTURES: Someone has to make the decisions on how to move resources to achieve goals. A central power structure means one individual has a clear picture of what's going on, which means removing that individual brings everything to a grinding halt. More decision makers means more stability if one goes down, but increases factionalization. Kill the head of the vampire's blood cult and watch the bloodsucker make a hard decision -- come out of the shadows and risk exposure or wait until the squabbles wrack the cult die down and a new leader takes hold?

SYMBOLS: Obvious symbols include corporate logos or religious symbols. Subtle ones -- an executive parking space or a reserved table at a restaurant -- can indicate prestige within the organization. Recognizing such symbols makes mapping out who's who in a crime family, for example, much easier.

RITUALS: Religious rites are an obvious element, but mundane routines are important to identify. If management meets every Wednesday and someone is missing, that tells a story. It's also a great bit of info to sell to an enemy organization to let them spend time and money on a raid that benefits you.

MYTHOLOGY: Organizations value stories because shared experiences strengthen bonds between members. Loyal members feel like family and love sharing positive experiences. The value of these stories illustrate behaviors to emulate and warnings of ones the group does not want. The colorful nickname a mobster gets is not just a fun story to tell at the strip club.

TACTICAL FACT-FINDING BENEFIT: FINDING THE ARCHBISHOP

Observing the congregation, studying the cathedral's iconography, and listening to the sermons with **Human Terrain** detects the undercurrent of fear, heresy, and dominance in the parish. A little subtle interaction (any Interpersonal spend) or a little longer spent in discreet observation (Surveillance, Difficulty 4) notes the patterns of avoidance centered on the name of the late Archbishop Tomas, and on the old shrine to St. Thomas the Twin in the hills. If you get there just after sunrise, you'll have a whole day to explore it without too much risk, and with a team pool of 12 points in any General ability.

SAMPLE SPEND BENEFITS

- The MP here will be happy to find you a safe house. After all, you made sure she won the election. Reduce your Heat by 1 while in town.
- If you've infiltrated one NGO, you've infiltrated them all. Gain a 2-point pool in any Interpersonal ability used among Guardian-reading do-gooders.
- This branch of the Camorra used the same anti-spyware in all of its hideouts. Gain a 3-point Digital Intrusion pool to teach them the dangers of lazy software piracy.

SAMPLE CLUES

- ⊕ The term Black Mass might be a little old fashioned, but the similarities between the Catholic Mass and the ceremony here are unmistakable.
- ⊕ These bodies were hastily stripped after being executed. Looks like a couple members of the DelGenX cleanup team got sloppy and contaminated themselves.
- The squalor of the lab's flat means most of the money gets kicked up the chain. Flipping one of the dealers shouldn't be too hard if you flash him a little folding money.

INTERROGATION

CONDUCTING A POLICE INTERVIEW

ASSUME EVERYONE'S LYING TO YOU. The truth will come out after a check and double check of alibis and statements. Even people completely innocent of crimes have things they don't want the police to know. The guard comes up when the badge comes out.

FIND AND EXPLOIT YOUR ANGLE. Getting cooperation means using leverage against a witness. Previous records are an easy one, but talking about friends, family and other things important to an interviewee opens doors.

NEVER UNDERCUT YOUR PARTNER. There's a reason Good Cop, Bad Cop is a classic. Each interrogator pulls in a different way. One uses the carrot and the other uses the stick. Switching interrogators also can open up a new avenue of questioning. People don't like to ask the same questions over and over; subjects lose the advantage of rehearsed responses.

IF HE'S TALKING, YOU'RE WINNING. The longer the witness is talking, the more likely they'll let an important detail slip. The longer they lie, the more likely it is they'll slip up.

WHEN IN DOUBT, LET THE LINE GO SLACK. Guilty parties often overwrite their alibis. The more complicated the story becomes, the more difficult it is to keep it straight. Talking to police rattles people. Silence after a meeting with the cops sets the interviewee on edge. People on edge do rash things that can break open cases.

For more information about integrating police procedural style into the GUMSHOE engine, check out **Mutant City Blues**.

TACTICAL FACT-FINDING BENEFIT: STOPPING THE TRAIN BOMBING

However you work it, **Interrogation** gets the locations of the explosives from the bomber. Disarming the bombs on the train (Explosive Devices, Difficulty 3) is a no-brainer, but the covert approach (Disguise or Infiltration, both Difficulty 5) keeps the cult from knowing their sacrifice is aborted. Expecting the train to explode as it pulls into Belgrade, the cultists are caught off-guard: the agents' Surveillance Difficulty to identify the cult watchers decreases by 2 in that scene.

SAMPLE SPEND BENEFITS

- The IT guy gives up the network access codes. You can take a one-time 3-point Digital Intrusion

pool to hack the system, or flip him into an asset (NBA, p. 112) and get in any time you want.
- The terrorist reveals the origin of the strain. Gain a 3-point Medic refresh to treat any agents felled by the disease.
- Once you get your information, your friends in the GSG9 will be happy to rendition him. It's always nice when German snipers owe you one.

SAMPLE CLUES
- ⊕ You get the demon's true name from his Renfield.
- 👽 The farmer finally admits the craft was moved from the crash site to the local airbase.
- Dr. Mandel gave up that information too easily. It's a trap.

INTIMIDATION

BATTLE TRANCE: Psychological warfare is a grand tradition that stretches back thousands of years. The fearsome masks and warpaint of old are mirrored in gas masks and camo face paint of today. This transformation might mean that, in the heat of battle, someone might not feel the pain of a wound. This lack of pain has a demoralizing effect on the opposition.

COERCION: Getting someone to do something they don't want to through threats of violence. People often are willing to endure violence against themselves to protect information. Threatening someone like a relative or friend with the same can make a target cooperative. Demonstrating a violent nature as an example can also get a target to do something out of fear.

GASLIGHTING: Psychological abuse involving the presentation of false evidence for the purpose of altering a target's perceptions. This often included denying evidence of physical abuse or telling a target what they see isn't real. The term comes from the play and film *Gaslight*, which involved the antagonist convincing the main character she is going insane.

SCARE TACTICS: Not every intimidation tactic requires violence. Openly displaying weapons can cause an aura of fear, or persuade people to move through an area quickly. Persons aware of an agent's background might find spending time with someone trained to kill to be uncomfortable. Showing up unexpectedly can put a target off guard. If they want an agent to leave an uncomfortable situation, they might be willing to do something in exchange.

TACTICAL FACT-FINDING BENEFIT: SHOCK AND AWE

You time your entrance into the fight for maximum psychological effect (Explosive Devices or Preparedness, Difficulty 4 and Shrink, Difficulty 5) to make the most of your **Intimidation**. The enemy all lose 4 points from their Shooting pools as they fire off their weapons in a panic.

SAMPLE SPEND BENEFITS
- ⊕ You quote just enough of the Roman Rite of exorcism to get the thing's attention. Your fellow agents can attack it at a lower Hit Threshold: -1 for each point of Intimidation you just spent.
- The lieutenant is more afraid of you than he is of his vor. Gain a 2-point Human Terrain pool to use his intel to ferret out the important members of his bratva.
- Semper fi, Marine. He may be 20 years older than you, but your fighting spirit inspires the old sergeant to join in the battle. Gain a full Stability refresh if he survives until dawn … and make a 5-point test if he doesn't.

SAMPLE CLUES
- 🕷 The Renfield keeps licking the cut on his hand. He's looking for strength from his master — and that tell will likely unconsciously warn you of its approach.
- 🔯 👽 When you face down that kidnapper, he actually exposes his throat and belly to you — are his reactions those of a dog, not a man?
- The DGSE agent squares off with you in the doorway for just a second and then relents to let you see her boss. He's embarrassed at her attitude, and attempts to be extra cooperative to make up for it.

LAW

ABILITY FOCUS: EUROPEAN FIREARMS LAWS

CZECH REPUBLIC: One of the least restrictive regimes in Europe. Handguns are available to anyone over 21 with a clean criminal record who passes the proper tests. Concealed carry is also allowed without a permit.

FINLAND: Outside of police, only specially licensed security are allowed to carry guns in public. Tighter laws passed in 2010 after some high profile school shootings.

FRANCE: A license for hunting or sport shooting is required to own a weapon. Guns are classified into eight categories with some limits within, such as fully automatic weapons. France limits the amounts of cartridges that can be purchased for a weapon per year.

GERMANY: The two-tier Federal Weapons Act is considered one of the strictest laws in the world. A firearms ownership license allows a citizen to own a gun for a specific purpose if they qualify. A separate license is required for every weapon. A firearms carry permit is issued to those who need to carry a gun in public. Several special weapons, ranging from switchblades to automatic weapons, are completely illegal to possess.

HUNGARY: Automatic rifles are banned. Other weapons require the permission of the Hungarian Police. Gun violence is rare here. Their first and only school shooting took place in 2009.

IRELAND: Licensure is required. Each license requires a medical check, two character references and the installation of secure storage in the home.

ITALY: Three different types of license are available; hunting, sport shooting, and concealed carry. Obtaining a concealed carry license requires proving a threat to the applicant's life. Having been shot in the past is one such example of proof.

POLAND: Poland's strict controls result in one of the European Union's lowest gun ownership rates. Owning a gun requires submitting a psychological evaluation, resume, clean criminal record, a weapons handling exam and a reason to own the weapon. The psychological evaluation must be retaken every five years.

SWEDEN: Specific weapons aren't banned — collectors can own machine guns, if they have a license. Licenses, however, require a purpose and the permission of the police.

UNITED KINGDOM: Tightening laws ban most automatic or self-loading firearms. Ownership of most firearms is regulated either by a Shotgun Certificate (SGC) or Firearms Certificate (FAC). The SGC requires secure storage, no criminal history, and no medical or psychological problems, after which all shotguns can be purchased on a single license. The FAC requires conditions for ownership to be set by the police, in practice a strict limit.

TACTICAL FACT-FINDING BENEFIT: MOVING A FIREARMS CACHE

Knowledge of the **Law** provides a way to certify the agents as collectors and licensed antique firearms dealers. Getting the weapons across the border requires inserting the proper licensure onto a cover identity (Digital Intrusion, Difficulty 4) and disguising the broken-down modern arms as collector rifles (Conceal, Difficulty 5; Difficulty 4 with Shooting 8+). In addition to any other benefits a stash of assault rifles might convey, the agents get two full refreshes of Shooting during the operation to reflect their superior firepower.

SAMPLE SPEND BENEFITS

- It's amazing how quickly people get rattled when you throw some legal terms at them. The secretary folds and lets you past just as if you'd used Intimidation — but the security guard just sees a polite conversation.
- Getting into the courthouse without proper ID means looking the part. Gain a 3-point Disguise pool to dress like you belong to a white-shoe firm.
- You helped McKenzie out of a wee legal jam when he was smuggling for the IRA. Reminisce in a flashback that in retrospect uncovers Conspiracy activity in Ireland or London or both.

SAMPLE CLUES

- ⊕ The priest claims to be an exorcist, but he's remarkably uninformed on canon law. He's either an impostor, or a freelancer, or both.
- ☉ The wiretap records include not just the observatory, but also the houses of three local UFO witnesses.
- Captain Prokovich has no jurisdiction here. If you reveal his presence to the local authorities, that should keep him occupied while you look for the Count's painting.

MILITARY SCIENCE

ABILITY FOCUS: SPECIAL OPERATIONS FORCES

ALPHA GROUP (RUSSIA)

AKA: Alfa Group, Spetsgruppa A
SELECTION PROCESS: A modern descendant of Soviet Spetsnaz training, Alpha began as KGB special forces and are still FSB troops. They train similarly to the SAS, but with an emphasis on absorbing pain rather than operational endurance. The Special Purpose Service, rumored protectors of high level government officials, often draws from the ranks of this group.
PRIMARY PURPOSE: Counter-terrorism.
NOTABLE ACTION: Moscow Theater Hostage Crisis (2002). Alpha Group pumped weaponized fentanyl gas into the Dubrovka theater to disable the 50 Chechen rebels that took 850 hostages there. The operation was successful, but 130 hostages died, mostly from inhaling the gas.

ARMY COMPARTMENTED ELEMENTS (UNITED STATES)

AKA: Delta Force, 1st Special Forces Operational Detachment-Delta (1 SFOD-D), Combat Applications Group, ACE
SELECTION PROCESS: Standard physical tests that turn into a series of marches featuring increased loads and decreased times. The psychological portion of the exam includes a barrage of questions where the recruit's answers are dissected directly in front of them.
PRIMARY PURPOSE: Intelligence gathering.
NOTABLE ACTION: Operation Heavy Shadow (1993). A Delta Force sniper is believed to have been responsible for the death of cartel kingpin Pablo Escobar.

GROM (POLAND)

AKA: Thunderbolt, Jednostka Wojskowa 2305 (Military Unit 2305)
SELECTION PROCESS: The truth test pushes recruits to physical and psychological limits. 75% of recruits are trained medics or paramedics. Proficiency in at least two languages required.
PRIMARY PURPOSE: Anti-terrorist and commando duties.
NOTABLE ACTION: Operation Little Flower (1997). GROM captured the war criminal Slavko Dokmanovic in Slavonia.

GSG 9 (GERMANY)

AKA: Grenzschutzgruppe 9 (Border Police Group 9)
SELECTION PROCESS: Minimum physical requirements include running 5,000 meters in 23 minutes, 100 meters sprint and jumping a distance of at least 4.75 meters. GSG 9 members cross-train with several units across the world.
PRIMARY PURPOSE: Counter-terrorist strikes, special police action.
NOTABLE ACTION: Operation Feuerzauber (1977). Terrorists hijacked a Lufthansa plane and landed in several Middle Eastern cities. During negotiations to release German Red Army Faction prisoners, the unit infiltrated the aircraft on the tarmac in Mogadishu and killed three of the four terrorists with no loss of hostages.

PONTIFICAL SWISS GUARD (VATICAN CITY)

AKA: Cohors Pedestris Helvetiorum a Sacra Custodia Pontificis
SELECTION PROCESS: Males between 19 and 30 years of age, at least 174 cm tall, with a high school diploma or professional degree. Recruits must be Catholic, single, and have Swiss military training with certificates of good conduct.
PRIMARY PURPOSE: High level target protection.
NOTABLE ACTION: Last Stand of the Guard (1527). 147 Guardsmen died defending St. Peter's from German invaders during the Sack of Rome, buying the Pope time to escape.

SPECIAL AIR SERVICE (GREAT BRITAIN)
AKA: 22nd Special Air Service Regiment of the Regular Army, 21st (Artists) and 23rd Special Air Service Regiments of the Territorial Army
SELECTION PROCESS: 200 armed forces members are chosen twice yearly to try out for the SAS and SBS. The final exam includes two endurance exercises known as the Fan Dance (a 24 km march up a mountain twice) and Endurance (a 64 km march). Thirty remain at the end of the gruelling selection process.
PRIMARY PURPOSE: Counter-terrorism and commando operations.
NOTABLE ACTION: Iranian Embassy Siege (1980). In the first mission that brought SAS into the public eye, the unit staged a daring 17-minute raid resulting in the death of one hostage and five of the six terrorists.

SAYERET MATKAL (ISRAEL)
AKA: The Unit
SELECTION PROCESS: Gibbush is the twice yearly recruitment process where interested members of the already hardened Israeli Defense Forces are run through many sleepless nights to prove their physical toughness and mental dedication. Recruits must complete a 150 km march to receive their red beret.
PRIMARY PURPOSE: Long-range reconnaissance, airborne operations.
NOTABLE ACTION: Operation Orchard (2006). Though not officially confirmed, Sayeret Matkal played an essential role in the identification of the Syrian nuclear facility destroyed by Israeli F-16s during this operation.

SPECIAL WARFARE DEVELOPMENT GROUP (UNITED STATES)
AKA: DEVGRU, SEAL Team Six
SELECTION PROCESS: All applicants are drawn from United States Navy SEAL teams. Candidates are in their mid-30s, in peak physical condition, with multiple operations in a SEAL capacity. Serious injury and death may occur during training. According to one source, 16 highly trained Navy SEAL soldiers applied and only two were accepted.
PRIMARY PURPOSE: Intelligence gathering, counter-terrorism.
NOTABLE ACTION: Operation Neptune Spear (2011). DEVGRU engaged and killed Osama Bin Laden, the mastermind behind the New York terrorist attacks on September 11th, 2001.

TACTICAL FACT-FINDING BENEFIT: RAID THE ABANDONED MILITARY BASE
Once you've penetrated the perimeter (Infiltration, Difficulty 5), **Military Science** identifies the most secure location for the vampire's crypt based on the pattern of fortifications and guard patrols (Surveillance, Difficulty 4). By striking directly for the crypt, you keep the guards off balance and channelized into predictable attack patterns: their Hit Thresholds all decrease by 1.

SAMPLE SPEND BENEFITS
- You spot a telling tattoo on the paramedic's arm. He'll patch up a fellow Ranger with no questions asked.
- You casually mention a few of the operations you were on. Gain a 2-point Intimidation pool when dealing with this information broker.
- The strategy of these gang rumbles is strongly reminiscent of Vlad Tepes' 1462 campaign against the Ottoman Empire: infiltration, ambush, night attacks, and "scorched earth" campaigns against the dealer network. Thanks to this insight into their likely vampire master, you can predict their next action and their likely line of retreat.

SAMPLE CLUES
- ⊗ For some reason, none of the Croatian gangbangers retreated through the park, even though it was by far their best chance to avoid a crossfire. Could that bank of rose bushes have anything to do with their odd tactical choice?
- The tattoo on the severed arm is of a stylized bat over a cross: the mark of Spetsnaz, Soviet special forces.
- This Israeli Army major has no unit insignia — and Sayeret Matkal personnel are not allowed to wear their unit insignia off base.

NEGOTIATION
LEAVE THEM AT THE ALTAR: Backing out of a deal at the last minute can get a concession or two. It can also lead to feelings of betrayal and a larger chance the other side will try to get one over on the back end.

THE CALL-GIRL PRINCIPLE: Most services are more valuable before they are performed. Satisfying a need is more important than already having done a favor. Offering new services is usually easier than trying to convince someone to go with a new provider.

GETTING AUTHORIZATION: A common delaying tactic is claiming to wait for a higher power to approve a deal. Appealing directly to that source speeds things up at the cost of upsetting the original broker of the deal. Let the higher power smooth over any hurt feelings.

BRING IN THE DANCER: This ranges from small talk before negotiations to turning to enjoy whatever show the meet provides. It's an attempt to control the situation and flow of information. Whoever does it wants to seem like they are in charge when they may actually be at a disadvantage.

TACTICAL FACT-FINDING BENEFIT: SCRATCHING THEIR BACK

Negotiation allows for a little side work to prove your usefulness to the *bratva* underboss. Sneaking in to Evenk's club requires a night approach (Infiltration or Disguise, Difficulty 4) and sending a quiet message to other rival gangs (Weapons or Hand-to-Hand; you get one round of surprise per point above 4 on the previous test). Once the Turk is eliminated, the underboss agrees to hit the cycle gang. When you hit the Angels, choose between: bringing allied *bratva* soldiers (one Thug per agent) along on your hit, or using the *bratva* hit as a diversion, giving you a team pool (4 points per agent) in any combat ability.

SAMPLE SPEND BENEFITS

- You let Kellan think she got one over on you. While gloating, she inadvertently reveals who she's really working for.
- Nicolae "Boom-Boom" threw in some extras he had lying around the warehouse. Treat his stash as a Cache (NBA, p. 94) and get one item per agent for 1 point of Preparedness apiece. If you want a rocket launcher, helicopter, or similarly dangerous, exotic gear, it counts as everyone's item and costs 1 point of Preparedness from each agent.
- The Libyans owe you for getting them their weapons. They can keep an eye on things here while you follow the clues back to Egypt.

SAMPLE CLUES

- The selling price was far too low. Chavez' demeanor changed completely after you said the word *sangre*.
- ⊗ You can't understand what it's saying, but it really seems to want that dingus you took from the warehouse.
- ⊗ A quick bribe to the morgue attendant gets you the name and office number of an endocrinologist who spends way more time with dead bodies than her specialty would indicate.

NOTICE

AWARENESS: Make use of the three main senses: sight, smell, and sound. These most common senses often are taken for granted. Training them well means being able to locate and focus on important details. Did that Audi have diplomatic plates? Is that the same perfume? Where do the echoes indicate an exit? Good awareness allows for quick processing of information as well as a rapid switching of focus.

OBSERVATION: Watching a scene too often lets the mind wander. Agents looking to hone their observation skills can use anything from the arrangement of junk on a shelf to a day at the art museum. Catching on to what's unusual in a scene opens up the possibility for clues. Who's not looking in the same direction as the other pedestrians? Who's not reflecting in the surveillance camera mirror?

DEDUCTION: Once the difference becomes clear, the reason for that difference needs to be discovered. This often means asking why until the answer is satisfactory. Change the theory to fit the facts, not the other way around.

TACTICAL FACT-FINDING BENEFIT: FIGHT WITH YOUR EYES OPEN

In the busy hotel kitchen, there are almost too many possibilities for improvised weapons and sudden distraction. Using **Notice** lets you pinpoint the most useful and surprising items: a pot of boiling bouillabaisse, a hot meat skewer, the door of the immense stainless steel freezer, the sous-chef who's obviously tweaking on meth. Every spend of a Notice point in this fight lets that agent refresh 3 points in one General ability: hurling the pot or grabbing the skewer refreshes your Weapons, opening the freezer door into a thug refreshes your Hand-to-Hand, diving behind the suddenly manic sous-chef refreshes your Shooting as you have time to slap in a new magazine. The player has to narrate the suddenly surprising action — Notice means it's timely and effective.

This option doesn't hold for every fight scene, but every few operations, it can be fun to throw the improv door open — and let a Bulgarian mobster run into it.

SAMPLE SPEND BENEFITS

- One of the men in the restaurant has a gun in his jacket — it's a setup. You can plot an exit from the room that keeps civilians between you and him, or you can try a quick Filch and leave with a gun.
- The crime scene was carefully faked. Gain a 2-point Criminology or Forensic Pathology pool to use solving the real murder.
- You've deliberately lost a few hands to get a sense of everyone's tells. Gain a 3-point Gambling pool at this table.

SAMPLE CLUES

- ⊗ It's -5°C in Moscow, and yet his breath doesn't show up in the subzero temperatures.
- ⊗ The policeman's eyebrows haven't moved once while he's talked.
- The dead man's pockets are missing one thing: his cell phone.

OCCULT STUDIES

ABILITY FOCUS: LEADING A SÉANCE

GATHER THE SUPPLICANTS: Three is the minimum number of people in a séance. More people means more spiritual power but also means a higher likelihood of a non-believer dampening the energy. The group involved in the séance is the circle.

CHOOSE THE MEDIUM: The best choice is someone with psychic abilities or great knowledge of the occult. Even someone whose knowledge of the séance is merely academic is more useful than an amateur harassing the spirits for love advice.

DECIDE ON THE TARGET SPIRIT: Spirits are usually connected to a place or a person. If the spirit is connected to a person, someone important to it should be part of the séance circle. If the spirit is connected to a place, the séance should take place near the important location.

SET THE TABLE: Set candles on a table in sets of three. The number should equal or exceed the participants in the circle. An offering should be set in the middle of the table. Food is a common choice; spirits don't see much home cooking on the other side.

DIM THE LIGHTS: Make the candles the focus of everyone's attention. Gather the circle around the table. Hold hands to connect everyone's summoning power.

SUMMON THE SPIRIT: The medium leads a chant to summon the spirit. Something along the lines of "(Spirit name), we gather here to summon you for guidance and wisdom from unseen worlds." Repeat the chant until the spirit makes itself known, such as by a sound or visual cue.

ASK QUESTIONS: The spirits may answer simple yes or no questions or speak through the medium. Begin with simple questions and proceed to complex ones. Spirits unable to answer questions may get frustrated and take it out on the séance group.

END THE CONTACT: If the spirit is amicable, thank it for its answers before ending the séance. If things get out of hand, end the séance immediately. Either way, breaking the circle, extinguishing the candles and turning on the lights end the ceremony.

TACTICAL FACT-FINDING BENEFIT: SURPRISING SATANISTS

The blood cult's liturgies and rituals follow the Satanism of the Abbé Boullan, a degenerate 19th century French priest, with additions based on the narcotic mysticism of Boullan's rival Stanislas de Guaïta. With **Occult Studies,** you predict when their next ritual takes place, what time it begins, and how long it will last. You can also predict when they'll be completely blitzed on hashish. Once you find their dark fane (Surveillance, Difficulty 4) you can

burst in at the most psychologically and pharmacologically destabilizing moment. Receive one round of surprise *and* 3 points in a team General ability pool for every point of Occult Studies you spend to pick just the right moment.

SAMPLE SPEND BENEFITS

- The séance was a sham, but Gordon bought it. You can use his dead daughter to manipulate him from now on.
- While telling the colonel's fortune with Tarot cards, your cold-reading and leading questions uncover three things the colonel is worried about. (Ask the Director up to three questions, or plant up to three suggestions such as "You will meet a man in a white jacket. He is a trustworthy guide.")
- You claim to have an incunabular copy of Hypnerotomachia Poliphili from the 15th century. An old book-hound like Dyson can't resist a chance to see it.

SAMPLE CLUES

- ⊛ All the terminology on the hard drive is alchemical, used in the "Chemical Marriage" to create the Red Elixir of immortality.
- ⊕ The body is staked to the pentagram in a way that brings to mind exorcism rituals practiced in southern Nigeria.
- ⊕ The chant the lead singer is leading the audience in is an authentic goëtic spell for summoning demons: she is far deeper into the scene than you thought.

OUTDOOR SURVIVAL

Contents of a basic survival kit:
- Bandana or any other similar cloth
- Compass LED flashlight
- Two 20-kilo garbage bags
- Butane lighter
- Matches in a waterproof metal case
- Magnesium flint striker (it's good to have multiple ways to start a fire)
- Folding metal cup
- Multi-tool knife
- Over-the-counter painkillers
- 9 meters of parachute cord or rope
- Protein bar
- Sharp belt (hunting or combat) knife
- Small solar blanket
- Whistle or other signal device
- Ziploc bag
- Sealable durable container in which everything fits

ESSENTIAL ACTIVITIES FOR OUTDOOR SURVIVAL

START A FIRE: Fire is essential to survival. Bodies need warmth, food needs to be cooked, and if signal rescue equipment doesn't work, signal fires might.

BOIL WATER: The quickest way to purify water. Having multiple hard containers means a larger amount of water can be boiled and stored.

PREPARE WOOD: A good fuel for fire as well as important for building a shelter.

CREATE A SHELTER: Either build one from gathered wood or secure a natural shelter. Keep your supplies dry.

GATHER FOOD: Hunt or gather additional supplies. Cook and dress game and make sure to store it out of the reach of predators.

TACTICAL FACT-FINDING BENEFIT: SET TRAPS AROUND THE REMOTE SAFE HOUSE

Using **Outdoor Survival** to get the "lay of the land," you find all the trails that any enemies could use to approach the remote safe house. On those trails, you rig snares, dig deadfall pits, and otherwise set booby traps (*NBA*, p. 98). Roll your Mechanics and Conceal "attacks" for those traps normally and deal out damage based on the fiendishness of your descriptions and the degree of success of your tests. When the Conspiracy strike team reaches the safe house, they are shocky, nervous, and inclined to fire at shadows – their carelessness increases all agents' Hit Threshold by 1.

SAMPLE SPEND BENEFITS

- It doesn't take long to find a good spot to set up your sniper rifle. Reminisce about your hunting days in a flashback, and take a 3-point Stability refresh as you reconnect with the great outdoors.
- You've dealt with exposure before. Gain a 3-point Medic pool to treat the symptoms.
- You know just the place in the woods to dump a body where nobody will find it for months.

SAMPLE CLUES

- 👽 The plants look like whatever came through here was putting out serious radioactivity.
- ⚙ 🐎 These horses are spooked by that thing's presence and are ready to bolt.
- ⚕ 🦇 That's weird – bats aren't native to this area.

PHARMACY

ABILITY FOCUS: THE 10 BIGGEST STREET DRUGS

CANNABIS: The most popular illegal drug in the world; mostly consumed as hashish in Europe and marijuana in America. Most hash enters Europe from Morocco; hashish, of course, was the sacrament and etymology of the original Assassins, the *Hashashin* of Alamut in Iran. Marijuana growers in America use sophisticated hydroponics and aggressive cross-breeding to derive ever-more powerful strains.

COCAINE: The Sinaloa cartel in Mexico, run by Joaquín Guzmán Loera, a.k.a. "El Chapo," dominates the global traffic in coke. Smokable cocaine, or crack, acts much faster than snortable or even injected coke. Cocaine stays in the bloodstream for up to 72 hours, although its byproduct benzoylecgonine stays in the liver (and thus, the urine) for eight days (after a single use) and as long as 12 weeks for habitual users.

HEROIN: If you include opiate painkillers like oxycodone, possibly more popular even than coke or hash. Over 90% of the global heroin trade originates with poppies grown in Afghanistan; most of the rest comes from Burma. Licensed poppy growers in Europe sometimes find their plants drained of sap by "opium vampires," implying that even the staggering amount of Afghan and Burmese heroin available still leaves demand unfulfilled.

METHAMPHETAMINE: Meth requires labs (or trailers) full of toxic, flammable chemicals to make, but the profit margin is huge, even at the relatively low prices it sells for (€40 per gram, on average). Meth, or crank, or piko (in Slavic-language countries), is a massive stimulant that pushes the body from increased awareness into full-blown mania, hooking users by creating a cascading release of dopamine. It's replaced cocaine as the stimulant of choice for all-nighters that turn into two-weekers. 95% of the meth in Europe comes from the Czech Republic, where it is called pervitin. Known as "Panzerschokolade" to German forces in WWII (who used it to keep alert), its military use has dwindled in favor of the less-dangerous Dexedrine.

AMPHETAMINE: Speaking of which, dex, bennies, and speed became staples of the European club scene in the 1990s and continue to be a major European street drug of choice. Manufactured mostly in the Netherlands, Poland, Germany, and Belgium, speed is increasingly popular in the Middle East, usually in tablet form as "Captagon."

THE NEXT FIVE: Ecstasy is the sixth-most used street drug, followed by LSD. The horse tranquilizer ketamine, or "special K," is an increasingly popular club drug (especially in Hungary and Hong Kong) despite (or because of) its tendency to produce out-of-body near-death experiences ("the k-hole") in overdose. The ninth-biggest drug is temazepam, a prescription anti-anxiety drug that produces a sort of super-drunkenness if taken to excess. "Jellie labs" in Russia and Eastern Europe produce "vitamin T" for a growing global market. Tenth on the list is qat, a plant chewed for the euphoric and stimulant effect of its active ingredient cathione. Common in Ethiopia, Yemen, and other Indian Ocean nations, it has followed those populations to immigrant and refugee communities in Europe and America.

TACTICAL FACT-FINDING BENEFIT: PARTY LIKE IT'S 1999

Using **Pharmacy** whips up a mild hallucinogen that can be inhaled. Half the team installs the concoction in the fog machines at the club (Mechanics, Difficulty 4) while the other half gets into position as clubgoers (Disguise, Difficulty 3). When the executives of Orion Industries show up in the VIP area, release the gas. Once they're rolling, the team (wearing breathing filters) gains a 10-point Filch pool to get any sensitive information they can in the next few hours: smartphones, tablets, briefcases, laptops, and wallets.

MORE TOXINS

These writeups use the toxin format from p. 81 of the **Night's Black Agents** corebook.

ATROPINE

Atropine serves as an antidote against a wide variety of nerve agents, but an overdose of the chemical can prove fatal.
ONSET: injected or taken orally; 1 round
TEST: Difficulty 5 Health
MINOR: Refresh one die +4 Health lost to a nerve agent; reduce Major effect of nerve agent to Minor
MAJOR: Roll one die +4, apply margin between that roll and damage lost to nerve agent as further damage, Hurt; must make another test in 10 minutes

BZ

The U.S. Army weaponized this hallucinogenic nerve agent in 1959. U.S. stocks were officially destroyed in 1989; stocks supposedly remain in some Middle Eastern arsenals under the name "Key 15." Doses of BZ cause muscle weakness and ataxia, vivid hallucinations (including folies à deux with other users), memory loss, and extreme emotional variability (paranoia, crying jags, panic, euphoria, laughter).

ONSET: inhaled or ingested; 30 minutes to 4 hours
TEST: Difficulty 6 Health (higher for increased doses)
MINOR: -3 Athletics, Shaken; lasts 10 minutes (or three rounds in combat time)
MAJOR: Totally incapacitated by hallucinations, Shaken, Hurt; lasts 1-4 days

DMSO

This chemical, dimethyl sulfoxide, allows other toxins to be transmitted by skin contact instead of through injection or other means. An agent must make a successful Filch or Hand-to-Hand test against the target's Hit Threshold to apply the DMSO and piggybacking toxin. The target then makes a standard Health test against the toxin.

LSD

Famously used in the CIA's MKULTRA mind control program from 1953-1973, in rules terms LSD can stand in for other hallucinogens such as ketamine, PCP, mescaline, lamia venom, and so forth. Each will have widely varying effects (and rules effects) depending on dosage, setting, purity, and other factors.

ONSET: usually injected or taken orally; 30-90 minutes
TEST: Difficulty 6 Health (higher for increased doses)
MINOR: -3 Athletics, Shaken; lasts 10 minutes (or three rounds in combat time)
MAJOR: Severely incapacitated (Shaken, +3 to all Difficulties) by sensory distortion and distraction; lasts 6-11 hours

VX

The U.S., U.K., and U.S.S.R. built up stocks of this nerve gas until it was banned by treaty in 1997. Some stocks remain, as bureaucratic and safety delays hamper rapid destruction. Japanese terror cult Aum Shinrikyo synthesized VX in 1994 and sprinkled it on the necks of chosen victims.

Use this writeup for other nerve agents such as sarin gas with less deadly effects (Minor: +4; Major: +9).
ONSET: usually inhaled; 1d6 rounds
TEST: Difficulty 7 Health
MINOR: +6 damage, Hurt
MAJOR: +13 damage; +6 every hour until dead or treated

SAMPLE SPEND BENEFITS

- You've been undercover enough times to know how to fake taking a hit ... or keep sharp and roll with the effects.
- Anything can be a painkiller if you balance out the ratios correctly. Gain a 3-point Medic pool after raiding the pharmacy.
- Give him about fifteen minutes before the Xanax kicks in. Gain a 2-point Reassurance pool when it does.

SAMPLE CLUES

- ⊕ The incense was laced with PCP to produce some vivid visions, but some of the survivors' descriptions stand out as uncharacteristic of drug-induced hallucinations.
- ⊛ The marks on her neck remind you of the scratches that meth users give themselves. Except this one is far, far worse.
- ⊗ The poor bastard was turned in the '70s or '80s; that's not a talon, but an eternal coke nail.

PHOTOGRAPHY

Fake photography has been around as long as photography. Pictures of august leaders' heads on trimmer bodies fill archives. Dictators' photographs feature men and women airbrushed out of the frame when they fell out of favor. Even Sir Arthur Conan Doyle was convinced by photographic images of faeries.

Detecting fake photographs is still very much an art. Human perception is still easily fooled. Each digital camera manufacturer's code is unique. Analyzing the data from a raw photo can trace the picture back to the device that took it. But most published photos aren't raw. Even genuine photos are still run through editing software to remove imperfections and reflections and edited for clarity. Once a photo hits software, it remains up to the expert to determine if a given change constitutes editing or deception.

Incorrect shadows can give away a fake. The shadows thrown by a light source are usually of a uniform length. Making sure they match is painstaking work. Perspective projection is another tip-off. Usually a faked photograph requires another photo for the original image. If the perspective of a picture is off by a few pixels, that indicates fakery. The compression of a photo is usually linear. If a picture is bigger than it should be on a hard drive, there's a chance it's been manipulated.

TACTICAL FACT-FINDING BENEFIT: NOW GIVE ME SUSPICIOUS

Working a miniaturized camera is an art in itself. Your **Photography** is up to it, however, as you mingle with the swells and beautiful people at the reception. When your teammate stages the distraction (secrete and detonate simulators with Conceal and Explosive Devices, both Difficulty 3) you get clear shots of Tibor's bodyguards responding. Knowing which guards react fastest, and how they're armed, gives your team a 10-point General ability pool when you ambush Tibor's motorcade the next week.

SAMPLE SPEND BENEFITS

- Your photos capture someone cheating in the casino. You can use this to put pressure on the cheater, or as an edge when gambling against her.
- The infrared lens detected some odd heat areas. Gain a 3-point Conceal pool to discover hidden spots in the manor house.
- You always keep backups of your photos. And backups of your backups. Treat this spend as a successful Preparedness test resolving the question: "Do we have a photo of that?"

SAMPLE CLUES

- ⊛ Why are the MP's eyes flashing like they are emitting an infrared signal?
- ⊗ You took 37 pictures; each time, her face is somehow blurred or obscured.
- In the lower left corner of the image, you see the reflection of the shooter in the cracked glass.

REASSURANCE

ABILITY FOCUS: TEN STEPS OF A CLASSIC GRIFT

The golden rule of the con artist is that you can't cheat an honest man. This isn't some Robin Hood pablum; the best scams make the target complicit in illegal activities. By doing so, the mark is far less likely to bring heat from the authorities to the grifter's doorstep.

PUT UP THE MARK: Research a well-to-do individual, and finding weaknesses to exploit.

PLAY THE CON: Gain the mark's confidence through the use of the roper's interpersonal skills. Meet the mark where their defenses are down, like at the club or a party.

ROPING THE MARK: Introduce another grifter as the "inside man" component of a profitable scheme. Often, the roper becomes the "outside man" and plays against the mark to make him trust the inside man more.

TELL HIM THE TALE: The inside man shows the mark his method for making a lot of money in a dishonest manner: e.g., inside knowledge of a fixed bet, or a program that buys stocks a millisecond before the prices rise.

THE CONVINCER: Show the mark that the method works and let him have a taste of the profits. This is the riskiest part of the con, since the mark could walk after getting a taste. If properly played, the marks rarely do.

THE BREAKDOWN: Figure out how much the mark can afford to lose. Add a ticking clock element; tell the mark they can only use the method a few times.

PUT HIM ON THE SEND: Send the mark away to secure the funding determined in the previous step. Sometimes, sending a grifter with him (or after him) to make sure he doesn't stray is the smart play here.

TAKE THE TOUCH: The bait and switch of the con -- the bet is too late, the program doesn't work. The mark loses the money.

THE BLOWOFF: Get the mark out of the way as quietly as possible. The "cops" bust in; the grifters kill each other (or the mark kills a grifter) in a fake double shooting.

PUT IN THE FIX. If need be, make sure the authorities are compensated, either by a bribe or a tip-off on the mark's criminal activities.

TACTICAL FACT-FINDING BENEFIT: GETTING INSIDE THE EXECUTIVE BOARDROOM

Reassurance convinces the receptionist that Giacomo is sick and you'll be substituting for him today. Letting in other agents via the back door, the team plants tear gas in the ventilation system (Explosive Devices, Difficulty 3) and the boardroom (Infiltration, Difficulty 4). Whenever the inevitable gunfight breaks out in the building, you can push the detonator at any time to reduce all the guards' Shooting pools by 4.

SAMPLE SPEND BENEFITS

- Even after decades of drinking blood, the idea of absolution strikes her in a way that bullets could not. She promises one final confession, to you alone, as you watch the sunrise together.
- Few people could make someone covered in blood laugh. The sound of his hearty laughter calms the whole room down and gets them paying attention to your plan to escape.
- You strike up a conversation about fishing with the customs agent after you notice a picture of him holding a rod and reel on his desk. Gain a 3-point Conceal refresh to distract him from finding weapons in your luggage.

SAMPLE CLUES

- You're the first person who hasn't told him he's crazy. He asks for a cigarette to smoke to calm his jittery hands. He seems happy to tell you about what he saw.
- Your soothing voice calms the child. In a clear voice, Piotr describes the monster that took his papa.
- Your calm demeanor lets Giorghiou believe he has nothing to fear from the Gendarmerie. He tells you which officers are taking bribes from the human traffickers.

RESEARCH

ABILITY FOCUS: SECRET ARCHIVES

VATICAN SECRET ARCHIVES (ROME): Documents date back to the eighth century. Famous documents inside include letters from Michelangelo and Henry VIII's annulment request. Only qualified individuals make it inside, requiring a letter of introduction from a recognized institute or well-known scholar. Applicants must also specify what they are researching and why.

THE ARCADIAN LIBRARY (LONDON): A privately owned library with several rare volumes valuable for both Christian and Islamic studies. The owner keeps his or her identity private even as exhibitions in the British Museum raise the profile of the collection. Studies are available through Oxford Press Publications. The library also sponsors a professorship at London University's Warburg Institute.

STASI ARCHIVES (BERLIN): Contains over 50 miles of shelved information accumulated by informers and agents of the East German Stasi during the Cold War. The archivists redact all personal information before letting visitors see items; anyone may see their own file. No former Stasi personnel are allowed unsupervised access. Many photos are of home and apartments the secret police searched while the occupants were away at work. Around 15,000 sacks of shredded documents remain unfiled.

BIBLIOTHEQUE D'ARSENAL (PARIS): Since 1936 a part of the Bibliotheque Nationale, the Arsenal library has been in continuous existence since 1757. Beginning as a collection of medieval manuscripts, over the centuries it has accumulated documents looted by Napoleon from other European archives, periodicals and plays, books seized from French noble houses and from the Bastille during the Revolution, the Imperial Archives, maps and plans, and a massive collection of occult works. Legendarily confusing and unorganized, it might hold any secret document produced in Europe since medieval times.

POST SECRET: A modern archive testifying to the anonymity of the Internet. People from around the world send in postcards with secrets that are posted at *www.postsecret.com* on a regular basis. Hiding a vital clue or hint on how to take down a vampire in plain sight could be the desperate move of a dying ally or the insurance of a treacherous lieutenant.

TACTICAL FACT-FINDING BENEFIT: IT'S TOO DARK TO READ

During the gunfight, reveal that you took time earlier to **Research** the building's electrical blueprints. You can short out the main power junction on this floor (Mechanics, Difficulty 3) if you can get to it — or you can try blowing it to hell with your H-K (Shooting, Hit Threshold 5) from across the room. When you take out the power, you not only get a round of surprise, but your teammates' night vision optics give you the advantage, raising your team's Hit Thresholds by 1.

SAMPLE SPEND BENEFITS

- You know just the expert to call: Ilona Gilbring knows more about Swedish political corruption than anyone else alive. Treat her as an investigative Networking (**NBA**, p. 32) contact with a pool as large as your spend.
- This horrendous Soviet-era microfiche reader might stump someone who hadn't spent the prime of their life hunched over microfilm spools in a red-brick Midlands university. Not only can you operate it, but you can figure out how to snap an image of the relevant pages with your phone.
- You know just the books to skim to make yourself an instant expert on porcelain. When you "accidentally" meet Mr. Lee at the auction, take a 2-point pool in Art History to impress him with your vast knowledge and to cement your false identity as a fellow collector.

SAMPLE CLUES

- Faerie legends share many traits with UFO sightings and abductions; your research in those musty folklore journals indicates a "fairy mound" near where the saucers were sighted. Now, you've narrowed your search down from a whole county to a hilltop.

- ⊕ Well, now, isn't that interesting. According to the records in the archepiscopal library, the Baron's great-great-grandfather was excommunicated for making a pact with the Devil. And there's no record here that anyone in that family was ever legitimately baptized thereafter. Did the family fake those baptismal records — or did they fake the descendants?
- The Rosenbach Library record shows that Haughton looked at the handwritten Dracula pages two days before she died.

STREETWISE

A GLOSSARY OF CRIMINAL SLANG

Akademiya: Literally "academy," used by Russian mobsters to mean learning new criminal trades while in prison.

Associate: Someone who works for or with a Mafia family but is not considered part of the organization.

Bratva: "Brotherhood." The generic word for a gang within, or subgroup of, the Russian Mafiya.

Class: When an outlaw biker shows "class," it's usually an act of extreme violence or shock to the general public.

Crash Truck: The large cargo vehicle, such as a van, truck, or bus that follows a motorcycle gang's trip route to collect broken down and wrecked bikes. It often doubles as a mobile headquarters.

Earner: A member of an organization that runs a business to funnel money to the don.

Ghost Payroll: Non-existent employees that funnel money to a Mafia family or allow members to appear to have legitimate jobs.

Krysha: Literally "roof," used by Russian gangs to mean protection money.

Omerta: The code of silence, more directly translated "manliness," attributed to the Sicilian Mafia. A member swears to not sell out the organization, to take punishments for senior members, and to repay bad behavior in kind. Similar codes have been adopted by other organizations.

One-percenter: In 1947, the American Motorcycle Association asserted that 99% of motorcyclists are law-abiding individuals. Outlaw gang members call themselves "the one percent" or "one-percenters."

Suka: In the Russian Mafiya, a snitch, literally "bitch." Applied to any mafiya member who works with the authorities in any way.

Vor v zakone: In Ukrainian or Belarussian, *zlodiy u zakoni*; in Georgian, *kanonieri kurdi*; in Armenian, *orenk'ov godj*; in Azerbaijani, *qanuni ogru*. Literally, "thief-in-law," perhaps better translated as "legitimate" or "lawful" thief, meaning one who has taken the oath and follows the Russian Mafiya honor code. The rough equivalent in the Russian Mafiya of the American Cosa Nostra "made man."

TACTICAL FACT-FINDING BENEFIT: THE BUMP AND RUN

When you use **Streetwise** to call up your old friend Marko who runs one of the biggest chop shops in town, he is willing to let you into the garage to work on your own cars. While there, you can "assist" with some of the repairs on the capo's fleet. When you hit the convoy in transit, the capo's pursuit vehicles just don't perform like they should; each driver on your team gains a 4-point Driving pool to outrun the damaged vehicles.

SAMPLE SPEND BENEFITS

- You would ordinarily have to take weeks to search all over Naples for the "salesman." But since you and Luigi go way back, he can have his soldiers keep an eye out and report back to you tomorrow night.
- You notice the girl at the party is running a long con on Herr Dorstmann. You can back the girl's play and hijack the con for your own benefit, warn Dorstmann and collect his gratitude, or tip the cops and get them to owe you one.
- Your use of criminal patter convinces Raul that you're connected. You can use his back room to lay low tonight.

SAMPLE CLUES

- ⊕ The tattoo of the dagger running through the neck from shoulder to shoulder means the victim was a sex offender who served some time. Perhaps Waldemar tries to feed off only those whom he feels have sinned, those humanity can lose with few repercussions.
- ☾ You've seen plenty of drug labs, but the piece of equipment on the table is far too sophisticated to be simply refining cocaine.
- If the 39 Crew and the 8-Jack-8 are fighting on the same side, they must both be desperate.

TRADECRAFT

A GLOSSARY OF ESPIONAGE JARGON

Acorn: Asset, sometimes only a potential asset.

Barium Meal: Easily traced "chicken feed" intel (or outright disinformation) provided to a possible leaker or mole.

Black-boxed: Refused information on sources of intel or the reason for an assignment. "You have no need to know" is a classic black-boxing.

Cannon: The black-bagger who steals back the bribe, bait, or nugget (q.v.) from an asset or target.

Clancy: Someone who has read too many Tom Clancy novels; an unrealistic wannabe.

Dry Clean: To lose a tail; to escape (or avoid) surveillance.

Dubok: Russian for dead drop (**NBA**, p. 111).

False Flag: To recruit an asset ostensibly for an organization not your own: e.g., the Russian SVR agent claims to be a CIA agent when approaching the American businessman in France.

Floater: Asset to be used only one time, possibly entirely without their knowledge.

Ghoul: Analyst who searches graveyards and death records for suitable false identities.

Jarking: British slang for bugging, tracking, or subtly sabotaging weapons.

Legend: Fictitious history and documentation of your cover identity.

Litter: Seemingly innocuous material (theater tickets, ATM receipts, American nickels, etc.) carried in your pockets or baggage to support your legend. Also, *pocket litter*.

Nugget: Bait or reward offered to a potential defector or asset.

Parole: Password or countersign.

Playback: To reverse the flow of information, usually after turning an opposition asset: the opposition gets bad intel, you get good intel.

Reactive Target: Someone who expects your approach and responds with violence.

Sleeper: An asset left alone in place, ready to be activated for a high-value operation.

Svinya: Literally, "swine." Russian intelligence slang for "traitor."

Trail Your Coat: Attempt to attract the attention of an asset or enemy agent.

Uncle: Headquarters.

Walk-in: Classically, a foreign national who "walks in" to the embassy (or CIA station), delivers intel, and sometimes (more often in the Cold War) wishes to defect.

Walking Back the Cat: Retracing or replaying an operation in reverse to find out what went wrong.

⊙ THE MOSCOW RULES

As befits their origin in the deepest freeze of the Cold War, the Moscow Rules have no official version, no canonical authority. They were simply what Western agents had to do in order to operate in the capital of a totalitarian police state. They are a little too LeCarré for a default **Night's Black Agents** campaign, because they tend to tamp down the action. But if you like things cold and dusty, you'll like playing by the Moscow Rules.

1. Assume nothing.
2. Never go against your gut. It is your operational antenna.
3. Everyone is potentially under opposition control.
4. You are always in enemy territory. Keep your head down.
5. Never look back. You are never completely alone.
6. Go with the flow. Blend in.
7. Vary your pattern and live your cover.
8. Any operation can be aborted. If it feels wrong, it is wrong.
9. Lull them into a sense of complacency.
10. Build an opportunity. Use it sparingly.
11. Don't harass the opposition.
12. Carry nothing that cannot be discarded or destroyed.
13. Keep your options open.

TACTICAL FACT-FINDING BENEFIT: SLIPPING THE NOOSE

Your **Tradecraft** identified the gray-haired man as former KGB from his counter-surveillance techniques, which means his dozen goons are probably former Spetsnaz. You likewise know that Spetsnaz wet-workers are trained to hit a location from all sides, through all entrances simultaneously. You can't possibly take on twelve hard-frozen badasses, but if you abandon the warehouse right now, you can roll over one fire team and escape. Not only does your whole team now face only three Spetsnaz, you get a team pool of 12 General ability points to reflect your tactical offensive surprise.

SAMPLE SPEND BENEFITS

- You set the rose in the window overlooking the MI6 station. Your old station chief will remember the signal and meet you at the café without informing the Circus — for now.
- Moscow Rule No. 2: "Never go against your gut. It is your operational antenna." Reminisce about your Cold War experiences. Then, when you head down to the waterfront, gain a 3-point Sense Trouble refresh.
- You call Bogdan and tell him that he'd better have more information tomorrow morning, and that you want him to get imagery from the SBU's surveillance cameras to confirm it. However, since you spoke in elliptical terms about "the flowers" and "fresh oranges," Bogdan got the message but whoever is tapping his phone didn't.

SAMPLE CLUES

- LeGrange used an old trick of setting a hair across the threshold of a closed drawer to see if someone opens it. The hair is dislodged.
- ⊙ These faked vampire killings in Zagreb remind you of something you heard at the Agency. An Air Force colonel named Edward Lansdale ran

psychological warfare campaigns in the Philippines and Vietnam for the CIA in the 1950s and 1960s. One of Lansdale's specialties was faking vampire killings to demoralize the Communist guerrillas — and his protégé Paul Kelly vanished in Croatia during the Bosnia war.

- ⊕ It's very strange to put a dead drop right under the holy water font, especially the way this one leaks. Unless that's the whole point.

TRAFFIC ANALYSIS

ABILITY FOCUS: DUMPSTER DIVING

One of the most least glamorous but most useful ways of gathering intelligence on a source is rooting through their trash. In most jurisdictions, when something hits the curb, it becomes public property unless a local law has been passed. If an agent picks up the trash before the garbage truck gets there, she can find out plenty of information.

RECONSTRUCTING SHREDDED DOCUMENTS: All that's truly needed is time, patience and clear tape. Even documents run through a cross cut shredder can be put back together eventually. Wear cotton gloves while sorting to avoid transferring fluids. Keep bags meticulously tagged. Often, shredded bags are specially marked. Separate the strips by bag location, paper size, paper texture, paper color, and computer font. Weigh the strips down and when they are assembled, affix them in place with tape. Make photocopies or scans — new imaging software can match torn ends and broken letters much faster than you can sort through them.

A FEAST OF INFORMATION: Take-out containers suggest where poisons can be applied and delivery guys impersonated. Plastic spoons, forks, and knives hold employee DNA. The absence of these items suggests meals prepared at home. A run of used tissues suggests a cold working its way through the office. Old training information offers names and titles of employees. Insights like this can help an infiltration, choose an extraction target, or locate the real facility the team needs to hit.

IDENTITY THEFT: Agents looking for cover identities can find them in the nearest apartment refuse bin. Pre-paid credit cards can still be activated and used for a short period of time. Bills have all kinds of personal information listed including ID numbers. Even junk mail for someone that no longer lives at the address can inspire an agent to build a legend off of a discarded mailing label.

TACTICAL FACT-FINDING BENEFIT: KILLING THE KRAKEN

Traffic Analysis identifies the central hub of the ketamine smuggling operation as a secure, well-guarded warehouse. The black-baggers get inside the port by mixing in with the laborers (Disguise, Difficulty 4) while the hacker changes the manifest and RFID on a barrel full of explosives (Digital Intrusion, Difficulty 4). The barrel they inserted gets routed into the warehouse as a normal shipment of bromine and then "erases itself" from the shipping computers. At your team's discretion, you can press a button and make the warehouse far, far less secure.

SAMPLE SPEND BENEFITS

- The guard gets up to use the bathroom 7 out of the 10 days he works that shift at 11:30. Gain a 3-point Infiltration refresh if you hit the secure door around that time.
- After analyzing the recordings, you've got a pretty good idea who is who in the bratva. Add two new names or connections to the adversary map for each point you spent.
- Your stash of flight log anomalies makes you a smash hit on the planespotters.com forums. When you need to track that CIA black flight, you've got a global network of folks to keep an eye out for the tail number YR-DRQ.

SAMPLE CLUES

- ⊕ There are four parishes named after St. Peter in the area, but only one currently without a cross (it's being restored by a local woodworker).
- ☣ The outbreak isn't following standard infection patterns. It seems to be connected to the lunar cycle in its peaks and valleys.
- There's only one place in 100 kilometers that rents hearses.

URBAN SURVIVAL

ABILITY FOCUS: THE BUG-OUT BAG

Hunting vampires is a dangerous game, even for trained field agents. Agents are advised to keep a bag packed with essentials for three days on the run. The bug-out bag is for cases where a safe house is compromised and a new base of operations is not immediately available.

WATER AND A WATER CONTAINER: Staying hydrated on the run is important, and a solid bottle is useful for holding other fluids.

NON-PERISHABLE FOOD: Even in an urban environment, stopping at a restaurant leaves a paper trail for pursuers to follow.

A LIGHTWEIGHT BLANKET: Useful for warmth or as a makeshift shelter.

SOLAR POWERED OR BATTERY-POWERED LIGHTING AND RADIOS: Flashlights light the way in out of the way hiding spots and a radio keeps you up to date on your levels of Heat. Unlike a smartphone, nobody can track or hack a transistor radio.

PERSONAL MEDICATIONS: Multivitamins, anti-diarrhea medications, and the pills the nice doc prescribed to keep the nightmares away.

A FIRST AID KIT: Soft-sided kits are the most flexible.

MULTINATIONAL CASH: Euros or dollars. Keep cash in a waterproof container. ATMs and plastic leave a paper trail. If you plan on crossing borders don't forget a passport.

WARM CLOTHES AND COMFORTABLE SHOES: Reversible jacket, sunglasses and ball cap to conceal your face, jeans or work trousers, and spare underwear. Rolling clothes optimizes space the best, so no tuxedos.

TOOLS: Multipurpose tools save space and have a variety of uses.

PROTECTION AND SELF-DEFENSE: Take a weapon of choice with you, ideally something that won't trigger suspicion if you're found with it: a claw hammer, for example. A good space-saving choice is a nice, heavy metal flashlight.

TACTICAL FACT-FINDING BENEFIT: SAFE HOUSE RAID

Urban Survival illuminates a route across the rooftops the gang overlooked. Getting on the roof involves a jump from the nearby roof (Athletics, Difficulty 4), or a silent shinny down a fire escape on the building across the air shaft (Infiltration, Difficulty 5). Anyone shooting down through the skylights in the roof gains +1 to their Hit Threshold and a round of surprise.

SAMPLE SPEND BENEFITS

- You know how to cut through the red tape in Athens: swear in French, and hint that helping you will annoy the Germans. Gain a 2-point Bureaucracy pool to speed up any essential licensures.
- You're in Kiev again! This will be just like old times. Reminisce about the good old days while chowing down on the best salo and onions in the world at Spotykach in Volodymyrska Street. God, you love this town. Refresh your Stability with a confidence die roll (*NBA*, p. 92).
- You know of an abandoned school where you can lay low for a few days.

SAMPLE CLUES

- 👁 The graffiti is clear -- this tenement used to be gang housing, but their tags are painted over with the red eye-L. The building is a nest of the infected.
- 👁 The look in the old woman's eyes tells you what the locals know. She faced these things when she was your age and she lived. You give her a packet of Gauloises and an unused Metro card and she tells you all about the infestation of '58.
- From the wrappers and trash in the corners, you'd say the killer was here for about two weeks waiting for a call from the smashed cell phone in the corner.

VAMPIROLOGY

ABILITY FOCUS: THE VAMPIRE SUBCULTURE

Beginning in the late 1970s, a subculture of self-identified "vampires" emerged within the Goth and BDSM communities and grew along with its two parent cultures. It blew up in the 1990s with the publication and popularity of the roleplaying game ***Vampire: the Masquerade*** and even moreso its live-action ruleset. Other influences include the Thelemite and neopagan religions; many vampires practice magickal rituals or "energy workings," and most New Age publishers have vampire grimoires and liturgies in their catalog. The modern "vampire community" (perhaps 10,000 people, and as many hangers-on) remains closely linked to its origins, with "vampire nights" common at some Goth and industrial clubs in America, Asia, and Europe, and dedicated "vampire clubs" in cities such as Toronto, Hamburg, Amsterdam, Tokyo, and New York. (Shanghai got its first vampire club in 2011.) Some vampires drink blood, usually consensually within a fetish or BDSM scene; a larger group self-identifies as energy vampires or psychic vampires. Many vampires, especially psi-vamps, avoid the scene and practice their habit secretively. Many self-identified vampires also avoid mirrors, sunlight, garlic, and other taboo items drawn from broader vampire pop culture. Other dedicated lifestylers wear tinted FX contacts or even special denture fangs – all potentially confusing to dedicated hunters of the true Conspiracy.

A GLOSSARY OF VAMPSPEAK

Ambient feeding: Taking energy from a crowd or group.
Beacon: The energy signature given off by fellow vampires, especially latent or potential ones. You spot a beacon with your *vampdar*.
Black hole: An energy vampire unable to stop feeding.
Black swan: A non-vampire familiar with, and accepting of, the vampire community.
Black Veil: The generally accepted code of conduct and ethics followed by conscientious members of the subculture.
Combo: A vampire capable of feeding on blood or energy: "I'm a psi/sang combo."
Donor: Someone who gives or sells their blood or energy to a vampire. Also *source*.
Fashion vamp: Someone who just likes to dress up as a vampire.
Grazing: Feeding indiscriminately; vampspeak for "slutting around."
Haven: "Vampire-safe" hangout space; usually a club, but it might be a coffee shop, apartment, bookstore, or the like.
House: A smaller social group within the subculture. A house might be a few roommates or a global "tribe." Major Houses include Kheperu, Sahjaza, Quinotaur, and Eclipse.
Human: A person who doesn't identify as a vampire. Also *mundane, mortal*.
Invisible: Someone expelled from the subculture. Also *sin nomine*.
Leech: Derogatory term for a blood vampire.
Lifestyler: Someone who lives the vampire lifestyle but who may or may not believe they need to drink blood or energy. Also *vampyre*.
Long Night: Vampire holiday, on the winter solstice.
Neo: Someone who "converted" to vampirism, rather than being born a (latent) vampire.
OSV: The Ordo Strigoii Vii is a large House of psi vampires; they disavow blood vampires.
Otherkin: A person who identifies as some other sort of supernatural being, usually a fae or lycanthrope. *Therians* are reincarnated animals, not supernatural creatures.
Parasite: Derogatory term for an energy vampire. Also *soul sucker*.
Psi-vamp: Energy vampire. Also *prana-vamp, pranic*.
Real vampire: A person who believes he needs blood or energy for his health. Also *HLV (human living vampire)*.
Sanguinarian: A person who believes he needs to drink blood; a blood vampire. Also *sang, sang vamp*.
Sanguinarium: The loosely affiliated clubs, organizations, Houses, businesses, authors, bands, etc.

who predominate in the vampire subculture. Some vampires avoid the Sanguinarium as too full of posers, fashion vamps, and wannabes.

Subs: What you drink or eat when you can't get blood: e.g., rare steak, hot sauce, chocolate syrup.

Twoofing: Suffering from a sudden attack of vampiric thirst or withdrawal symptoms. Also *vamping out*.

White swan: Someone familiar with, but hostile to, the vampire community.

TACTICAL FACT-FINDING BENEFIT: THE REMINGTON ALLERGIST

Knowledge of **Vampirology** gives you a wide variety of possible banes to try out. Cleverly, before tracking the thing to its lair, you spent a night hand-loading shotgun shells (Shooting or Mechanics, Difficulty 2) with rock salt, aloe vera, minced garlic, hawthorns, rose oil, silver shot, holy medals, and splinters from nine different kinds of wood. When you start blasting away in a memorized sequence, you do only -2 damage with most of the hits — but the first 6 you roll on your damage die is the shot with the true bane in it. It does damage as a normal shotgun shell, plus any damage from the bane itself (*NBA*, p. 139), plus giving the team one round of surprise while the creature reacts with impotent rage. To remember which load had the effect ("was it ten shots, or only nine?"), make a Preparedness test at a Difficulty of 3, adding +1 to the Difficulty for every 3 points of Health or Stability lost *by the shotgun wielder* during the fight. If you succeed, you know something that can kill vampires, or at least royally tick them off. (The team may not get that round of surprise in future combats, now that the fiends know the agents know their weakness.)

Obviously, if the vampires in your campaign don't actually have a true shotgun-usable bane that Vampirology might suggest, this TFFB provides nothing but a false sense of confidence: everybody on the team gets a 3-point Stability refresh before the battle or retroactively if they activate this TFFB during the scrap.

SAMPLE SPEND BENEFITS

- Learning about vampires means learning about blood. Gain a 2-point Criminology pool to read the blood spatter evidence.
- Checking over the CCTV feed from the park, you see a white carriage horse shy and rear in the bridle path, near that statue. In Albanian folklore, a white horse refuses to pass a vampire's resting place.
- There are others out there who know the truth. They are just as deadly and paranoid as your team, but by revealing a few select secrets of the undead, you can convince one of them to meet you one on one and compare notes.

SAMPLE CLUES

- ◉ The aliens come from a red dwarf star — maybe they, like fictional vampires, are sensitive to ultraviolet light, the kind our sun emits in greater quantities than their home star.
- ◉ ◉ This man's throat was simply torn out. The vampire that did this must have been starving, or rabid. It will almost certainly strike again tomorrow night.
- Rumors persist of an annotated copy of *Dracula* that's been passed down through intelligence channels when government agents run afoul of real vampires.

GENERAL ABILITIES

For each General ability, this section provides specific uses, information, and techniques to increase both the seeming plausibility and the technothriller flavor of your agent's badassery. If the ability can be used investigatively (which most General abilities can, if you try hard enough) each writeup includes some sample clues similar to those in the Investigative abilities section.

Each of the General Abilities includes one or more **new cherries** for agents to choose if they so desire. Players who want to switch cherries should discuss the change with their Director the next time an opportunity to spend experience arises. Cherries that never found use can be easily wiped away. Ones that came into play can be switched once the Director and the player arrange a mutually agreeable fiction. Perhaps Mr. Blanc's devilish luck ran out after that close scrape in Budapest. Now, he throws himself back into games of chance, honing his abilities to detect lies.

Some Directors may also allow more than one cherry in a skill. High-octane series featuring supercompetent agents suit this possibility best, but any game can benefit at the discretion of the Director. Multiple cherries in a single skill follow this rule:

- When a General ability reaches 8 rating points, pick the cherry you want to use. It does not change.
- You can add a second cherry (if available) when you have 14 rating points in that ability.
- You can add a third cherry (if available) when you have 20 rating points in that ability, and so forth.

◉ As in the corebook, in a Dust mode game only the cherries marked with the Dust icon are available.

Finally, all Directors interested in increasing the success rate of their players' actions should see the optional Mastery rule in the nearby box.

ABILITIES ■ GENERAL ABILITIES

37

OPTIONAL: MASTERY

This rule radically reduces the chance of total failure on ability tests.

It may be used for tests of any General ability in which your rating is 8 or above. When you spend from that pool to add to an ability test, you may spend 1 point to instead get an extra die. As with all other spends, you must choose to take the extra die or the extra point before you roll any dice. Roll both dice and keep the larger of the two results; add any other spent points to get your total result.

Beatrice has Shooting 9. She takes a careful bead on the Renfield with her Glock and squeezes the trigger. Her player spends 3 points: the first to get an extra die, and the next 2 to add to her result. She rolls a 1 and a 4 on the dice, so she dumps the low die (the 1) and adds 2 to her higher result (the 4) for a total of 6. That beats the Renfield's Hit Threshold of 5, so Beatrice's shot hits the blood-fiend.

You may only get one extra die per roll. You never add both dice. Rolling a 6 on either die is a "natural" or "unmodified" 6 for the purposes of other rules, maneuvers, and cherries.

☾ This option is not available in Dust mode.

🔥 This option cannot be used for Stability tests in Burn mode.

This optional rule can be used in any GUMSHOE game modeling cinematically competent characters (such as **Ashen Stars** *or Pulp-mode* **Trail of Cthulhu***), or in campaigns or play groups where failure is more than usually annoying.*

That said, it should never be used for Stability tests in **Trail of Cthulhu***.*

ATHLETICS

ABILITY FOCUS: PARKOUR

Derived from *parcours*, French for "journey." The "art of displacement" was developed by the Belle family as a way to make the most efficient movements in dangerous situations. Parkour is actually a conservation of movement, making sure every move propels the *traceur* (runner) forward. Speed, focus, and intent are the keys to parkour. Freerunning, a similar modern movement technique, is more acrobatic in its expression.

SOME PARKOUR TECHNIQUES

BODY ROLL: By landing and rolling to dispense the momentum of a jump, a *traceur* can make longer jumps and farther falls without injury.

CAT JUMP: Jump with your arms extended, to land with your arms or hands on the top of the obstacle and feet touching the obstacle. Also called the *arm jump* and *saut de bras*.

CLIMB UP: To climb a wall from the cat jump, use your legs to propel you, not your arms to pull you. Push in, not up, with your feet. Move explosively and smoothly; don't struggle with the wall. Hop your hands forward, then lean over the wall.

DEMI TOUR: Hit a rail or wall with both hands, pull up, pivot on your left hand and drop over the wall into a hang. Also *turn vault*.

MONKEY: Vaulting an obstacle with your legs between your arms, an excellent way to get more distance or clear large objects. Also called the *Kong vault* and the *cat pass*.

PASSEMENT: A vault over an obstacle featuring minimal contact with the object. One or two hands at the most.

TIC TAC: To gain height and change direction by pushing one foot off an object or obstacle.

TOP OUT: Swinging your legs over an edge after a wall climb rather than setting foot on the wall.

UNDERBAR: Jump feet first through an opening, grabbing onto the bar or lintel above you to propel your torso through.

WALL PASS: Running toward the wall, converting your momentum to height by running up the wall, catching the top of the wall with your hands, and pulling yourself over the wall. Also *passe muraille*.

INVESTIGATIVE SAMPLE CLUES

- ☻⊕ This descender was never actually engaged. This guy didn't rappel down the walls at all, he floated down them.
- The world record for the long jump is under 9 meters. It's ten meters to that roof. And yet she jumped it.
- The man in the khakis has gym muscles, not combat muscles. He's not a real mercenary.

NEW CHERRIES

These cherries are available to characters with 8 or more rating points in Athletics.

ROLL THROUGH THE PAIN

After a failed Athletics roll, you may spend points from your Health pool to turn the failure into a success. You may spend Health for Athletics on a one for one basis. You may not spend your Health below 0 in this manner.

⚇ RUNNERS INTUITION

Spend 1 pool point of Athletics to size up another character's athletic ability, constitution, or degree of fitness. The Director will tell you if your opponent's Athletics *rating* is greater than, lesser than, or within 1 point of your rating.

CONCEAL

ABILITY FOCUS: STASH SPOTS

THE FALSE STASH: Consider splitting whatever valuables you have into two spots. Leave a smaller stash in an obvious place. Make sure the fake stash is large enough to convince any thief that there's no reason to continue searching.

FROZEN ASSETS: Anything unaffected by the cold can be wrapped in aluminum foil -- or ground beef! -- and put in the freezer. Thieves are unlikely to raid the fridge while ransacking the safehouse.

FRAME JOB: Searching often leads to take a picture off the wall, but only trained investigations search the picture itself. Thin documents fit between the matte and the picture.

THE PLANT: Fake plants don't need water, but they can have important items buried in the soil.

THE TOY BOX: Burglars rarely toss kids' rooms since they are cluttered and rarely hold valuable items. Stashing important items inside a toy, especially if there are a lot of toys to provide cover, will keep it hidden in plain sight.

THE LIBRARY: Bibliophiles can stash documents in the pages of a book. Shelves might be cleared looking for safes or stashboxes, but few have the time or energy to leaf through every book.

COMMON CONTAINERS: Aspirin bottles, coffee cans, or anything else common in a household. Cereal boxes are a favorite of drug users.

INVESTIGATIVE SAMPLE CLUES

- ⊕ ☠ There is garlic powder all over this car trunk. That wouldn't work to mask smells from drug-sniffing dogs ... but it might hide something from a vampire shapeshifted into a dog or a wolf.
- 👽 You catch a look at the screen of the airport baggage X-ray. You've seen everything imaginable go through one of those, but you've never seen this kind of moiré pattern, even from radioactive metal.
- The narcotic was pressed into potato chip form and hidden in the Pringles tube.

NEW CHERRY

This cherry is available to characters with 8 or more rating points in Conceal.

BUG STASHER

When you plant an electronic listening device and spend 1 Conceal pool point, it won't be found without specialized equipment and a major SIGINT-agency level sweep unless someone who knows it's there reveals its existence.

DIGITAL INTRUSION

It's more than just defeating their code with yours. Other methods include:

WIRETAPPING: The Internet makes extensive use of phone lines. Phone lines are vulnerable to wiretapping. This includes both diverting data and copying it and listening in on VoIP electronic phone calls. Wireless networks are also vulnerable if the WPA or WEP key is cracked.

PHISHING: Masquerading as a trustworthy entity to acquire user names, passwords or important numbers like credit cards or social security. Phishers send out emails pretending to be an ISP looking to update contact information, or banks asking to verify a large purchase the target didn't make. *Vishing* is voice-phishing, using VoIP to fake calls from seemingly trusted numbers.

KEYSTROKE LOGGING: More commonly known as keylogging. Keylogging tracks the strokes on a keyboard through various methods. Knowing which keys are pressed when makes discovering passwords, browser contents, or anything else easy. Multiple software keyloggers exist that can be installed or even "infected" onto a target computer. Hardware keyloggers can be plugged into the back of a tower or installed inside the casing of a laptop. Acoustic keyloggers detect the subtle differences in the sounds of keys being struck.

WARWALKING: Moving your location in search of an open WiFi network. The better your antenna and the better your sniffing software, the less you have to move, but you should stay on the move anyway. One tip: Kids who play Pokemon have their controllers on all the time. Find a family with a kid who plays Pokemon and you have an always-open door.

SOCIAL ENGINEERING: One of the biggest jokes in IT departments around the world is the computer problem classified as PEBKAC: Problem Exists Between Keyboard and Chair. The human element is the weakest link in most systems, because humans forget security procedures, use lazy passwords like "password" on secure systems, or pay bills on unsecured wireless networks.

INVESTIGATIVE SAMPLE CLUES

- By analyzing the code and the shortcuts the hacker used, you can identify him as a Chinese hacker who wants you to think he's Ukrainian. That means Chinese MID most likely — you know the names of the four men most likely to use that dodge.
- This so-called Swiss bank account interface is a mockup, running over a keylogger most likely. They're faking the transfer to get the mark's account number.

- ⊕ They left all these obsolete drives and machines in place, but they replaced the CRT monitors with brand-new LCD screens. Is it because CRT monitors emit ultraviolet light, and LCD monitors don't?

NEW CHERRIES

These cherries are available to characters with 8 or more rating points in Digital Intrusion.

THE HEAD OF A PIN

You are constantly aware of people when they enter their passwords, PINs, or other safeguards near you. If you can see a target type in their password, you can use it later. It doesn't matter what precautions they take to protect it -- you can guess it from finger position, or a reflection from the window, or a picture of their wife on the desk, or whatever amazing deduction sounds plausible.

👽 MR. CLEAN

You make a point to wipe all electronic traces of your contacts. Any digital devices you create can't be traced back to you. You spend your off-camera time deleting hard drives and cracking cell phone carrier databases for fun. An agent may leave a device in the field that can give up information, but only from the last time you handled it for a wipe.

DISGUISE

The principles of altering your appearance are fundamental, regardless of the specific technology or techniques you use to attain them.

FIGURE OUT WHAT STANDS OUT: Decide upon your most noteworthy characteristics. Ask two fellow agents what they think they are. Ask two complete strangers, one man and woman, what stands out. Compare the lists. The top five are things that need to be changed.

GO THE OTHER WAY: If you have short hair, wear a wig. If you have a penchant for color, wear dark clothes. Wear bulky, padded clothes to look heavier. Make yourself taller with lifts. Make yourself shorter by slouching. Wear square or boxy glasses to mess with facial recognition, both software and human.

A DISTRACTING DETAIL: Draw attention toward something. It can be anything from a fake scar to a larger bust line. People looking at your diversion aren't looking at your face.

QUICK CHANGE: If there isn't enough time for a full disguise, you can change a few things to throw off pursuit. Wear a wig with different colored hair from yours, and junk it as soon as you're out of sight. Wear a ball cap pulled over your eyes, and toss it or walk through a stadium-bound crowd. Wear a reversible jacket, light under dark. Ideally, wear layers: colored shirt over gray t-shirt. Every time you leave your watchers' sight, you should be able to change your profile. Pull a ball cap or a work shirt out of your jacket to make yourself thinner, and then put it on or throw it away.

INVESTIGATIVE SAMPLE CLUES

- You stand around outside the club in a red vest, and Yuri's mistress tosses you the keys to her Lamborghini. One planted tracker later, and you know where he spends his off hours.
- ◉ That dye job is decent, but the hair under it is broken and white — which is weird for such a youthful looking face.
- ◉ The cosmetic dentures left behind are designed to conceal two extra teeth.

NEW CHERRIES

These cherries are available to characters with 8 or more rating points in Disguise.

◉ INNOCENT BYSTANDER

If you are in disguise, you may also spend Disguise pool points on any Surveillance test to observe, follow, or surprise (*NBA*, p. 60) an enemy, or to unexpectedly Jump In (*NBA*, p. 75) to combat.

◉ JUST THE HELP

You specialize in looking nondescript. If you're wearing a service uniform, jumpsuit, rented-looking tux, or the like, your Difficulty on any Disguise test is reduced by 1.

DRIVING

ABILITY FOCUS: AGGRESSIVE DRIVING MANEUVERS

BOOTLEGGER'S TURN: Vehicles with a handbrake allow for a quick 180-degree turn. Invented by Prohibition-era smugglers who used it to spin around and zip past pursuers on the other side of the highway.

DRAFTING: Two vehicles moving quickly together move slightly faster than one vehicle alone. The lead vehicle disrupts the air as it speeds, leaving less air resistance for the trailing vehicle. The trailing vehicle forces high-pressure air into the lead vehicle to push it forward.

DRIFTING: Intentionally oversteering into a corner causing the rear wheels to lose traction while controlling the angle of exiting the curve with the front wheels. Drifting allows a car to take a turn while losing a minimum of speed. Common in European racing and street racing everywhere.

PIT MANEUVER: The Precision Immobilization Technique was adapted from the dangerous bump and run technique of dirty stock-car racers. The pursuit vehicle pulls parallel to the quarry vehicle being chased. The pursuit vehicle steers into the back quarter panel of the quarry vehicle, causing the quarry to spin and come to a stop. This maneuver is best used with two pursuit vehicles so one can watch over the quarry while the vehicle that performed the PIT has time to recover.

INVESTIGATIVE SAMPLE CLUES

- ◉ Celine is still angry at getting fired from her driver's gig by the ambulance service. A little gearhead bonding and he spills all the gory details about his passenger on the fateful night in question.
- The trunk on that model isn't big enough to hold a body. Makarov's lying.
- ◉ The route programmed into the BMW's GPS isn't nearly the fastest, but it does avoid every church in Wroclaw.

NEW CHERRY

This cherry is available to characters with 8 or more rating points in Driving.

◉ DEFENSIVE DRIVING

While you're at the wheel, you and your passengers add 1 to your and their Hit Threshold against attacks from outside the vehicle; foes throwing objects (such as grenades) at your vehicle add 1 to their Difficulty to hit it. Opponents in a chase or contest of Driving add 1 to their Difficulty on attempts to ram your vehicle, run it off the road, or similar direct attacks.

EXPLOSIVE DEVICES

ABILITY FOCUS: PLASTIC EXPLOSIVES

Plastic explosives have been around since 1875. They played a part in World War II, often used in British commando raids. The simplest plastic explosive from the period was Nobel's 808, also known as Explosive 808. The famous von Stauffenberg plot to blow up Adolf Hitler involved a briefcase filled with Nobel 808 captured from British SOE agents. Another WWII-vintage explosive called HMX could be mixed with flour: pancakes made with the mixture were edible, but could also be used as demolitions.

Most plastic explosive (or plastique) is very stable and cannot be set off through physical shocks. Gunshots won't trigger it, nor will it explode if set on fire. The only way to set it off is when a detonator set into the explosive is triggered, usually by det cord, or by an electric or electronic detonator. (Some plastique can be triggered with a blasting cap.) Plastic explosive is useful in demolition because it can be fit into cracks, gaps, and holes inside important structural points.

C-4 (or C4) is the most common plastic explosive used by the U.S. military, especially for making shaped charges. It is plasticized RDX, and off-white in color. Developed for use in Vietnam in the 1960s, it replaced Explosive 808 in Western arsenals. Supplied to American client states for decades, including Iran and Saudi Arabia, it is omnipresent in terrorist arsenals. Britain and China use a slightly more volatile (and thus more reliably explosive) formulation of the same mixture, called PE4 in Europe; Pakistan also manufactures the Chinese version.

Semtex is the most common plastic explosive used by contractors and construction companies. Known for its distinctive orange color, it is a blend of PETN and RDX. It was developed in Czechoslovakia in the 1950s, and has been manufactured there since 1964. The Czechs supplied it to Communist states, terrorist movements, and rogue governments for 25 years, most famously shipping 700 tons to Khadafi's Libya between 1975 and 1981. It is waterproof, highly malleable, and has a stable shelf life of about five years.

INVESTIGATIVE SAMPLE CLUES
- ⊛⊕ This bomb is a WWII-vintage design, although it uses modern explosives. The builder must be very old, and very set in his — or its — ways.
- ⊕ There is absolutely no trace of any accelerant in this arson scene, except for a vague scent of sulfur. It's as though the fire came out of nowhere.
- ⊛ This blood spray isn't from the victims — it's from the bomb casing. The bomb was a delivery system, to aerosolize whatever was in that blood.

NEW CHERRY
This cherry is available to characters with 8 or more rating points in Explosive Devices.

MAESTRO OF DESTRUCTION
Your wiring diagrams belong in the Louvre. The only way one of your bombs can be deactivated without your cooperation is if the EOD man also possesses this cherry.

FILCH

ABILITY FOCUS: PICKPOCKET TEAMS
Whether it's a neo-Fagin using children in Singapore to soak up loose tourist cash, or a precisely timed lift to get the thumb drive off the *capo* at his birthday party, a coordinated *wire mob* can get sensitive material into important hands with nobody the wiser. The working parts of a *wire mob* are:

The mark: The target of the pickpocket team.
The steer: The person that chooses the mark and runs the operation.
The stall: The person who distracts the mark. Popular choices include mistaken identity, a seemingly innocent bump, asking for directions, or the always classic spilled drink.
The shade: The person who prevents the mark from noticing the lift. The shade might use their own body or an object like a newspaper or a coat.
The dip: The person performing the actual lift.
The duke man: The person who takes the item the dip lifts to keep the rest of the team clean.

A one man *wire mob* is known as a *cannon*, a title of high esteem amongst pickpockets. For those *cannons* who prefer to work solo, here are a few tips for good lifts:

- Let the mark's momentum help you. Instead of pulling the item, grab the item and get the mark to move on her own. It will slip out into your hand.
- Wait for (or create) a diversion. If the mark is watching something else, he's not watching his wallet. Another person interacting with the mark is the best diversion possible.
- Brush against the mark once to locate a wallet, passport, or other specific target. It's harder to detect two brief touches than one lengthy pass.
- Get an accomplice to shout "My wallet's gone!" Most people will instinctively flinch to check their valuables and give their location away for a later lift.
- Approach the mark in a peripheral manner. Coming at someone from directly in front or behind puts them on the defensive.

NEW CHERRY
This cherry is available to characters with 8 or more rating points in Filch.

A LIFT IN TIME SAVES NINE
You may retroactively declare that you lifted a palm-sized or smaller item from a scene or character encountered in this session. You must still succeed at the Filch test against what would have been its normal Difficulty; the item must not have been visible "on screen" or used after your ostensible Filch opportunity. This is the Filch-specific equivalent of In the Nick of Time (***NBA***, p. 33).

GAMBLING

ABILITY FOCUS: EUROPEAN CASINO TABLE GAMES

BACCARAT: Baccarat is the game of choice for anyone with a license to kill. Baccarat is played between the player and the banker. There are three outcomes: the player wins, the banker wins, or there's a tie. Players choose to bet on either the player or the bank. *Chemin-de-fer* is the original version created in France.

KALOOKI: A relative of gin rummy. Popular in the United Kingdom. Cards can be played as sets (3 or more of the same value) and runs (3 or more of the same suit in order). Payouts occur after every hand, though if a player lays out a run of an entire suit, which gives the game its name, they get a special payout.

PAI GOW: A Chinese game that mixes dice and tiles. Bets are laid out and then the dice are rolled to see how tiles are dealt. Each player, up to 6 gets four tiles. The tiles must be assembled in the strongest possible combination of pairs. Each pair is compared to the dealers pair. If the player loses both hands, the bet is taken. If one pair wins and one loses, the bet is a push and the player keeps the money. If both hands win, the player receives a payout equal to the bet less a 5% house commission.

INVESTIGATIVE SAMPLE CLUES

- ⊗ There have been persistent rumors that Krytshchkyn has been doping, but no examination has ever found steroids or other PEDs in his blood. Which in itself is unusual for a boxer who began in the Soviet Olympic program.
- ☻ Every machine the Stranger sat down to play paid out a big jackpot. Electromagnetic fields affect slot machines. Maybe it's time to build us a Faraday cage.
- That's the third big pot she's folded out of with decent cards. She doesn't have the killer instinct to be a killer, and her poker face isn't good enough for a long bluff. If she's involved, it's peripheral, and she might not even like the smell on the periphery. We can flip her.

NEW CHERRIES

These cherries are available to characters with 8 or more rating points in Gambling.

ALL IN

You're not just lucky, you play fast and loose with everything, scoring adrenaline on a win. You drive faster, bet your last dollar, and push the physical envelope a little more than most.

Once per session, you can take a 3-point refresh of any General ability, including Gambling. You must have a rating in that ability, and its current current pool must be 0. If your refresh takes you above your normal rating for that ability, you lose the excess points.

> *Desmond has Explosive Devices 10, but has spent all those points burning avgas and setting off claymores to disrupt a ghoul attack, giving him a current pool of 0. Fortunately, he has the All In cherry; when he really needs to disarm that fuel-air explosive, he can refresh 3 points in Explosive Devices before making the test.*

The Director may ask you to justify the ridiculous turn of luck that gives you that boost.

⊙ EVERYBODYS GOT A TELL

Your lengthy study of faces across the green baize pays off in more than one fashion. You receive 1 free rating point in Bullshit Detector.

HAND-TO-HAND

ABILITY FOCUS: MARTIAL ARTS MIXER

Hundreds of styles of unarmed fighting exist around the world. Most practically trained fighters don't stick to one style. Mixed martial arts allow for maximum flexibility. Cross-training makes every agent unique and able to adapt to the techniques any opponent might use in the field. The following list is not exhaustive by any means, but highlights mixed martial arts that combine styles in new, deadly ways.

For more detailed rules for martial arts use in GUMSHOE, see the ***GUMSHOE Zoom: Martial Arts.***

BRAZILIAN JIU-JITSU (BRAZIL)

OFFENSIVE TECHNIQUES: Submissions, joint locks, chokeholds

DEFENSIVE TECHNIQUES: Grounding, positional strength, sweeps

FAMOUS MASTER: BJJ founder Hélio Gracie famously battled the judoka Masahiro Kimura in 1951. He fought until Kimura dislocated his elbow and broke his arm in two places. Even then, Gracie did not tap out; his corner threw in the towel. That lock is now commonly known as the Kimura lock.

JEET KUNE DO (U.S.)

OFFENSIVE TECHNIQUES: Hand strikes, foot strikes, grapples

DEFENSIVE TECHNIQUES: Movement, blocks, trapping

FAMOUS MASTER: Bruce Lee developed these techniques in 1969 after feeling that other martial arts made practitioners too rigid. He built JKD as a way to attack by defending, or to strike while an opponent was preparing to attack.

KRAV MAGA (ISRAEL)

OFFENSIVE TECHNIQUES: Targeting vital areas, ending fights quickly, integrating knife attacks

DEFENSIVE TECHNIQUES: Counterattacks, situational awareness, preemptive attacks

FAMOUS MASTER: Imi Lichtenfeld developed the system in the late 1930s to protect Jews in Bratislava. Following his emigration to Israel, he taught the techniques to what would soon become the Israeli Defense Force.

MODERN ARMY COMBATIVES (U.S.)

OFFENSIVE TECHNIQUES: Hand strikes, knee strikes, submissions

DEFENSIVE TECHNIQUES: Ground fighting, takedowns, disengaging into firearm range

FAMOUS MASTER: Matt Larsen received an induction into the Order of Saint Maurice for his mixture of Muay Thai, sambo, and judo techniques taught since 2007 to all Army Infantry personnel.

MUAY THAI (THAILAND)

OFFENSIVE TECHNIQUES: Knee strikes, foot strikes, elbow strikes, grapples

DEFENSIVE TECHNIQUES: Clinches, neck wrestling, redirection

FAMOUS MASTER: The Art of Eight Limbs' most famous master, Nai Khanomtom, defeated ten Burmese champions in 1774, winning his freedom and two wives. Thai fighters celebrate March 17 as Boxer's Day in his honor.

SYSTEMA (USSR)

OFFENSIVE TECHNIQUES: Rib slaps, bone and joint strikes, joint locks

DEFENSIVE TECHNIQUES: Ground fighting, leg locks, takedowns

FAMOUS MASTER: Mikhail Ryabko learned "the Spetsnaz martial art" from one of Stalin's former bodyguards in 1961. The term Systema has been used for many different martial arts and training styles; as used in the Spetsnaz it has much in common with Vasili Oshchepkov's Combat Sambo style.

INVESTIGATIVE SAMPLE CLUES

- 👁️👽 When that guy grabbed you, you were sure of two things: you were dead meat if you didn't break that lock in the next two seconds; and you've never felt any muscles that move like that.
- ⓧ The sumo purify their ring with salt before a match. It looks like the yokozuna kept the vampires out of his bedroom the same way.

- Look at the calluses on the corpse's hands. He's spent serious time breaking boards at a dojo somewhere — ask around and we might find out who he was and who he sparred with.

NEW CHERRY

This cherry is available to characters with 8 or more rating points in Hand-to-Hand.

HAYMAKER

You may roll two dice when doing unarmed damage and choose either die. If you choose the higher of the two dice rolled, you must spend Hand-to-Hand points equal to the difference between the rolls.

INFILTRATION

DEFEATING CCTV CAMERAS: A security camera becomes much less useful if it is unable to record the face of an intruder. A head lamp with an IR bulb defeats most cameras without a IR lens. The light reduces a face to a glowing blob. In a pinch, a laser dot pointer or laser pen pointed at the camera will also scramble the visual.

SURVIVING A GUARD DOG ATTACK: Freeze. Don't make eye contact. Don't smile — the dog may misinterpret this as baring of teeth. If the dog bites, push into the mouth rather than pull; pulling just makes the teeth tear more flesh. Strike the dog in its most vulnerable parts.

CUT THE POWER: Most home security alarms have a 24 to 48 hour backup battery. Checking out lost household power is a low priority if nobody is home. Flip the breakers to the house, wait 48 hours, then come back and take your time while the targets are on vacation.

BUMP KEY: Most modern locks can be opened with this item. A bump key features peaks that are all cut to the lowest groove. When struck with a hammer while inside a lock, the force causes the top pins to jump into place. Top line locks have protection against bump keys.

NEW CHERRIES

These cherries are available to characters with 8 or more rating points in Infiltration.

BONO CANE

For whatever reason, dogs just love you, and you like them. Spend 1 pool point of Infiltration to bypass guard dogs, either by stealth or by pure charisma. This cherry has no effect on transformed vampires, ghouls, Renfielded hounds, or the like.

ESCAPE ARTIST

You missed your calling by not playing Vegas. No matter how you are bound, locked, tied up, given enough time unobserved you will get free. This doesn't mean you can't be captured. In fact, that may become a viable plan for your team to get you on the inside of a secure facility.

MECHANICS

Using tools as weapons still calls for tests of Weapons or Shooting, but it's the grease monkey or the wire rat who actually carries this arsenal around with her.

Attacking using a tool with an asterisk (*) takes Shooting instead of Weapons.

For a mounted tool like a table saw, use Smashes or Throws (*NBA*, p. 76) to shove or force opponents into the spinning blades of death. Combine them with Feints (*NBA*, p. 74) for extra effect.

INVESTIGATIVE SAMPLE CLUES

- ⊕ Maybe you can't read the Korean writing on the control panel, but a ground-penetrating radar is a ground-penetrating radar, right? This one certainly seems to show a lot of tunnels centered on that tomb.
- The aircon compressor feeds were cut. They were done in a way to look like an accidental break caused by wear or metal fatigue, but it was intentional and professional. That's how the bratva got access: they must have walked right in wearing air-conditioner repairman outfits.
- ⊕ That's weird – MacLean's flask has a second compartment underneath the bourbon. Since when does he drink water? And why did he spot-weld that crucifix to the bottom of the flask?

NEW CHERRIES

These cherries are available to characters with 8 or more rating points in Mechanics.

DEMOLITION MAN

You may spend your Mechanics pool for Explosive Devices tests when rigging a vehicle or other large machine to explode.

TRAPMASTER

When you build a non-explosive booby trap (*NBA*, p. 98) you may spend 2 points of Mechanics to ensure it does two instances of damage (roll twice) instead of one when it successfully catches an opponent. You only need to spend after the trap is triggered.

MEDIC

A good first aid kit that can serve four agents should contain the following:

- 2 absorbent compress dressings (13 x 23 cm)
- 25 adhesive bandages (assorted sizes)
- 1 adhesive cloth tape (10 meters x 2.5 cm)
- 5 antibiotic ointment packets (approximately 1 gram)
- 5 antiseptic wipe packets
- 2 packets of aspirin (81 mg each)
- 1 blanket (space blanket)
- 1 breathing barrier (with one-way valve)
- 1 instant cold compress
- 2 pair of nonlatex gloves (size: large)
- 2 hydrocortisone ointment packets (approximately 1 gram each)
- Scissors
- 1 roller bandage (8 cm wide)
- 1 roller bandage (11 cm wide)
- 5 sterile gauze pads (8 x 8 cm)
- 5 sterile gauze pads (11 x 11 cm)
- Oral thermometer (non-mercury/nonglass)
- 2 triangular bandages
- Tweezers
- First aid instruction booklet

Before going into gunfights, adding extra dressings, bandages, gauze, tape, antiseptic, and painkillers is probably indicated.

TOOLS AS WEAPONS TABLE

TOOL	DAMAGE MODIFIER	NOTES
Box cutter, oil spray*	-2	**BOX CUTTER:** Doesn't do much damage, but draws blood **OIL SPRAY:** Forces Athletics test against Difficulty equal to your Shooting total; succeed or fall down for -2 damage, lose next two attacks
Auger, chisel, flashlight, hacksaw, hammer, hatchet, hedge clippers, nail gun*, pliers, rake, screwdriver, shears, socket wrench, soldering iron, tire iron, trowel	-1	**NAIL GUN:** Close range maximum, can use Autofire **SOLDERING IRON:** Add another -2 for burning damage
Crowbar, hand power saw, heavy wrench, mattock, maul, oxyacetylene torch, plasma cutter, post-hole digger, pick, power drill, sand blaster*, shovel, sledgehammer, tree limb loppers	+0	**LOPPERS:** +2 damage if used to sever a limb (Called Shot) **OXY TORCH, PLASMA CUTTER:** Does double normal fire damage **SAND BLASTER:** Close range maximum
Axe, chainsaw, large power saw, lawnmower, scythe, table saw	+1	
Arc welder	+2	**ARC WELDER:** Only at Point-Blank, emits strong UV and blinds unprotected onlookers as flash-bang

Syringes, ammonia inhalants, salt tablets, hand sanitizer, anti-malarials, hemostatic bandages, military morphia syrettes, and other exotic items might be in an agent's first aid kit as well, depending on the kindness of the Director and the vagaries of Preparedness.

NEW CHERRY

This cherry is available to characters with 8 or more rating points in Medic.

ON YOUR FEET

You may take one round to give an unconscious agent a chance to get back in the fight. She receives a bonus to her Consciousness roll equal to any points you spend in Medic.

PILOTING

ABILITY FOCUS: SURVIVING A PLANE CRASH

PLANNING TO FAIL: Make sure your seat belt is securely fastened. Wear long sleeves and long pants on a flight to protect from glass, metal, and the elements. Keep anything important on your person at all times. If it's too large to carry that way, be prepared to lose it or to spend time recovering it later.

GET SECURE: Extend your arms, cross your hands, and place them on the seat in front of you. Place your head against the back of your hands. Tuck your feet under your seat as far as you can. If you have no seat in front of you, bend your upper body over with your head down and wrap your arms behind your knees.

GET OUT: Fire is a likely danger thanks to the mix of leaking fuel and flammable objects. The toxic fumes from burning pieces of the plane are more likely to kill you than the flames. Stay low and keep moving. Don't attempt to recover any luggage. Anything sensitive can be recovered at a later time. Infiltrate a crash investigation site instead of hunting around a burning, poisonous time bomb for that briefcase four men died for in Stuttgart.

GET AWAY: The first 90 seconds after a crash are called "golden time." If you can get out of the plane, stay calm and get away in that time frame, your chances for survival are significantly better. The farther away from the plane you can get, the less likely you'll be killed if it explodes. Seek cover behind a large rock or other solid formation to protect yourself.

INVESTIGATIVE SAMPLE CLUES

- ⊛ A sudden fog descended over the tower that night. No flights were able to land, but the air traffic controller on duty said that the Alucardia executive jet took off anyway.
- ⊛ No known aircraft can make sudden high-speed, right-angle course changes like that.
- You used to fly the Sheik's jet to the Riviera for him. You know just which terminal Abu Anfal is likely to use at NCE.

NEW CHERRY

This cherry is available to characters with 8 or more rating points in Piloting.

⊛ MOVE AROUND THE CABIN

You really know your way around cramped quarters, even when they're moving up and down unpredictably. When on a plane or boat, your Difficulty for all Athletics feats, and the Hit Threshold of anyone you attack with Hand-To-Hand or Weapons, is decreased by 1.

PREPAREDNESS

BRASS KNUCKLES: Slipping a solid item in your fist can give you an advantage (damage -1 instead of -2) in a Hand-to-Hand contest. If a roll of coins is not available, make a fist around a set of keys. Make sure the sharp edges of the keys protrude out from between your fingers.

BURGLAR ALARM: Wedge rubber door stops under a hotel room door. Set up the office chair in front of the door. Stack the room glasses on the chair so that any motion from the door will dislodge them. This way, even if someone attempts a quiet entry into the room, the glasses fall and alert the occupants.

COVER IDENTITY: Collect business cards wherever you go. Take them from desks. Pick them up from the flyer-choked lobbies of coffee shops. Scoop out handfuls from those fishbowl "get a free meal" drawings at restaurants. While an ID like this won't survive much scrutiny after the fact, having a business card to whip out on an introduction can lower the defenses of a witness faster than an hour of well-spun story.

SILENCER: A thick towel wrapped around the gun can muffle the sound (for effects see **NBA**, p. 103). A 2-liter plastic bottle taped to the barrel also works. Improvised silencers like these greatly lower accuracy and stopping power (-1 to damage, +1 to foe's Hit Threshold).

NEW CHERRIES

These cherries are available to characters with 8 or more rating points in Preparedness.

CHECK YOUR OTHER LEFT POCKET

You may spend Preparedness on behalf of other agents in the field. The Director may require a brief flashback scene where you give your teammate the piece of equipment along with an eerily prescient explanation of why he or she will need it.

⊛ HOARDER

You learned long ago the virtues of stay-behind equipment. The Difficulty of all your Cache rolls is lowered by 1.

SENSE TROUBLE

ABILITY FOCUS: THE COOPER COLOR CODE

Developed by firearms instructor and former U.S. Marine Lt. Col. "Jeff" Cooper, the Color Code describes various levels of situational awareness. By knowing these levels exist and giving them names, an agent can perform useful analysis of his own mental state and the state of his surroundings. Even asking the question "what Color am I in right now?" helps focus the mind away from distraction and toward any possible dangers. The colors don't refer to the level of danger in the environment, but to the mindset of the agent.

WHITE: Unaware of danger, unprepared for combat, and unready to take action. Usually caused by exhaustion, distraction, or the false sense of security that comes from being a normal civilian. Analysts thinking about the deeper problem and unused to fieldwork might walk around in Condition White.

YELLOW: Relaxed alert status, aware of the potential for danger in a situation or location. You know that you might have to fight or take other sudden action. Watch your six and pay attention to possible anomalies – less traffic than normal, two men in identical sunglasses, a glint from a rooftop, a missing reflection in a shop window, and so on (see *NBA*, p. 141). Model the scene as a predator; think "if I were ambushing someone here, who and where would I be?" Listen to your "hunches," your "Spidey sense," your gut instinct. Good agents are always in at least Condition Yellow in the field, in strange cities — anywhere except their place of Safety, in fact.

ORANGE: Specific alert status, aware of a specific possibly dangerous person, object, or anomaly. While keeping up your general awareness, you focus on the potential immediate danger and set an invisible line that, if crossed, must result in action. "If that car turns off on this dirt road, I'm being tailed." "If that shadow is a gun barrel, I need to duck and return fire." "If that woman doesn't pass the cathedral doors, she's a vampire." Your mindset shifts to "if I have to take that opponent out, how can I do so?"

RED: Aware of an immediate threat and ready to take action. The invisible line in your mind is crossed, and you are putting the tactics you devised to use on a specific target. Perhaps you're calling for backup. Perhaps you're drawing your gun. Perhaps you're unscrewing the flask of holy water. If you don't plan to attack the target, you should be running away now.

NEW CHERRY

This cherry is available to characters with 8 or more rating points in Sense Trouble.

⊙ HAWKEYE

Always looking for threats means you're always looking. You receive 1 free rating point in Notice.

SHOOTING

AUSTRALIAN PEEL: A firing retreat from overwhelming force. The point shooter fires repeatedly to suppress the enemy, then "peels off" and runs back down the line, tapping the second shooter, who now becomes point and immediately continues the suppressing fire. This continues until the fire team is out of ammunition or out of range of the foe.

BIATHLETE BREATHING: Take three long, controlled breaths before taking an aimed shot. Breathe in through the nose and out through the mouth to settle heart rate and steady aim. Take the shot at the end of the breathing cycle. There are seven seconds before lack of oxygen affects vision and induces muscle tremors. If the shot can't be lined up, start the cycle over again.

CROSSING THE BORDER: Throwing a gun from your off-hand to your dominant hand, usually after drawing two pistols and emptying the first.

DOUBLE TAP: Firing two rounds in quick succession. The controlled pair uses the natural recoil of the first shot to put the second shot higher up on the target.

ISOSCELES STANCE: Proper pistol firing stance. Both feet parallel slightly wider than shoulder distance apart, pistol held with both hands in front of the body. This stance allows for maximum absorption of pistol recoil for a faster reset between shots. The *Harries stance* is similar, with a flashlight in the weak hand, supporting the strong hand.

MOZAMBIQUE DRILL: A shooting technique where the shooter puts two shots center mass, takes a moment to assess the hits, and then finishes off the target with a third shot to the head. "Two to the chest, one to the head, leaves anybody dead." Also known as the Failure to Stop Drill.

NEW YORK RELOAD: Replacing an empty gun with a second, fully loaded gun instead of reloading the primary weapon.

PUSH/PULL DIALING: Adjusting the dial on a scope while keeping the shot lined up is tricky. For a standard right handed shooter, pushing forward will move the point of impact down or to the left. Pulling back on the dials moves the impact up or to the right.

ROAD-AGENT SPIN: Present the gun butt-first to a foe as if surrendering it. Then open your hand, and as the gun barrel falls and rotates along your finger, fire the gun upside-down. Good for only a single shot, and in Dust mode only effective with single-action revolvers.

INVESTIGATIVE SAMPLE CLUES

- ⊗ These silver bullets aren't hand-loads, they were machined industrially, most likely in Austria. Someone with serious resources sent this dhampir.
- ☻ I tell you, I saw the muzzle flash. That bullet curved in mid-air. Bullets don't curve in mid-air unless something moves them.

- The shot had to have come from that tenth-floor window, three buildings back. All the roofs slope here, so it's the only decent sniper's nest along the angle of incidence, and even then the shooter must have been very, very good.

SHRINK

POST-TRAUMATIC STRESS DISORDER: A severe anxiety disorder that stems from psychological trauma. Victims re-experience the traumatic events through nightmares and flashbacks. They often avoid things that remind them of the events, like locations, objects, or sounds. Some victims can't or won't sleep to out of a fear of triggering a flashback. These symptoms often occur up to a month after severe psychological trauma as severe anxiety disorder. (See *NBA*, p. 84.)

SELF-MEDICATION: The use of drugs to treat self-diagnosed disorders or symptoms, or the intermittent or continued use of a prescribed drug for chronic or recurrent disease or symptoms. The choice of a drug often reflects the lack of coping mechanism the victim needs to feel whole. It is not a random selection.

STOCKHOLM SYNDROME: Traumatic bonding in which hostages express sympathy for their captors. Extreme cases involve the prisoner defending the hostage taker, or informing on other captives. According to the FBI, one out of four hostages display evidence of the syndrome. Some evolutionary psychologists believe the roots of capture-bonding underlie sociological phenomena including battered wife syndrome, cult behavior, military/fraternity hazing, BDSM, and vampiric dominance.

TRAUMA TRIGGER: An experience that triggers a reminder of a traumatic event. Triggers themselves need not be intense experiences. Visual experiences are commonly trauma stressors, thanks to the realistic portrayal of violence in film and television. Eliminating a trauma stimulus involves experiencing it in a safe environment to reconnect it to everyday life.

NEW CHERRIES

These cherries are available to characters with 8 or more rating points in Shrink.

ANGER MANAGEMENT

After talking with someone (or reading a complete psychological workup on them), you know how to push their buttons. You may make a Shrink test to incite them to anger — to distract them, to goad them into attacking, to make a spectacle of them, or for any other reason. Your basic Difficulty for this test is 4; to get them angry at someone besides you (to urge them to attack some other foe, for example) your Difficulty is 6. The Director may alter these values depending on the target's specific psychological hangups, the likelihood of your desired reaction, the amount of time you spend poisoning their mind, and the quality of your roleplayed taunt.

This cherry does not work on supernatural, vampire-controlled, alien, or other nonhuman creatures.

TALKING CURE

You are incredibly skilled in managing other agents' mental health, particularly after shared trauma. Your Difficulty for all tests to treat fellow agents' mental illness (see *Head Games*, *NBA*, p. 85) is one lower than normal.

When you spend 2 points of Shrink on psychological triage (*NBA*, p. 85), the recipient gains 3 points of Stability.

After a brief scene of roleplayed therapy (hypnosis, psychoanalysis, etc.), you can increase another agent's Stability pool by 2 and refresh your own Shrink or Stability by the same amount.

🔥 This cherry is not available in Burn mode games.

SURVEILLANCE

DETERMINE A CHOKE POINT: Most buildings feature an area everyone must pass through to exit. An elevator, a lobby, or the entrance to the parking garage make good choices for choke points.

ALTER YOUR APPEARANCE: Often, following a target requires multiple attempts to get from the place of origin to the new location. A distinct hat or color distracts from the face. If the target doesn't remember your face, subsequent attempts to shadow will be easier. (See p. 40.)

LET THE RABBIT COME TO YOU: Set up at the choke point. Waiting there makes it less likely the target will think they are being followed. Normal targets fearing surveillance expect to be followed from the beginning of their journey and take precautions when they leave. Only those with counter-surveillance training stay vigilant all along the route.

FOLLOW THE RABBIT: If the rabbit is driving, follow in your own vehicle at least three car lengths behind. If the rabbit is on foot, follow on foot. If the rabbit takes a cab, note the cab number. If you lose the rabbit, you can get the location of the drop-off by contacting the cab company.

USE A THREE-MAN TEAM: The shadower closest to the rabbit has the eye. The second team member follows behind the first member so the eye can pass between them as necessary. The third member follows in a parallel course along the street. If the rabbit turns or doubles back, the team passes the eye and readjusts. In addition, the rabbit doesn't keep seeing the same face behind him.

AVOID EYE CONTACT: Making eye contact is the surest way to let the rabbit know you are watching. If that occurs, immediately break off the shadowing, either by passing on to another team member or trying again another time.

NEW CHERRIES

These cherries are available to characters with 8 or more rating points in Surveillance.

FACE IN THE CROWD

Though you may lose your quarry, you are never blown. You may start over at another time.

⚫ TAIL LIGHTS

You may also spend from your Driving pool for Surveillance tests while in a vehicle following a target.

WEAPONS

ABILITY FOCUS: KNIFE GRIPS

FENCER'S GRIP: Grip the handle between forefinger and thumb, pointing the blade at the foe. This allows for the greatest movement of the blade, especially in slashing attacks or keeping the fight open. A solid block, or a swing that hits some nearby scenery, can break this grip and potentially disarm the wielder.

HAMMER GRIP: Grip the handle using all fingers in a fist, pointing the blade upward out of the fist, like holding a hammer. Tilt the wrist to point the blade at the foe. The most basic, versatile grip, allowing for thrusting, cutting and parrying, but vulnerable to attacks to the hand.

ICEPICK GRIP: Grip the handle using all fingers in a fist, pointing the blade downward out of the fist. This grip is most useful for penetrating thick coats or soft armor. This grip can't be used to parry or block. It also opens up the attacker for a counterstrike to the chest.

MODIFIED SABER GRIP: As the hammer grip, but the thumb rests on the flat of the knife. This puts the blade in a horizontal slashing posture by default, and unlike the hammer, allows the wielder to lock his wrist for a strike.

REVERSE GRIP: Similar to the icepick grip, though the blade is laid along the forearm of the attacker. Most useful for concealed attacks and close up work. It also has some use for blocks and defense, but most knife fighters don't use knives to parry.

NEW CHERRY

This cherry is available to characters with 8 or more rating points in Weapons.

RIPOSTE

If an attacker rolls an unmodified 1 on a Weapons roll *and* misses when attacking you, you may take advantage of his weakness by immediately striking back at him. Without rolling an attack test, spend Weapons pool points. The attacker loses 1 point of Health for every point you spend, up to the maximum normal damage possible for your weapon.

TRICKS OF THE TRADE

A RESOURCEFUL SPY MASTERS A VARIETY OF techniques to handle various threats in addition to the more straightforward approach of repeated punches and kicks punctuated by gunplay.

This section lays out more options for agents in the form of new maneuvers, and for Directors in the form of customizable achievements. Adaptive tradecraft expands the universe of covert action to some really off-the-hook uses of off-the-shelf technology. And the "Cartagena Rules" accompany, adapt, and expand upon the "Bucharest Rules" from the corebook (*NBA*, pp. 116-117) for even more high-energy, proactive play.

NEW THRILLER MANEUVERS

Players love to wring every possible advantage out of the rules. When you're fighting vampires and playing badass secret agents, that's just good thinking. The new thriller manuevers here play up that fantasy of competence, and add more potential action for non-combat activities as well. Like the maneuvers in the book, they add to and expand the agents' resources, their options, and their resilience.

Directors should be ready for that, either by adding another few Renfields to the node or by keeping an eye on refresh rates and pool levels as these maneuvers come on line.

Like Gear Devil, Martial Arts, Parkour, and Technothriller Monologue in the corebook, maneuvers that provide a refresh can normally only be used *once* during a scene, chase, or combat. The specific maneuver writeup will give details, but the Director can always restrict them further: from once per fight, say, to once per session or once per operation.

And as always, all these maneuvers are completely optional. The Director can reject any of them as she sees fit, to preserve the flavor of her game or her sense of even cinematic realism.

⚫ Most of these maneuvers are not available in Dust mode games. Look for the Dust icon for maneuvers generally compatible with low-fi spy-fi.

NON-COMBAT MANEUVERS

ALIBI

PREREQ: Disguise 8+

You are so skilled at appearing like someone else, so capable of mimicking another person's mannerisms and appearance that you can, in character, convince a mark or his associates that something plausible did or didn't happen as needed. "In character" means "while pretending to be someone else," whether short-term (flashing a phony badge and using CopTalk) or long-term, as with a Connected Cover.

Once per session, you can spend 1 point of any Interpersonal ability (if you can't think of the right one, use Reassurance) and 3 points of Disguise to convince your target.

- "Mickey, don't you remember? I was just down in the vault. I came up here to ask you if the combination was 22-34-5 or 16-4-33."
- "Was he sweating a lot? Because rabies victims sweat a lot. It was probably just rabies."
- "What do you mean you saw me in the parking lot? How the hell could I be in there if I was downstairs with Carlos?"

This maneuver doesn't implant false memories or erase true ones. It solidifies a doubt one way or the other. You can't use it to say "Johnnie shot you, I was in the loo" if the crew boss saw you shoot him, but you can use it to convince him that "Johnnie shot you, I was in the loo" if you shot him in the back but Johnnie might 'ave dunnit.

BLENDING AGENT
PREREQ: Surveillance 8+

A character with a Surveillance *rating* of 8 or higher can earn a 3-point Surveillance refresh, once per session, when you describe the details she picks up on in the crowd around her that tell her what the surveillance on her trail is doing or when you describe how she stays unnoticed. That gives her the edge to outmaneuver them. For example:

- "The CCTVs offer good picture but a crap turning radius, so if I keep moving laterally, I'll stay a vague blur until I reach the edge of its POV, then I can stroll underneath it."
- "Once I'm on a line toward the east exit, I slow down but do not deviate from that line. I'm a traveller, scrolling through tweets on my phone. I chuckle and shake my head but I do not look up. I'm a traveller."
- "When I see the mobile units on approach, I set down my coffee and tie my shoe for eight seconds. Then I drop my pen, fumble after it like an idiot for six seconds, and come up elsewhere in the crowd, back on the move."

At the Director's discretion, such surveillance talk may grant a 4-point refresh instead if it adds such detail and nuance to the sequence that others players marvel.

Pre-write such descriptions, if you like, to give your character the savvy ability to vanish in a crowd at a moment's notice.

CALCULATED RISK
PREREQ: Preparedness 8+

Your ability to plan is unmatched, going so far as to even account for remote possibilities in response to responses from responses. While the plan is being executed, when a new element arises seemingly not accounted for in the plan, once per operation (or per Infiltration thriller contest; see p. 81) you can counter the new element with an ad hoc narration:

DIRECTOR: "Because of Sergei's visit, the guards have upped their timetable by ten minutes."
YOU: "I planned for this. The playoff game will be on in the office, and during that distraction, we can still disable the motion sensors."

You receive a 3-point Preparedness refresh representing your resourcefulness. If your counter was especially inspired or effective, the Director may give you a 4-point refresh.

Don't use this maneuver when you could use In the Nick of Time (*NBA*, p. 33), unless you really need the refresh.

CARD UP THE SLEEVE
PREREQ: Gambling 8+

Once per session, you may spend 3 points of Gambling to reroll one Gambling test. If you do, your character cheats to succeed. You may take either of the two rolls. If your *second* roll is a 1, someone noticed you cheating, but you automatically succeed.

DANGER ZONE
PREREQ: Sense Trouble 8+

Your sense of danger borders on the supernatural. Your every sense paints a picture of your surroundings whether you're "in country" or in a country club. Once per session, you can try to explain to your blundering colleagues how you know what you know, and gain a 3-point refresh to Sense Trouble:

- "My time spent with the Chiricahua shamans expanded my awareness to see beyond seeing."
- "We had days like this in Afghanistan, days when every rock shone with a premonition of danger."
- "The bullet hole in my shoulder hurt like hell this morning. Death is coming."

If your borderline four-color explanation sufficiently illuminates your surroundings or sparks your fellow players' paranoia, the Director may grant you a 4-point refresh.

Feel free to scout ahead and write down especially revelatory ideas on index cards if need be. However, once you've established your agent's past, evocatively riffing on the dangers you evaded back then should be fairly simple.

🌑 This maneuver might not fit the tone of Mirror mode games, in which death often comes as an unpleasant surprise.

DIGITAL JUDO
See p. 81.

FOR YOUR EYES ONLY
PREREQ: Surveillance 8+

When you get eyes on a target, you hunt him until you know him. The intel you provide is an analyst's dream: reliable, actionable, and insightful. After succeeding in a test of Surveillance against a target, you can compose a deep-level dossier on the target by spending 3 pool points of Surveillance and 1 pool point of an appropriate Investigative ability: Human Terrain, Notice, Photography, Streetwise, or Tradecraft. The time needed for the initial surveillance and dossier prep will vary depending on the nature of the target and the Director's sense of dramatic timing, but likely averages out to 1-3 days.

All those who read the dossier gain access to a team 1-point dedicated pool usable as any Investigative ability against the target (it points up promising leads for Research, notes target interests for Flirting, hints at shady activities to spark Cop Talk, whatever) and to a team 2-point pool for any General ability use against the target. If the target is not on the adversary map (*NBA*, p. 113), the team can add him to it.

You may invent ad hoc and then highlight crucial details about your target that you turned up in your surveillance:

- Zlatan doesn't like to be touched.
- Clarissa Meyer spent three hours in the British Museum looking at Hittite sculptures.
- Quways al-Ubar always sits in the same booth at the falafel shop, back to the wall, four bodyguards.

If the Director accepts a detail, you can add 1 point to each pool per detail, up to a total of 3 Investigative pool points and 4 General pool points. Yes, this means that last detail has hit the point of diminishing returns. It's unwise to add details that conclusively demonstrate (in your own mind, at least) that your target is or is not a vampire. Such details often turn out to be mistaken or misinterpreted. The Director will reject details that make future hits too easy ("for a terrorist mastermind, he sure does trust street vendors"), so it's best to err on the side of drama and excitement.

GREASE MONKEY
PREREQ: Mechanics 8+

Once per session, you can gain a 3-point refresh of your Mechanics pool by narrating in precision-ratcheted detail what you're doing and how you're doing it:

- "If I adjust the timing belt and clear the spark channel, we can get an extra 50 rpm out of the motor."
- "Just loop another few turns of wire around that rheostat and pop it in there, and we can crank up the power as much as we need to."
- "I can pry off the governor and drill an extra hole in the manifold to turbocharge the bus, seeing as it's pulling a straight eight instead of a four-stroke diesel."

At the Director's discretion, descriptions that should come with their own Allen wrench may merit a 4-point refresh.

Feel free to blueprint your description ahead of time, on index cards perhaps, if it helps sort out your narrative tool box.

LIKE SMOKE
PREREQ: Athletics 8+ *or* Infiltration 8+

Infiltrators with either Athletics or Infiltration *ratings* of 8+ can earn a 3-point Infiltration refresh once during any sneak when they describe some move or stunt that would astonish onlookers if it weren't so stealthy:

- "Once the guard is past, I slide a vent cover away and unfold myself from the shadowy compartment beyond, which should be too small for anyone my size to fit inside, and yet."
- "I'm pinned to the ceiling by leg strength at the corners of the corridor and a grip I've got on the Exit sign. The patrol strides by beneath me."
- "The flashlight beam cuts across my face, shadows playing on my features. Double take. When the guard flashes the beam back in that spot, I'm gone."

Especially chilling or clever descriptions that captivate or delight the other players earn a 4-point refresh, at the Director's discretion.

Players are free to write out such descriptions in advance; it's only their characters that have to be so quick on their feet.

M4D SK1LLZ
PREREQ: Digital Intrusion 8+

Once per contest (*not* per test) of Digital Intrusion, you can earn a 3-point refresh of that ability by dropping some cybernetic leetspeak expounding upon the awesomeness of your digital kung fu or the dramatically impenetrable behavior of the tiny green letters on your screen.

- "These guys are good enough to use a 5585-X as their base firewall, but I'm good enough to reconstruct their password cache while their WHOIS query is resolving."
- "The Steranko system uses a rotating blowfish encryption algorithm and heuristic AI to map the intruders in real-time."
- "Start slow, probing a few low-level systems for a few hours, and plant the key-logger and signal-monitoring spyware. When I kick the attack into overdrive and their security staff starts logging in from home to see what the hell's going on, they show me passwords and authorization keys. It's like perching on their shoulder as they walk right in the door."

At the Director's discretion, jargon more impenetrable than an overclocked tower nest running Fortinet NG5000-series ware in parallel might be worth a 4-point refresh.

Obviously, you're going to store your best hacker monologues on your jailbroken phone, but the point is go ahead and code them ahead of time.

QUICK CHANGE
PREREQ: Disguise 8+

Once per chase, you can earn a 3-point refresh of Disguise by describing how you gather the necessary components for the next disguise or what details you steal from nearby people to alter your own body language for a short time. The actual donning of a disguise may not be necessary to use these 3 points; simply blending in with passersby is enough for now.

- "As we pass, I slip a ball cap out of a stranger's open duffel and hide it under my jacket, ready to deploy in a moment."
- "I fall in alongside a trio of chums talking about their college days, just far enough from them to be one of them from the outside, buying myself a good twenty paces toward the washrooms."
- "At the café patio, I pick up a few dirtied plates, toss a napkin over my shoulder, and bus those dishes inside the building to buy myself some time off camera and maybe seek out a back door."

If the Director feels the detail evoked by this description is particularly sly or convincing, she may award a 4-point refresh instead.

Go ahead and write Disguise descriptions in advance, if you can. Your prep is your character's improvisation.

RUN AND HIDE
See p. 84.

SAFETY'S ON
If you discover or notice a firearm on a person (not in hand) and succeed in a Filch test against him, you can spend 1 point from either your Shooting or Filch pool to deactivate the weapon without letting its owner realize you've done so.

The Difficulty of the Filch test, as normal, depends on circumstances including the owner's Alertness modifier, if any. The usual result of a successful deactivation (e.g., switching the safety to "on") is one round in which the opponent is unable to fire his weapon. For weapons without safeties (such as most revolvers and all Glocks), you must spend 3 points, but you unload the weapon completely.

This is *not* a combat maneuver — flicking safety switches is too delicate for that! To grab a foe's weapon in combat is a Disarm move (**NBA**, p. 73).

SIGNATURE WHEELS
PREREQ: Driving 8+

If you have a Driving rating of 8 or more, you may spend 5 build points to grant yourself Signature Wheels: one make and model (or just a make for boutique marques) of car from which you can pull top performance. You might make anything from an Aston-Martin to an Audi S8 to a Ford Focus your Signature Wheels, although the Director and other players may mock you if you pick something like a Trabant. Luxury cars may be harder to come by on the run, requiring higher Network Difficulties or Streetwise spends to find reliable chop shops: just something else to keep in mind. To "stumble upon" a car matching your Signature Wheels in a position to be stolen may require an Urban Survival spend, depending on your car and the city.

While driving your Signature Wheels, every full 2 points of Driving you spend count as a 3-point spend.

This applies not only to the particular car you own, but to all other cars of that exact make. If a Mini Cooper is your Signature Wheels, and you crash yours into a tank barrier in Ankara, the new Mini Cooper you steal in Swindon still provides you the enhanced spend.

You may take Signature Wheels in one sports car and one other make of ground vehicle.

VERBAL TRAUMA UNIT
PREREQ: Medic 8+

Once per session, you can gain a 3-point refresh of your Medic pool by uttering a brief narrative description of your actions surgically sliced from medical drama:

- "He's tach-ing! Very thready pulse, shocky, eyes dilated … flesh cold and moist … Damn it to hell, I won't lose another one. Not today!"
- "I pop the top from the syrette and smoothly insert it into her armpit, right where the axillary vein goes over the trapezius."
- "My hands greasy with blood, I tear the duct tape with my teeth and then whip it around Jensen's thigh. My eyes are far away, however, seeing only the basement in Sarajevo where I first felt life slip through my fingers."

At the Director's discretion, descriptions so bloodily graphic or antiseptically detached as to amount to vampiric porn may earn a 4-point refresh.

OPTIONAL RULE: FAMILIAR FOE

You have done battle with a particular enemy before. Not a generic mook, not just one class of opposition, no matter how distinctive. A Familiar Foe is a named opponent, be they the "Wizard of Waziristan" or the "second Lieutenant of the Death's Sword Brigade, Johannes Klonsveldt." Each agent gets a maximum of one Familiar Foe per campaign. The agent can pick a suitably badass-appearing NPC during play, or construct her nemesis in collaboration with the Director during character creation.

The agent is free to declare their pre-existing history, pending Director approval, so long as their invented fiction does not conflict with or otherwise alter the power(s) of the foe, if any.

> "I know this guy, the Killer of Kuala Lampur. We met in Jakarta in 2004. He doesn't like me very much since I gave him that scar on his chest from when I used the flagpole to pin him to the table."

A Familiar Foe might tie into an agent's personal arc (**NBA**, p. 37) or her Drive in some fashion.

A Familiar Foe, because of the history between the characters, is both more and less of a challenge.

The agent gets a 3-point dedicated pool for use with any Investigative ability, when that ability is used to uncover something about the Foe. This pool refreshes between operations, like other Investigative abilities.

The Director should similarly keep the Familiar Foe's knowledge of the agent in mind when plotting Conspiracy responses using the Vampyramid.

When in a direct contest with a Familiar Foe:

Both the Foe and the agent **reduce their Hit Threshold** or other contest Difficulty by 1, indicating that both know the styles and tactics of the other.

Both Foe and the agent **minimize the first instance of damage** done by their opposite number in any combat directly between them. Hand-to-Hand or Weapons hits do only 1 point of damage maximum; Shooting hits do damage as fists (-2) with 1 point the minimum.

> Jack and his Familiar Foe Roman Szabo are in a gunfight, blazing away with their Glocks at each other. Szabo's first shot hits Jack, and the Director rolls a 4, subtracts 2, and Jack loses 2 Health. "Is that all you got?" rasps Jack. His return fire misses, however. In the second round, Szabo's shot at Jack does normal damage, but Jack shoots a mook (doing normal damage) who threatened to flank his team mates. On the third round, Jack finally hits Szabo, but rolls a 2. Subtracting 2 makes the total 0, so Szabo loses the minimum, 1 Health. "You never could kill when it counted, Jack," Szabo taunts.

This models an intense fight, allows utterance of lines like "You've slowed down since Beirut," and prevents anticlimactic one-and-done potshots or sniping ambushes from ruining the arc.

These utterances needn't be improvised; you can crib from *Gray's Anatomy* (book or show) in advance, then adapt your medical doubletalk to the injury.

WATCHING THE WATCHERS
See p. 83.

COMBAT MANEUVERS

These maneuvers, like other Thriller Combat Maneuvers, are entirely optional. None of them are compatible with Dust mode games, although Mark and Execute is the closest to realistic.

MARK AND STRIKE
PREREQ: Infiltration 8+

When you succeed in an Infiltration test to surprise or ambush an unaware target (*NBA*, p. 60), you may spend Infiltration as well as combat ability points on your first attack.

> *Beatrice has an Infiltration pool of 8, spends 4 on the Infiltration test to surprise a skulking Renfield, rolls a 3 and beats the Difficulty of 6 (4 plus the Renfield's Alertness Modifier of +2). On her first round of combat, she can spend 2 from her remaining 4 pool points of Infiltration, plus 2 from Weapons, for a total spend of 4 on the Weapons test to drive home the teak bayonet she lovingly lathed the day before.*

You may use Mark and Strike throughout Player-Facing Combat (*NBA*, p. 64).

ONE-TWO PUNCH
PREREQ: Hand-to-Hand 8+ or Weapons 8+

You are fond of the brutal one-two combination, the coup de grace. After the preparatory jab or slash comes the blow at full strength: the jaw-aimed uppercut, the elbow strike to the temple, the leg sweep — or the plunge of a stiletto or stake into the heart.

After two successful blows in a row (either in successive rounds or with Extra Attacks, Jump In, etc.) against the same target, you can:

- spend 3 Athletics pool points
- narrate your most recent blow ("I wrench his arm all the way around" "I straight-arm him in the throat")
- increase your rolled damage by +2
- refresh 1 point in the combat ability you used for the second blow

You cannot use One-Two Punch against the same foe twice in a row. You must either attack someone else, spend a round doing something else, or miss to "restart the count" for a One-Two Punch.

PERFECT DROP
PREREQ: Sense Trouble 8+

A character with a Sense Trouble *rating* of 8 or more is so attuned to danger that she can act in a combat before the fighting has really even broken out. This option interacts with the Sense Trouble cherry Combat Intuition (*NBA*, p. 34) like this: Once per session, when determining initiative, you can spend 3 points from your Sense Trouble *pool* to treat your *rating* as if it were 3 points higher than it is, thereby getting the drop on your foes.

> *Jack has Sense Trouble 9 and Shooting 8. He makes a Sense Trouble test to notice the Renfield wetworker Carmen coming into the hotel, spending 2 points from his pool for a Sense Trouble pool of 7. Jack suspects (rightly) that her Shooting is higher than his. Ordinarily, she would win the initiative and get to fire first. But Jack spends 3 more Sense Trouble points (lowering his pool to 4) to raise his rating to 12, beating her Shooting of 10, and thus beating her to the draw.*

To do this, describe *how* your character knew things were about to turn ugly. If you act fast enough, you might end a fight or an alarm before it can begin.

- "It's the snap on the holster before the gun comes out, that's what gives him away."
- "I know what he's up to as soon as he holds his breath for that half-second. Before he can choose between baton and radio, I'm on him."
- "I hear his stomach rumble before he comes around the corner, so I'm ready for him."

It's fair game to write sample details before you use them and then see if they work in the moment.

THROWN CLEAR BY THE BLAST

Any explosion you can fly away from is a good explosion. You can spend Athletics points to "roll with the shock" or "dive behind the cement mixer" or "be thrown clear of the blast" or whatever excuse you wish to make for your palpable violation of the laws of physics. When you spend points, you can move your agent's damage up a row or over a column on the Explosion Damage table (*NBA*, p. 67).

If you spend 4 points of Athletics, your damage moves up a row. You take damage as if the blast were one explosive class smaller: from class 4 (truck bomb) to class 3 (land mine), for example. If you wind up in the "Annihilation range" of a class 1 or 2 explosion as a result, treat it as Damage range with a further +2 damage modifier.

If you spend 6 points of Athletics, your damage moves over a column. You take damage as if the blast were one range rank farther away: from Annihilation range to Damage range, for example.

In very, very cinematic games, you may spend as many Athletics points as you'd like, as long as you spend them in whole increments as above.

Even in those games, the Director is very unlikely to let you escape the effects of a class 5 or 6 explosion with such antics.

You can *never* spend yourself completely "out" of a blast: you will always take damage at least as if you were in a class 1 explosion or the Debris range or both.

After the dust clears, the Director may rule that your agent was hurled (or lies curled) anywhere she wishes, regardless of the range of damage you took. Kindly Directors will allow you to suggest a likely outcome.

NIGHT'S BLACK AGENTS — DOUBLE TAP

ACHIEVEMENT REFRESHES

Modeled on the achievements, trophies, badges, medals, etc. available in many computer games, this optional rule can amp up the badass quotient — and the thriller genre quotient — of your game even further. They are meant as hot rewards in play for following genre into danger and fun.

The basic rule of an Achievement is this:

- when an agent meets the criteria for an achievement
- and the player provides a colorful bit of roleplaying or hot-dogging
- the agent gets a 3-point refresh of whichever General ability seems most appropriate.

This may be the ability used to reach the achievement, or the dominant ability in a scene: a player who scores with a *Dead Man Walking* during a chase might refresh Athletics instead of Sense Trouble, for example.

Some achievements, such as *Armchair Sportsman,* can be fulfilled by Investigative abilities. To receive a refresh for such an achievement, the player must spend 1 pool point from a relevant ability.

Many of the achievements have fairly loose criteria, or criteria potentially entirely up to the players — "the last match in the box" for *Prometheus,* for example. For these achievements, players should aim to really bring it on the roleplaying, showboating, or colossal explosion. Directors should only negate an achievement if the player is being abusive, if the achievement seems completely pointless or shoehorned into the story, or if the achievement would badly damage the dramatic or horrific tone of the scene. Don't spend forever arguing about an achievement; when in doubt, just grant the refresh, add two more mooks to the next combat or 6 more Health points to the bad guys in this one, and move on.

The Director can make as many or as few of these achievements available as she wishes. She may also customize her own, either to reflect beloved clichés and genre moments from favorite films, or to reinforce the modes or themes of her campaign. She should write up a list of the approved achievements, or print them out on index cards and keep them handy.

In any case, any given achievement can only be triggered once per operation. Achievements exist to provide a wide menu of thematic genre moments, not an endless button-mashing sequence.

Some of the achievements suggest potential plot elements, clues, tactics, or scenes for the time-pressed Director or one who is seeking a few twists for her game. For players, this list includes plenty of cool stunts, heroic actions, and otherwise idiotic escapades that you could aim for and, of course, improve upon.

⚫ Achievement refreshes are almost never suitable for Dust mode games, although awarding 1 extra experience build point at the end of the operation for a suitably Dusty achievement (*Janus,* for example), won't completely overbalance the game.

ACHIEVEMENTS

A GOOD VINTAGE: Find incontrovertible proof that your target has been "alive" for more than a hundred years.

AMATEUR HOUR: Use the local rent-a-cops to distract the enemy from your true operation.

ANGEL FALLS: Swan dive into water from a height that most would consider fatal.

ARMCHAIR SPORTSMAN: Identify key information about a target's background purely from their fighting style, e.g., "That throat strike is a favored technique of French Foreign Legion paratroopers."

BARACUS: Fit armor plating to a civilian vehicle.

BIG-BA-DA-BOOM: Overestimate the amount of C-4 required for your Explosive Devices test by at least a factor of two. (The Director almost certainly awards this achievement after the fact and after the damage roll.)

BIRDMAN: Infiltrate an enemy compound via parachute or hang glider.

BOOTHROYD: Custom-build a gadget that is used to turn a final showdown in your favor, e.g., a silver-tipped TASER.

CHEF DE PARTIE: Have a shootout in or foot chase through a working commercial kitchen.

CORNERING ON RAILS: Complete a successful driving maneuver despite having four blown tires.

DAS TRUNK: Escape a submerged road vehicle.

DEAD MAN WALKING: Encounter the bad guy you iced on the previous op.

DEAD MAN'S HAND: Use a severed hand to open a palm lock. Also available in the *I've Got My Eye on You* variant.

EVERYONE'S A CRITIC: Break into Interpol's Ten Most Wanted as a result of your activities.

FAKIN' BACON: Impersonate a cop.

FULL FATHOM FIVE: Survive an underwater fight without SCUBA gear.

GOIN' UNDERGROUND: Infiltrate a fortified target location by using long forgotten sewers, tunnels, or catacombs.

GORDON RAMSAY: Mix easily available household chemicals into something that explodes.

GUAVA HALF: Kill a bad guy with a weapon improvised from something innocuous.

HARD LANDING: Jump from a bridge onto a moving truck/train below.

HEISENBERG: Get trapped in a situation where you are forced to run two simultaneous false identities in the same city.

The Camorra know you as Scialfione but the Colombians who happen to be in Naples for the drug summit at the same time know you as Ortiz. Try not to get both Scialfione and Ortiz invited to the same meeting!

HERMÈS HOLDOUT: Get out of a situation using a weapon concealed on your person in an unusual place: stiletto in your stiletto heel, Kel-Tec P32 in your garter belt or inseam, piano wire in your bikini strap or necktie. No points for shoulder, ankle, or small-of-back holsters.

HI HO SILVER: Escape your pursuers on horseback – in a city.

HUSH PUPPY: Clear an area of mooks using a silenced gun – before any can react. Double your Shooting refresh if you are not using the Player-Facing Combat rules to accomplish this.

I'VE GOT A BRIDGE TO SELL YOU: Successfully pass off tractor parts, talcum powder, or blocks of newspaper when your mark thinks he is buying arms, drugs, or dirty money.

INSIDE JOB: Plant evidence that fatally compromises the position of a node leader on Level 3 or higher of the Conspyramid.

IT IS A PRESENT FROM MY COUNTRY: Meet a native of the obscure town/village/nation used in your current Cover at the most inopportune moment.

IT'S ALL IN THE REFLEXES: Catch a thrown weapon and return it to its origin. (Difficulty equals 2 plus the total Weapons result (roll plus spend) of your foe; roll damage after making this test.) Successful completion almost certainly surprises your opponent, giving you a free action.

JANUS: Confront the mole in your org with incontrovertible proof of his guilt.

KRESKIN: Establish a Cover as a psychic or spirit medium, and back it up with a mentalist stunt. This could use excellent psychological techniques (Shrink or Bullshit Detector can provide a "cold reading") or it could be based on in-depth Research (with or without Digital Intrusion) of your mark's family, medical, and hidden personal history. ("No one could know that about me!")

LITTLE BLACK DRESS: Gatecrash an embassy ball.

LE MANS: Radically improve the performance characteristics of a standard car, e.g., adding twin turbos to a Smart ForTwo.

LE PIQUE-NIQUE: Destroy an open-air restaurant during a chase by driving a vehicle through it at high speed. (Preferably an establishment with few elderly customers.)

LIFELINE: Climb to safety from a high window using knotted sheets, a fire hose, or other improvised line.

LOOK NO HANDS: Drive a vehicle with your knees or feet (Driving Difficulty +3) because you are otherwise engaged fighting another occupant of said vehicle, or shooting at pursuers or your quarry.

LUCKY PUNK: You have exactly the same number of rounds left as you do bad guys.

LUCKY SEVEN: Fleece a casino to fund your ongoing fight against evil.

MAX SCHRECK: Successfully impersonate a vampire.

MINCEMEAT: Provide entirely convincing false data to a mark that completely throws them off your plans or leads them in a direction of your choice. This is likely entirely the Director's call.

MOTHER SUPERIOR: Impersonate a religious figure of any sort.

NIGHT SHIFT: Steal human remains from a mortuary, morgue, funeral parlor, or graveyard.

NOT SO VERY DIFFERENT, YOU AND I: Go up against an opponent who has had exactly the same training/martial arts master/service background.

ON THE COUCH: Psychologically manipulate an enemy agent and turn him to your control.

ONE-ARMED MAN: Complete your theft/intrusion/termination while

NIGHT'S BLACK AGENTS — DOUBLE TAP

leaving cast-iron evidence that implicates someone else.

PROMETHEUS: Use the last match in the box to do something epic.

RADIO FREE EUROPE: Gain total access to and control over your enemies' communications system.

RAMMING SPEED: Use a speedboat to take out a target on land.

READY PLAYER ONE: Use an RPG to destroy a moving helicopter.

RED OR BLUE: Stop a countdown clock with less than 10 seconds left.

REICHENBACH GAMBIT: Fake your/your group's death to throw pursuers off your tail.

ROCKEFELLER: Acquire enough cash that it requires more than one person to carry. (10,000 bills weighs 10 kg.)

SMOOTH OPERATOR: Lift, clone, and return a target's ID/credit card/cell phone without them noticing.

SURF'S UP: Traverse the entire exterior of a moving train or tram; this achievement is upgraded (double refresh) to *Hang Ten* if you are fighting as you do so.

THE REGIMENT: When challenged, you know the color of the boathouse.

TORINO: Engineer a massive traffic jam to your benefit.

WALKING ON AIR: Use the air-conditioning ducts to move around a building without anyone remarking on how very unrealistic that is.

WATCH THE BIRDIE: Replace the live footage of a security camera with your own footage either by hacking, physically "looping the tape," or using mirrors or a picture in front of camera.

WEISSMULLER: Swing between buildings, ledges, or the like using improvised material like power cables, comms cables, or washing lines.

WILD GEESE: Take "one last job" for someone who is not (or does not appear at the time) part of the Conspiracy.

YOJIMBO: Engineer a violent showdown between two competing criminal factions.

AD HOC ACHIEVEMENTS

If an agent does (and ideally survives!) something really impressive, heroic, superhumanly skillful, or just plain lucky *and* the play group can come up with a name that describes it succinctly whilst nodding towards the genre source material then it becomes a new achievement, complete with a refresh.

Julia's character Anika van der Waals, previously of Dutch Military Intelligence Service (MIVD), has just decoupled a freight car from a moving goods train. She brakes the slowing tank car (which contains thousands of liters of highly flammable liquid) to bring it to rest in path of the on-coming private train being used by the vampire lord. Anika just manages to scramble to safety as the fireball engulfs the viaduct.

Julia reckons this is worthy of an achievement — mounting a moving train, decoupling a freight car, braking in the right spot, and escaping — so she calls it *Chemin de Fer*, a lovely nod both to the railway and to a certain Mr. Bond's preferred type of baccarat.

Her Director agrees, and she takes a 3-point refresh in the Mechanics ability she used to decouple and brake the freight car. If Julia had used Driving to brake the freight car and Mechanics to decouple it, she might refresh either. Although she used Athletics to dive free, everyone agrees the freight car is the key element of this achievement.

ADAPTIVE TRADECRAFT

Good spies are great at thinking on their feet. Spies sucked into the blood-soaked world of *Night's Black Agents* must adapt even further. Tradecraft is the name given to the tips, tricks, and improvised equipment that keep agents alive to fight another day. Changing these techniques to hunt vampires requires lateral thinking, the right equipment and the devil's own luck. When you're a spy who becomes a vampire hunter, you use every advantage you get. This section discusses how to adapt Tradecraft techniques for the silent war against vampires and their minions. Each entry also includes alternate General and Investigative abilities that you can use to this end besides Tradecraft.

You can use the abilities as noted, or you can spend points to get more intel. Examples of suggested benefits from spends incorporating those actions are also included to stoke the imagination … or give the Director ideas on how to fight back.

DETERMINE WHEN THE CAR LEAVES

TRADECRAFT: If the enemy is wise to watchers and sweeps for spy eyes, purchase a cheap analog watch. Remove the wristband. Make sure it is set to the correct time and working. Wrap the watch in duct tape to protect the face. Locate the subject's vehicle in the parking lot or garage. Put the watch underneath one of the car's tires, to be crushed when the car moves. Return the next day to retrieve the watch. It will display the time the target left in their car.

ALTERNATE ABILITIES: Mechanics, Urban Survival

SUGGESTED BENEFITS

- You retroactively set the watch during an earlier visit. "Yeah, while you were flirting with that security guard, I found Stavros' Lexus and wedged this under the tire."
- Confirm the target leaves when it works best for the brilliant plan.

"Natalia leaves 30 minutes before sunset. If we want to get the hostile before sunrise, that's our window."
- Put together the vampire's itinerary for the evening. "Thursday nights he … it feeds at the discotheque. Creature of habit."

FAKE AN INJURY

TRADECRAFT: Skewer a few pieces of cardboard on a thumbtack. Put the tack in your shoe for a small nagging reminder of pain of an ankle injury. Tape a flexible metal ruler on the back of your knee to alter how you walk for a knee injury. Simulate a back injury by wearing a back brace reversed to give yourself a stooped over look.

ALTERNATE ABILITIES: Disguise, Diagnosis

SUGGESTED BENEFITS

- Convince an opponent to underestimate your condition. "Go easy on me? I'm still feeling the effect from last night's bout."
- Mislead potential followers. "No, the guy we're looking for has a limp."
- Lure a predatory vampire into thinking you're a weak victim. "The old fake limp gets them everytime. Get the pliers and the cloves of garlic."

CONCEAL LIQUIDS ON YOUR PERSON

TRADECRAFT: Go into any drug store and pick up cheap sample bottles. Alternately, raid the hotel mini bar and empty the small liquor bottles by your preferred method. Refill the bottles with more volatile liquids like acid, gasoline, or holy water. Small bottles such as these can get into otherwise secure locations such as airplanes. Plastic bottles can also be squeezed for a limited squirt effect.

ALTERNATE ABILITIES: Conceal, Chemistry

SUGGESTED BENEFITS

- You can walk into a secure room with gasoline. "Just hand sanitizer, boss."
- Burn your way through a lock. "When they said extra strength formula, they probably didn't have this in mind."
- Combined with a Hand-to-Hand Called Shot (+3 to Hit Threshold), jam your bottle full of holy water (or garlic oil, etc.) into a vampire's mouth. "Here's a juicy treat for you, sucker!"

MONITOR A NEGOTIATION

TRADECRAFT: Acquire two cell phones. Call one phone and leave the connection in place. Hide one phone on your person and carry one into the negotiation. At some point during the negotiation, leave to go to the bathroom, leaving your phone on the table. While out of the room, use the phone still on you to listen to the conversation going on in the room, since the negotiators will think you left your phone with them.

ALTERNATE ABILITIES: Conceal, Electronic Surveillance

SUGGESTED BENEFITS

- Reveal a bit of info they thought you didn't know. "Marceau is going to be quite upset you lowballed him to cover my costs."
- Get the location of the stash. "Go to the warehouse and bring him his cut from the diamonds."
- Detect who in the meeting is a vampire, if they don't register on electronic recording devices.

MAKE A CONVENIENT WALL SAFE

TRADECRAFT: Shut off the electricity in the location. Unscrew the plate covering a wall socket. Disconnect the wiring. Stash the items of value in the wall behind the socket. Replace the socket and screw it in for security. Items roughly the size of a deck of cards can be hidden this way, as well as small firearms.

ALTERNATE ABILITIES: Conceal, Mechanics, Preparedness

SUGGESTED BENEFITS

- Pull a weapon from the wall of the safe house. "I couldn't find a cookie jar I liked so I keep the guns here."
- Stash something on another site for later. (This will require insulated gloves, since you usually can't cut off the power.) "These night vision goggles don't fit in this tuxedo pocket."
- Booby-trap something valuable by reconnecting the wires. "Okay, it's behind the wall socket. You got what you wanted, now leave."

PWN A WEBCAM

TRADECRAFT: Many laptops, tablets, and phones come complete with webcams. Multiple programs exist to allow remote control of webcams. Loading these programs can be as easy as popping in a thumb drive for a few seconds or visiting a website for a few moments while the laptop's user is away. With devices like tablets and phones being carried everywhere, you can monitor a subject much more consistently.

ALTERNATE ABILITIES: Electronic Surveillance, Digital Intrusion, Filch

SUGGESTED BENEFITS

- Turn the laptop into a motion sensor. "Target leaves at 8 AM, returns at 4 PM"
- Record a sensitive meeting. "Now, *that's* an internship."
- Get the layout of the vampire's lair. "Looks like the coffin is hidden in the closet."

SEE IN DARKNESS QUICKLY

TRADECRAFT: Eyes normally adjust to darkness over a 20-30 minute period. Wearing red-tinted glasses helps your eyes adjust ahead of time. Wear the glasses and remove them when you enter the dark area.

ALTERNATE ABILITIES: Outdoor Survival, Surveillance

SUGGESTED BENEFITS
- Eliminate or reduce darkness penalties. "They can't see? They can't shoot back!"
- Track a subject in the evening without needing lights. "Keep the headlights off."
- Attack a vampire using red-filtered flashlights to reduce glare. "He can't target us."

GET IN WITHOUT A TICKET

TRADECRAFT: Trade shows, sports venues, hotel functions, and concerts generally require most smokers to pursue their habit outside the building. (Yes, even in France, since 2008.) Scope out the exit the smokers use. Wait until the event is underway; most security is concerned with people sneaking in at the start of an event rather than the middle. As new smokers cycle out, chat them up, offer and light cigarettes. When your new friends head back inside, join them. If security hassles you, tell them you left your badge or ticket in your seat. If security looks extremely tight, use the smoking huddle to lift a badge or ticket.

ALTERNATE ABILITIES: Infiltration, Flattery, Filch

SUGGESTED BENEFITS
- Shock a public figure by your appearance at the gala. "No further questions, Senator?"
- Scope out a building before a heist in two days. "Nice ceilings. We can probably mount a rappelling rig and not scratch the marble."
- Pocket some internal documents from a conspiracy front. "The Red Phoenix Initiative sounds harmless enough."

WRITE IN INVISIBLE INK

TRADECRAFT: Write a short message using a medium that becomes invisible when dry, get the message to the recipient, who then uses an activator to reveal the message. Writing the message on a blank piece of paper makes it more notable. Better to write the message on something else, like a receipt or junk mail, to hide its true purpose. A recognition code (e.g., three tack holes in one corner, or a code word in the cover text) indicates the presence of an invisible message to the recipient.

Classic medium/activator combinations include:

- eye drops/UV light
- lemon juice/iodine solution
- baking soda in water/purple grape juice
- crushed laxative in rubbing alcohol/ammonia-based glass cleaner
- diluted urine/hair dryer

Long-time deep-cover agents or asset handlers may have a specific or specialized chemical ink/activator combination they use.

ALTERNATE ABILITIES: Cryptography, Notice

SUGGESTED BENEFITS
- Send important messages hidden on mundane paperwork. "Kerensky always files his expense reports on time."
- Discover the name of a vampire written on the back of a receipt. "If he was bleeding so badly, why did he go to a pharmacy and buy eye drops?"
- Entrust a message to be held until other agents arrive. "Miss, I want you to hold onto this 100 euro note until someone asks to see it. Let them look at it, and then it's yours to keep. Can I get more coffee when you get the chance?"

COMMUNICATE DESPITE MONITORING

TRADECRAFT: Prisoners of war in Vietnam developed a tap code in which they laid out the alphabet on a 5 x 5 grid (merging *c* and *k* into one letter). By tapping out a rhythm of two sets of taps, one determining the row and the other determining the column of the letter, they sent messages to other prisoners without the guards catching on. They later refined the system to use coughs, hacks, sniffs, sneezes, and clearing the throat to get the messages out in a more natural manner.

ALTERNATE ABILITIES: Cryptography, Notice

SUGGESTED BENEFITS
- Leave a mundane voicemail with a hidden message. "Must be cold season in Minsk."
- Hide a password in the beats of an unfinished backing track, or a techno song on an iPod. "And here I thought he just had no rhythm."
- Communicate to a fellow agent while under the domination of a vampire. "She couldn't say her master's name, but she kept clicking her pen in a certain way."

HIDE DOCUMENTS

TRADECRAFT: Most thieves and operatives look under the bed or in your luggage. Hotel safes are also very easy for a professional to open because the locks are standardized and rarely changed. Take a large plastic freezer bag, put the documents (or other light item like a thumb drive) inside, and safety pin it to the top of the drapes. Make sure the bag can't be seen from either inside the room or through the window. A determined investigator given enough time will find anything in a hotel room, but someone on the clock will only hit the obvious places and move on.

ALTERNATE ABILITIES: Conceal

SUGGESTED BENEFITS
- Feed the conspiracy false information by hiding it in easier-to-find places.
- Present evidence of burglary and other crimes. "I took the liberty of coating the inside of the safe with a paint only visible in UV light. Gentlemen, present your hands."
- Monitor your room and catch the thief red-handed. "Hey, as long as you're looking under the bed can you see if the remote for the TV is down there?"

BUILD A BULLETPROOF BRIEFCASE

TRADECRAFT: "Bulletproof" is something of a flexible term. Attach armor plates (like those in a ballistic vest) to the inside of a briefcase with adhesive Velcro strips. The heaviest plates (ESAPI, weighing 3.25 kg apiece) can stop a .30-06 rifle firing armor piercing rounds. The real trick is getting the case up to protect your torso or head in time.

ALTERNATE ABILITIES: Military Science, Mechanics, Preparedness

SUGGESTED BENEFITS
- You switched cases before the meet. "You think I'd really bring the cash to the underground Albanian fight club?"
- The weight of the case pulls an opponent off guard. "Here, catch!"
- The documents inside were protected from the blast. "A sniper *and* a bomber? Were the Chechens having a sale?"

PRETEND TO DRINK

TRADECRAFT: In a public situation, order a drink with a Coke or other non-transparent chaser. Appear to swallow the tainted drink and then spit it into the chaser. Bartenders often have a chaser like this handy at the bar so they can appear to do a shot with a patron but not get drunk. If a chaser is not handy, seek out the nearest glass of water or potted plant to spit the drink into. Use a flask or sample bottle if you have one on your person. If another vessel is unavailable, keep a sponge taped to your wrist and spit it out there. Drinking from a bottle? Put your thumb over its mouth.

ALTERNATE ABILITIES: Filch, Reassurance

SUGGESTED BENEFITS
- You never drank the vampire's blood. "I kept it in my mouth until I went into the bathroom to freshen up."
- Pretend you are passed out to listen in on a sensitive conversation.
- Keep a sample to take back to the lab. "There were enough tranquilizers in that vodka to knock out an elephant."

TAKE FINGERPRINTS IN THE FIELD

TRADECRAFT: Common substances can be used to lift fingerprints. Use talcum powder on dark surfaces. Use copier toner on light surfaces. Remove the fingerprint using clear adhesive tape. Matching the fingerprints to a database usually requires a bit more legwork, but most spies have ways (such as Cop Talk or Digital Intrusion) of getting into a database easily. Even without access to a criminal database, building their own database of fingerprints can help the team keep track of the members of the conspiracy.

ALTERNATE ABILITIES: Criminology, Filch

SUGGESTED BENEFITS
- Get into a secure location using the lifted prints. "We can construct some fake fingertips out of latex to complete your disguise."
- Blow a cover identity. "Or, should I say, Alexandria Andretti?"
- Prove someone is a member of a vampire cult. "The next time you drink the Eternal Ocean from a chalice, you should wear gloves."

NIGHT'S BLACK AGENTS – DOUBLE TAP
STANDARD OPERATING PROCEDURES

There are times in every operation when you just get stuck. You may be out of obvious options, you may be over-planning, you may be suffering from analysis paralysis, or you may be at a loss as to the best strategy for confronting your vampiric nemeses. If your Director is particularly sadistic, you may even be hesitant to move because the stakes are too high and you're afraid that any move might be the wrong move.

THE CARTAGENA RULES

When play slows down, you should fall back on the *Bucharest Rules* (**NBA**, pp. 116-117), and you should consider the following guidelines. They're named the *Cartagena Rules* after a particularly spectacular playtest mission that left Cartagena in Colombia on fire and in the midst of a murderous drug war, with car chases and exploding helicopters drawing the unwanted attention of the authorities, but we'll say this: play never bogged down once.

COMMANDER'S INTENT

A common problem with any team of agents is over-planning. Players become obsessed with gathering as much intelligence as possible and with mapping out each stage of their anticipated assault, despite the fact that no plan ever survives contact with the enemy. In fact, it's remarkable if a plan is still on track ten minutes into its execution; there are just too many contingencies to take into account, especially when a good Director is experienced at keeping agents on their toes.

The result? Hours of relatively tedious planning immediately thrown out the window in exchange for an adrenaline-fueled scramble. The scramble's usually much more fun, but it's hard for most players to forego preparing at least a minimal plan.

This happens with real-world military commanders as well. The U.S. military now uses a concept called "Commander's Intent" (CI). It's a simple, clearly-worded statement of intent that appears on the top of every order, stating the plan's goal and the operation's desired result.

This is true both for high-level and tactical level operations. For a short-term operation it may be "clear the warehouse of enemy combatants and empty their vault." For a longer-term strategy, it may be "capture a vampiric-tainted creature and keep it alive long enough to question."

In a complex operation, the Commander's Intent helps keep combatants focused on the end goal. How you reach your goal matters less than remembering what the goal itself is. To develop a CI, fill in two blanks: *"If the mission accomplishes nothing else, it must…"* and *"The single most important thing we must do during this mission is …"* Think of the first as the end state: what does victory look like? The second is the core activity: what key thing will bring about that victorious end state? Then write it down, keep it visible for all players, and use it as a touchstone.

YOU'RE ALREADY PREPARED

It is worth noting that **Night's Black Agents** is a game that makes over-planning unnecessary. The Preparedness ability (and high levels of Mechanics), the Nick of Time (**NBA**, p. 33) and A Lift in Time Saves Nine (p. 41) cherries, the Calculated Risk maneuver (p. 50), and TFFB spends from Investigative pools (**NBA**, pp. 107-109) mean that an agent can smoothly adapt to new situations without bother or fuss. Trust your creativity and use your abilities; you'll have a more exciting game than if you'd spent hours working out a plan.

NOBODY DOES IT BETTER

Don't forget your MOS. The nice thing about a MOS is that it still succeeds, often spectacularly, even when you've completely expended all your points in that pool. There's some logic to saving your MOS for the most dramatically appropriate moment; when you're out of Shooting and your foe has you on the ropes, it's reassuring to know that you can still manage to slide your pistol into his open mouth before pulling the trigger.

In addition, every player treasures the look on a GM's face when they use their MOS to accomplish something completely unexpected. In one playtest adventure, a player used their Preparedness MOS and their entire Shooting pool to use a rocket-propelled grenade at the best possible time; in another, a well-timed Weapons MOS allowed an agent to throw a wooden stake with spectacular results. Do likewise.

CHOOSE THE MOST AWESOME ALTERNATIVE

If you have an array of equally good (or equally bad) choices in front of you and can't come to a decision, pick the most awesome alternative. Sometimes it helps to say "in an action movie, which would the hero pick? What's the most cinematic approach?" Then follow that path. (In a Dust mode game, ask "What would George Smiley do?" instead.) Even if it ends up being somewhat sub-optimal tactics, it gets you moving and usually gets the Director on your side. Regardless of how it develops, you're likely to end up with a memorable and spectacular dénouement.

GET THE LAY OF THE LAND

You hit a new location, touching down at the airport without any illegal equipment. What's the process for establishing yourself in a new city? It depends on how long you'll be there and what your goal is, but a few procedures always make sense. Consider establishing a safe house using your Network, or with other Abilities (**NBA**, p.112). Head there once you re-equip yourselves with standard weapons (**NBA**, p. 94). Call local contacts if needed and gain local intel beyond what a newspaper or the internet can provide. Using Human Terrain, ask the Director which local movers and shakers might interfere with your operation. If appropriate, you may even want to glance at a real-world map to get a quick lay of the land.

Once established, dig up clues on your target. Hacking skills are useful here, as you can use Research and Digital Intrusion to dismantle and display your enemy's online life. Accounting lets you trace their money trail, Architecture gives you floor plans of the buildings they're living in, and Electronic Surveillance allows you to tap into their supposedly secure internal video cameras. Expect that they'll have secrets you won't be able to find right away, but you'll have a fine start to your operation. Knowing where to strike is always a good first step.

HACK THE EXPOSITION

Interpreting clues is more fun than the process of gaining them. Sometimes you want many clues quickly in order to keep the plot moving. An agent with Digital Intrusion, as well as Research, Accounting, and other computer-related Investigative skills, is the Director's best friend. This skill set allows the Director to say, "You identify her image on the airport security cameras. You trace her flight to Vienna, re-identify her on the Viennese security cameras, track her on the traffic cameras out of the city, and know roughly what country town she must be hiding in." It also allows the Director to efficiently say, "You trace the wire transfer through five shell companies. Most people would never have been able to track it back to Drocas Industries, but you're not most people."

Basically, some clues are best found quickly in order to move the action forward. Don't be afraid to try using several of your Investigative abilities at once to make this possible.

WHEAT FROM CHAFF

There will be times when you find an abundance of possible clues, so many that your possible options become overwhelming. Don't panic. An advantage of GUMSHOE is that you can take each clue in turn, following it to see where it leads, and if it peters out or heads in the wrong direction you can always come back to it later. Best of all, good Directors give several different paths to the same end. You only need to find one set of clues that gets you to your objective, not all of them.

ASK ABOUT RED HERRINGS

There will be times when you suspect that a clue is a red herring, and you worry that your team is about to go down a rabbit warren of wasted effort as you follow the trail of someone who turns out to be a shoe salesman in New Jersey. Don't be afraid to ask the Director, "Are we safe putting this clue aside for now, under the theory that it isn't relevant?" Many Directors will tell you flat-out that you're on the wrong track. Even in a Mirror game, a red herring wastes time that could be spent luring you into trusting traitors. They want to see the game move forward as much as you do, so take advantage of this when you're otherwise stuck.

FOLLOW THE CLEAR LEAD

You will occasionally discover a single, miraculously clear lead. It may be that the bad guy has slipped up, it may be that you're so good you tracked down the real trail, it may be that you're running short on time in the game session and the Director wants to skip to the action.

When this happens, don't dither. Keep moving forward, and keep an eye open to make sure your targets haven't laid a trap for you.

NEVER TURTLE UP

The most important advice is to keep moving forward. GUMSHOE gives you clues for free if you're asking for them with the right ability. If you can't gain any intelligence from the thug you're questioning, he isn't going to give you any information; if you don't find pertinent information in the assassin's financial records, it isn't there to find. Keep moving, keep checking possible data and interpersonal trails, and you'll track down the next link in the chain.

PHONE A FRIEND

When in doubt, use your Network. It's particularly useful if you need information that's best obtained with an unavailable Investigative Ability. If you need a quick and accurate information dump, there's nothing like being able to call your old colleague in a local government agency who happens to be an expert on the matter. Likewise, if you need a massive garbage truck to block the road and stop a fleeing suspect, but you don't have the manpower (or Preparedness) to arrange it, calling your mobbed-up Network contact who happens to know some guys who own a local waste management firm will solve the problem neatly.

SUPPORT OTHER PLAYERS

Some players are more comfortable pulling out spy genre conventions at the drop of a hat, and levels of player expertise varies. Always be thinking about how to make the game more fun for the other people at the table. That may mean considering cool questions that could be answered with their abilities, or engineering ways for them to use their specializations in unexpected ways. If you're the player who manages to keep your wheelman involved and useful in an operation with no driving, you're going to make the game more fun for everyone.

WHAT'S THE WORST THAT CAN HAPPEN?

You may be paralyzed with inaction because you can't move on your enemy without drawing attention by local authorities. It's bad tradecraft, but some operations are worth risking exposure. There will be times when the best course of action is to do something entirely unexpected. Blowing up an unhallowed church in downtown Budapest, for instance. You'll draw Heat, likely lots of it, but it's always an option when you can't find a more subtle approach.

When it occurs you have a few options. You can find a real group to blame your activities on, create a fictitious group's electronic history using Forgery and blame your public mayhem on them, or just leave town for a while. Just always know where the exit is.

RETREAT IS AN OPTION

Sometimes the only legitimate course of action is to retreat. Perhaps your vampiric foe has you outflanked or is threatening to expose your cover. Sometimes the only tactic that kills your enemy involves too many innocent deaths. When that happens there's no shame in dropping back and regrouping, if for no other reason than it lures your enemy into a false sense of security.

THERE ARE DIFFERENT KINDS OF PRESSURE

Shadowy conspiracies thrive on the darkness. If you're unable to take down your target with physical action, either because you can't get to them or you don't know what they're vulnerable to, consider a political or social takedown instead. Glaring public exposure, political blackmail, sudden bankruptcy, massive inconvenience ... these are all other methods to achieve goals against a foe. If your enemy isn't flying because you hacked the U.S. government's do-not-fly list, she becomes more vulnerable when travelling by train. If your target has spent decades building up a popular and well-known public persona, dismantling it and ruining their reputation will send them into paroxysms of rage. Angry people – and angry vampires -- make mistakes. Leverage that to achieve your goals.

MATERIEL

A GOOD AGENT NEVER GOES INTO THE FIELD unequipped. And while resourcefulness can provide gear and tactical advantages on the fly, preparation is the key to victory. Preparation produces positive results, as the saying goes, and behind every good spy is a gadget-savvy sidekick, a well-endowed quartermaster branch, and government wonks with a passel of collegiate degrees and sixty-million-dollar grants to burn.

Here the materialistic spy will find more spytech, rules for tricking out vehicles, and even more types of bullets and bombs and things that go "bang" in the night.

MORE GEAR

The following section lays out yet more wonderful toys for the postmodern agent. It follows the organizational pattern of the corebook Spytech section, breaking gear down by the general task (and usually the General ability) for which it is designed.

Whether this equipment is "standard," or available in a Cache or with Preparedness, is up to the Director. Likewise, the Director can move Difficulties, provided ability pools, or any other value in this section up or down to match her campaign's "realism" level. By default, most of it is at the very least exotic – some of this gear is downright cinematic.

Fortunately, there's a rule for that.

THE Q RULE

This rule covers only devices and gadgets that you or the Director strongly believe don't actually exist outside the fevered imagination of scriptwriters and thriller novelists. If you can find something like it with a real-life price tag on the Internet somewhere, it's just a Preparedness test. Also, the Director has to be willing to allow it in her campaign. Some gadgets are simply impossible, or too campy, or violate the game's tone.

Describe, ideally in the form of a flashback, the implausible gadget you claim to have been issued (or built, or found in an abandoned weapons lab, or whatever). Spend 12 total points from Preparedness and whatever ability the concealed gadget uses (e.g., a bomb in a pen would cost 12 points from Preparedness and Explosive Devices). You now have, on your person, a gadget meeting your specs. For wilder games, lower the cost to have a gadget: Daniel Craig has a laser-watch for 12 points (Preparedness and Shooting); Sean Connery has a laser-watch for 9 points; Roger Moore has a laser-watch for 6 points.

COMMUNICATIONS

Communications equipment overlaps with Surveillance equipment in many cases. As a general rule, if you're using it to penetrate enemy communications networks, it probably requires a test of Digital Intrusion or Surveillance, or a spend of Electronic Surveillance. If you're using it to protect your own network, or to communicate with your own team, it may require a one-time, 1- or 2-point spend (of Mechanics or Electronic Surveillance) to set up, but is presumed to work until blown up, shot to pieces, or hastily abandoned in a Varna safe house.

AUDIO JAMMER

This black box, about the size of a wallet, produces either white noise or low-level interference to disrupt bugs and focused microphones. With a Difficulty 3 Mechanics test, it can be rigged into a bug detector, perfect for sweeping potential safehouses or hotel rooms, wherever agents find themselves needing privacy.

SCRAMBLER

This device alters a radio signal at the point of transmission in order to make it unintelligible to receivers that lack the appropriate descrambling technology, ensuring the privacy of a communication between parties. The method of encryption can be cryptographic, digital, or incorporate the use of spread spectrum signal generation. An agent must possess the Electronic Surveillance ability to set up a scrambler; activating a scrambler is just flicking a switch.

Overcoming a target's scrambler depends on the means of encryption, but always requires a lengthy sample of scrambled communications, or just gaining access to an enemy's receiver. A transmission that has been cryptographically altered requires dedicated cracking software, and a 1- or 2-point Cryptography spend. A digitally scrambled transmission or spread spectrum signal transmission requires a Difficulty 5 to 7 Digital Intrusion test to defeat; building a descrambler is a Mechanics test with a similar difficulty. Commercial shortwave and digital descramblers are available, but don't necessarily defeat anything more robust than police scanners. Really, it's much simpler to steal a walkie-talkie.

Spread spectrum signal generators provide a Digital Intrusion or Surveillance contest advantage against an opposing signal jammer when sending out a transmission.

TIME-LIMITED MESSAGE DISCS

Useful for recording messages, dead drops, or other sensitive materials, these self-playing minidiscs are one-use only, consuming themselves in a hiss of smoke (or flame, Director-depending) once the message is played through once. The messages may be of any length or complexity, perfect for disposable "burn after reading" briefings.

DISGUISE

Wearing a disguise always requires a Disguise test to bring off confidently, although piggybacking is allowed for groups of disguised agents. Also, if a superior disguise artist succeeds in making you up after a suitably difficult Disguise test, you might only have to spend 1 or 2 points of Disguise to keep your cool and avoid touching the fake moustache all the time.

Acquiring a fake ID badge usually devolves to Forgery or Filch; passing a fake ID is usually a fairly easy Disguise test or even a 1-point spend if the ID is good.

Standard Equipment: Baseball cap, blank badges and ID cards, bronzer, brushes, contact lenses, costume jewelry, eyeglasses, eye pencil, false mustache and brows, gloves (latex, leather, and thinfilm), glue, hair color, hair extensions, heel lifts, insignia and patches, jewelry, makeup, neckties, paint, plastic inserts, putty, reversible jacket, spirit gum, sunglasses, talcum powder, temporary tattoos, throat spray, wigs.

FACIAL MASKING TECHNOLOGY

This unit is roughly the size of small suitcase, and requires an external power supply. Starting with a set of source photos (a 1- or 2-point spend of Photography or Research), the self-contained latex spray and prosthetic apparatus produces a three-dimensional mask of the target. The machine takes anywhere from five to thirty minutes to produce an individual mask, but using the mask (and assuming you have the proper wig or dental implants) subtracts 3 from the Difficulty of specific impersonations.

Although the above is cinematic tech at its finest, the CIA does reputedly have a technology called "Dagger" that creates a paper-thin mask wearable for specific missions. Most likely, Dagger masks create "generic" faces to allow an agent to escape surveillance, but you never know — Hollywood makeup and SFX artists have been working with the CIA for at least 40 years. Barring that, a Dagger mask is one-use, and cannot stand up to rain, heavy physical activity, or being punched in the face. It provides 5 pool points of Disguise or Surveillance to escape enemy searchers; when the pool is empty, the mask is too badly degraded or sweaty to keep using.

VOICE SYNTHESIZER

A thin collar of carbon with a round disc wraps around the throat, most often worn with a facial mask (see above) to mimic the voice. Accompanying software (usually running on a smartphone or nearby transmitting computer) mirrors speech pattern and inflection, ensuring that whatever the agent says sounds like the original voice. Using a voice synthesizer subtracts 1 from the Difficulty of specific impersonations (4 from the Difficulty of voice-only impersonations). A 1-point Mechanics spend allows you to rewire the device to "throw" the voice, making it seem as though it comes from some other location.

Again, this is fairly cinematic technology, but basic voice-changing technology is decades old. Simply altering speech into unrecognizability is an app available on most smartphones; a small disk that does the same thing can be screwed into telephone receivers for devotedly retro agents (or agents in devotedly retro Balkan nations). Applying computer software to change an agent's voice to a specific voice print may still be on the edge of possibility, but off-the-shelf programs exist to change male voices to female, old voices to young, and make almost any other alteration you can imagine. The illusion still breaks down face to face in the real world, of course.

EXPLOSIVE DEVICES

See the corebook for:
- rules for the Explosive Devices ability (**NBA**, p. 29)
- explosive classes and damage effects (**NBA**, pp. 67-68)
- booby trap construction (**NBA**, p. 98)

EMP WEAPONS

EMP (Electro-Magnetic Pulse) weapons kill any electrical devices within range by generating an intense and fluctuating magnetic field. This field induces a powerful electric current in any conductive object. So, wires, power cables, antennae, electronics, even metal pipes within the field get supercharged, and they'll pass the power spike onto anything connected to them. A powerful EMP weapon can permanently fry all electrical systems in a whole city. Powering down an electrical device protects it from a low-level EMP, but not a big blast.

Now, the classic way to generate a big EMP effect is to detonate a nuclear bomb, ideally high in the air to maximize the area of effect. Back in the good old days of the Cold War, the U.S. feared the Soviets might try to knock out the whole eastern seaboard with a single high-altitude nuke.

Of course, nukes are overkill in most situations, and there are other ways to generate a smaller EMP burst. A flux compression bomb – a finicky combination of bomb and an electrical armature – can kick out a strong enough pulse to fry a city block. Building such a device requires both Explosive Devices and Mechanics (both at Difficulty 5), not to mention some expensive and exotic components. Flux compression bombs are one-shots, but do have the virtue of being vehicle-portable. Other ways to generate a pulse, like a Marx generator, can be reused but need an awful lot of juice to run.

When using a NNEMP (non-nuclear electromagnetic pulse) weapon, the trick is calibration. (This may require a Physics spend.) Generate too weak a pulse, and you only fry the electrical systems closest to you. Too strong a pulse can cause a lot of collateral damage – the power spike might fry systems across the city. Also, remember that the pulse expands in all directions – unless you stick your own gadgets in a Faraday cage to shield them, they'll also be destroyed. off a sizeable EMP is also going to be treated as a terror attack (+4 Heat at least), as the authorities are twitchy about infrastructure these days. Also, remember that switching off electronics may suit older vampires perfectly -- they come from an era before telecommunications and blinkenlights, and would be quite happy to return to the Dark Ages. A city without street lighting is a vampire hot buffet.

Finally, the new non-lethal hotness is directed-EMP (more technically HERF: High-Energy Radio Frequency) weapons – a gun that zaps the electrical systems of whatever it's pointed at. Aim at a car, fry the ignition and control systems. Aim it at a phone, disable it. Aim it at a laptop, fry it. Theoretically, you can make one of these with the guts of a microwave oven and a few big capacitors (Difficulty 5 and about an hour's work), but the effectiveness varies wildly depending on the target. Directed-EMP weapons are less power-hungry than their big brothers, but still require several minutes to recharge between firings. They are human-portable, but not remotely concealable: think of a radar gun with a microwave oven on it.

While man-portable, reliable HERF weapons remain on the edge of reality for now, larger EMP weapons already exist. The U.S. Army has tested broader-focus vehicle-mounted HERF weapons. When fired at a crowd, the targets feel feverish and hot (effective temperature 54°C), imposing a -3 penalty to Athletics and forcing a Difficulty 5 Health test to remain downrange of the HERF. (Targets who fail also become Shaken.) That particular weapon has a 500-meter range, but in theory such weapons could focus their effect anywhere within line of sight from a parabolic or planar array.

BINARY EXPLOSIVES

Tannerite, H2, and other binary explosives usually blend ammonium nitrate and ammonium perchlorate with other compounds. Until mixed, they are inert; once mixed, they become explosive (class 1). They can be left in powder form, but are more useful mixed into clay or thick paint. Such explosives are great for taking out doors, hinges, and small barriers to entry, and in emergency combat situations.

They usually require impact (such as a bullet strike) to set them off, but an Explosive Devices test (lower Difficulty with a Chemistry spend) can create binary explosives that detonate on an electrical spark, flame, or after five seconds of evaporation exposes a trigger chemical such as sodium to air. A higher Difficulty test increases the mixture to a class 2 explosive.

GRENADES

Hand-loading grenades with anti-vampire payloads such as holy water, garlic oil, silver nitrate, wood fragments, etc. is an Explosive Devices test at Difficulty 4. You can modify one grenade per hour at that Difficulty; adding one additional grenade per hour increases the Difficulty of the test by 1. On a failed test, the best possible outcome is a whole bunch of inert grenades.

Grenades modified to deliver a non-explosive, non-shrapnel payload do class 1 damage, not class 2 damage. Grenades that simply replace their normal fragmentation payload with silver or other metallic shards do normal damage.

Some other examples include:

BELL GRENADE: This grenade is about the size of a bell pepper. Detonating it produces not a concussive force, but rather a loud clanging, jangling, or tinkling sound. It can best be compared to a sound-only flashbang (agents refer to it as a "jinglebang"), projecting a ringing tone of silver bells – perfect for disorienting foes (who must make a Difficulty 5 Health test or be deafened and surprised for a number of rounds equal to their margin of failure) and demoralizing those things sensitive to the ringing of bells. It does no other damage.

BONE GRENADE: This grenade is a canister, lined with blessed bone fragments. Once detonated it produces a hail of razor sharp bone shards, which do full damage against unarmored open targets, but class 1 damage against targets under cover or wearing armor. Ideally, of course, the blessed bone shards are also the target's bane and do damage as other banes.

See the list of rifle grenade ammunition on p. 77 for more inspiration.

LAND MINES

You think modifying grenades to deliver a different payload is hard? The parallel test for land mines (or Claymores) is Explosive Devices at Difficulty 6 with working or black-market mines; Difficulty 5 with decommissioned or safe-stored mines from a military stockpile. (Increase all Difficulties by 1 for cluster mines or similarly tricky munitions.) You can modify one land mine per two hours at that Difficulty; adding one additional mine per two hours increases the Difficulty of the test by 1.

Land mines modified to deliver non-explosive, non-shrapnel payloads do class 2 damage, not class 3 damage. Mines that simply replace their normal fragmentation or canister payload with silver or other metallic shards do normal damage.

INFILTRATION

ANTI-INFRARED CLOTHING

When attempting to infiltrate a location, hide from snipers, or sneak behind a hideous creature of the night that can see into the infrared spectrum, anti-IR clothing can be of great benefit. This clothing absorbs or masks infrared radiation and gives a contest advantage to Infiltration checks where the opponent is using night-vision technology or can see naturally at night. In some cases, it might negate a foe's entire Alertness modifier.

This technology goes back to WWII; in modern use, it might involve metallized fibers in the weave or chemical treatments for the cloth.

ANTI-SURVEILLANCE ATTIRE

An unrecognized agent is a living agent. Remaining hidden and anonymous is necessary for covert operations. Sadly, cameras are ubiquitous in modern society. From surveillance devices placed throughout the city to random citizens capturing cell phone images, it is increasingly probable that an agent might leave evidence that can be run through facial recognition software. Anti-surveillance attire, typically in the form of casual wear like T-shirts, hoodies, or jackets, contains imagery and patterns that interfere with pattern recognition software, effectively concealing the identity of the agent from passive computer searches. Anti-surveillance attire grants the wearer a 3-point pool that can be used for Infiltration, Surveillance, or Disguise spends against computerized visual surveillance.

While the specific notion of clothing designs to thwart surveillance software remains cinematic, carefully applied makeup can bollix at least current facial recognition software. Applying such makeup is a Difficulty 7 Disguise test.

EMMU CLIMBING GLOVES

These gloves, similar in construction to weightlifter's gloves, are covered in adhesive pads wired with tiny coils that create electromagnetic micro-vacuums with other surfaces creating adhesion on any solid surface or texture. Using a rolling/rocking motion of the hands the wearer is able to climb or scale surfaces otherwise impossible. One warning, though: It is possible that given extreme temperatures or stress (say, supporting your entire weight by your fingertips) that the gloves may fail to adhere. Check with your Director often while climbing.

Magnetic gloves that work on steel-frame buildings already exist; for glass surfaces such as, say, the Burj Khalifa in Dubai, the cinematic gloves above or human fly cups (**NBA**, p. 98) remain the only option. Using these supertech gloves lowers the Difficulty of a climb by 2 versus human fly cups: from Difficulty 9 to 7, say.

FREQUENCY SCANNER

This remote control device scans along the 315-430 mhz bands to deactivate whatever car alarms are within a 10-meter radius. With a 1-point Mechanics (or 2-point Digital Intrusion or Driving) spend; it can be set to activate the alarms instead.

Most garage doors, gates, and other automatic barriers work on fairly sophisticated signal spreading systems with a rolling code. Cinematic spies can use frequency scanners to sniff and hack these codes (with a Digital Intrusion test), but an Infiltration test can usually defeat the keypad more simply.

RFID SNIFFER

RFID tags are in everything from cars to ID badges to phones to credit cards to pets to electronic keys to anything inventoried in a big box store or warehouse. They listen for an interrogation signal and transmit their coded number in response.

This device, about the size of a coffee-table book (easily concealed in a backpack or briefcase), sends out a series of interrogation signals, then scans for 13.56 MHz outputs characteristic of RFID tags, records the tag's specifics, displays them on a screen, and writes them to a memory card. From there, making a cloned tag is simple, and creating a perfect duplicate ID or credit card, for example, is just a Forgery spend away.

Available commercially over the Internet, it takes a Difficulty 5 Mechanics test, a 1-point spend of Data Recovery, and one day to build an RFID sniffer from relatively common electronics. Such a sniffer works only within 2 meters of the tag. An even smaller sniffer, about the size of a trade paperback, works within 35 cm of the tag.

WRIST LASER

As noted, this is the sort of thing the Q Rule (see p. 63) covers.

Designed to look like a wristwatch, this cutting tool can be used to slice through nearly anything, given enough time. As a weapon, it works only up to Close range. Its limited damage (-1) makes it at best a quick close-quarters distraction.

Need it be said, the most powerful handheld cutting lasers are still only 5 watts, compared with the standard cutting laser output of 1500-6000 watts. Using a big cutting laser to open a vault or burn through a steel coffin is completely (well, mostly) realistic, but such devices weigh 80 kg or more and require mains power and heavy duty cooling or heat sinks. That said, you can build a 5 watt cutting laser with the DVD burner, heat sink, and power supply of a desktop computer, which is enough to burn through plastic, set fires, and blind aircraft.

CAR HACKING

If you're in some little podunk former Soviet satellite or Third World country, then you can steal a car using the time-honored methods passed down from the ancestors. Pop the door lock by sliding a coat-hook down the window, hotwire the ignition, drive off. There are eight-year old kids who can do all that in thirty seconds; you can do it with a Difficulty 2 Infiltration test (or the Open Sesame or Grand Theft Auto cherries).

In the West, though, we're not driving cars any more. We're driving computer networks with wheels. To steal one of those means you've got to get a bit technical – unless you take the easy approach, and steal the owner's keys first. You don't even have to keep the keys. Modern cars have a data port, the On-Board Diagnostics port, located under the dashboard. If you can get access to that port for five minutes with a laptop, some specialist software and a Difficulty 4 Digital Intrusion test, you can hack the car and upload whatever malware you like. You could, for example, program the brakes to lock at a certain speed, or alter the readout on the fuel display so the driver runs out of gas without realizing it, or override the door locks so the driver gets trapped inside. You could even insert your own subroutine allowing you to override the driver and take remote control of the car like an RPV. Or, more prosaically, you could gain access to the door-locking mechanism and inject your own code so you can open the car with your own keyfob later on.

Things get trickier if you can't get physical access to the owner's dashboard or his keys. Spoofing the unlock code is doable, but it isn't easy. The best approach is to build a small RFID sniffer (see facing page). Pop this gadget in your coat pocket, put it near the keyfob (say, by standing next to the owner for a few minutes at a party), and the decoder keeps demanding the keys respond with the unlock code. It'll take some time for the decoder to find the right challenge, but once it does, you've got the secret code to unlock and start the car.

You can also use two antennae – put one near the keys, and the other near the car, and the car thinks the keys are nearby. On some models, you can then just pull the handle to open the car; on others, it just disables the alarm so you can finish the job with Infiltration.

With social engineering, you can talk a car open. If the owner's signed up to OnStar or a similar service, then with a basic knowledge of the owner's personal data and a convincing (Reassurance spend) story, you can claim you locked your keys in the car and need the nice operator to send the unlock code.

You can also use GPS systems to track a car's location (Digital Intrusion, Difficulty 4), but you need the car's VIN (Vehicle ID Number), which can also be obtained with a short-range RFID sniffer. Some cars also boast a remote-shutdown feature. If your car gets stolen, the car company can send a signal that automatically slows the car to a stop, then freezes the engine. Hacking the car company network to override a specific car requires a Digital Intrusion test at Difficulty 6, but remember that anyone who's remotely paranoid will certainly have disabled this feature already.

MECHANICS

Unlike most of the other General abilities, "standard equipment" for Mechanics varies too widely to be handwaved. A full machine shop doesn't just materialize wherever an agent happens to be, after all – and different machine shops are required for different sorts of construction and repair.

That said, a commercial (or criminal) auto garage holds most of what an agent needs for most missions, and a quick trip to the hardware and home supply superstore will finish the inventory nicely. For more electronically focused Mechanics work, a TV or computer repair shop supplies the (minimal) heavy or specialized tools.

Regardless of the above, an agent with a decent rating in Mechanics can have an Arduino, batteries, a crimping tool, driver set, multi-tool, pliers, power drill, screwdrivers, soldering iron, spudger, tape measure, tweezers, wire cutters, wire stripper, wrench set, and assorted minor hardware (bolts, diodes, nails, nuts, screws, wires, etc.) in his go-bag for most missions without needing to invoke Preparedness.

3D PRINTERS

While not quite the magic build-anything device of futurist legend, 3D printing technology can make the creative agent's life much easier. The primary use for 3D printing in the field is manufacturing specialized parts that would otherwise have to be stolen (leaving traces) or sourced (leaving different traces). Using a 3D printer is fairly simple. Designing a printed object from scratch is a Mechanics test; wire rats or helpful assistants with Chemistry, Research (to pull up pre-existing programs and blueprints), or similar abilities can lower the Difficulty.

CONSUMER GRADE 3D PRINTER

This desk-sized unit (perfect for safehouses and forger's dens) can create a reasonable facsimile of most three-dimensional objects and prototypes.

CINEMATIC RULES: Using a 3D printer with a 2-point Forgery spend creates duplicate items (diamonds, guns, antiquities) that can reasonably bypass cursory inspections. They cannot pass specialist examination.

PROFESSIONAL GRADE 3D PRINTER

Most consumer grade 3D printers use ABS plastic or similar agents for the manufacture of small objects by an extrusion process. More sophisticated printers use selective laser sintering and other techniques to create more useful objects from a broader array of materials. A professional grade 3D printer can be set up to manufacture objects out of carbon fiber, thermoplastics, paper, plasters, titanium, and other metals. Such a printer requires a permanent home, ventilated work space, and industrial power, and is at least twice the size of a desk-sized unit.

CINEMATIC RULES: Professional grade 3D printers can be used for forgeries in the same manner as consumer grade printers. Additionally, a professional grade printer may be used to manufacture readily usable equipment: bullets (including silver, hollow-point, etc.), knives, and so forth. Even in the non-cinematic world, 3D blueprints for a single-use plastic .380 caliber pistol exist; material strength is the only real barrier to printed submachine guns, for example.

Building an object requires a spend from a related ability and a test of Mechanics. The more complicated the object, the higher the spend or the higher the Difficulty. In general, a 1-point Investigative spend equals a 3-point General spend.

> *For a 3-point Piloting spend and a Difficulty 4 Mechanics test, Ivan could print a working UAV that could be used for surveillance. Or, he could spend 1 point of Piloting but increase the Mechanics test Difficulty to 6. Or, he could make a 1-point Physics or Military Science spend to design the UAV and manufacture it with the original Difficulty 4 Mechanics test.*

Abilities such as Chemistry, Vampirology, Shooting, Occult Studies, or Diagnosis could allow for the manufacture of a wide array of equipment. The only obstacle is the acquisition of ingredients; Network is usually more reliable than Streetwise. The metals and organic compounds used in professional grade printers are in granular form and quite expensive: agents with steady funds will drop to insufficient funds for the next few missions.

SURVEILLANCE

BLUEJACKING SOFTWARE

This software can be installed on an agent's smartphone or laptop computer and allows agents to hijack a target's Bluetooth capable device. An agent can make a Difficulty 5 Digital Intrusion test to remotely implant phone cloning, data mining, and buglike surveillance software into the target's Bluetooth capable device. For remote implantation, the agent must be within 15 meters when using a handheld device and 100 meters with a laptop computer. The software can also be physically installed by flash drive into the target's device, which may be done with a Difficulty 4 Filch test or an Infiltration test into the location where the device is kept.

SIM CARD COPIER/READER

This USB stick can duplicate a cell phone's SIM card, cloning all information and making it possible to create multiple phones with the same number and contacts. It's also useful for overhearing phone conversations. It requires access to the phone to be cloned; the phone should use UTMS architecture (see *Cloning a Mobile Phone*, p. 17).

A 1-point Electronic Surveillance spend allows an agent to clone an existing phone and overhear the calls it makes and receives, as well as its browser history and text messages, both sent and received.

If the agent has this device, access to the phone in question, and a rating in the Electronic Surveillance ability, the Director should provide any core clues accessible from the target phone without a spend.

VEHICLES

JETPACK

On the cusp of practicality since the 1950s, a typical jetpack allows an agent to fly 200 meters, with a maximum ceiling of 35 meters, before it runs out of hydrogen peroxide fuel. The absolutely best (powered by jet fuel) test models promise 9 minutes of flight time and a ceiling of 75 m, for a potential range of 15 km. You begin to see why jetpacks have fallen out of favor as secret agent vehicles this century.

Jetpacks have Speed -1, Maneuverability -1. They fall between a speedboat and a Humvee on the Vehicles table (**NBA**, p. 101).

In 2004, the Swiss pilot Yves Rossy invented an avgas-burning four-engine jetpack mounted on a carbon-fiber wing (2.4 meter wingspan). Rossy's jetwing requires the pilot to wear a fireproof suit and a parachute for braking, but it can cross the English Channel at Calais (6 km) in 9 minutes, reaching a top speed of almost 300 kph. In an extremely cinematic game, the agents might be able to build a jetwing (Difficulty 6 Mechanics test) given the necessary components. (The wing, at least, can be 3D printed.) In which case, of course, the Conspiracy has had production milspec jetwings all along – plus a squadron of camazotz.

Jetwings have Speed +1, Maneuverability +1. They fall between a racing motorcycle and a sports car on the Vehicles table (**NBA**, p. 101).

PERSONAL INFLATABLE PROTECTION SPHERE

This translucent nylon and Kevlar shell, worn uninflated as a thick belt, expands at the pull of a tethered cord to encase the wearer in an inflated bubble (2 meter diameter) of body armor. Designed to protect the wearer and her possessions while in hostile territory, the bubble provides 360-degree protection from most small arms fire and projectiles (armor -2). It is not rated to withstand explosive or concussive forces, or slow cutting (armor 0). From inside the sphere, the wearer can "roll the ball" at a slow walking pace – or *much* faster on a steep slope! An inflated sphere reduces the wearer's damage from falls by half. The wearer cannot fire a weapon out of the sphere without deflating it and trapping herself.

Believe it or not, something very similar to this device was actually patented in 1988. It is based on the avalanche airbags worn by some climbers: at the tug of a ripcord the airbag inflates and uses the fluid dynamics of the avalanche to "sift" the wearer to the top of the snow.

PARAGLIDER

Great for those moments when you need to bail out of a speeding vehicle, cross a ravine or escape from a window, this one-agent ripstop polyester or nylon wing folds up small enough to be harnessed under a tearaway jacket (with a 2-point Conceal spend) and used during dramatic escapes. (In the real world, make your dramatic escape at least 150 meters from the ground, or 60 m if you're using a static line tethered to the building.) It uses a "ram air" airfoil inflated by the onrushing wind to maintain lift and steerability; a paraglider can stay aloft for hours and cover hundreds of kilometers. A successful Preparedness test to have a paraglider includes a vario-altimeter (or a vario-altimeter app on your smartphone) for finding altitude and detecting air temperature.

Someone with a slot of Piloting assigned to paragliders has a contest

MATERIEL ■ MORE GEAR : SURVEILLANCE TO VEHICLES

advantage against a flier using only Athletics to direct their sail. Such a slot also applies to BASE jumping parachutes, which have a similar design but less maneuverability, lift, and range. Apply a contest advantage to the airfoil most suited to the immediate task.

Paragliders have Speed -1, Manuever +1. Small, cinematically concealable paragliders fall between a cabin cruiser and an APC on the Vehicles table. Larger paragliders and steerable airfoil parachutes (such as those used by various special forces) fall between a scooter and a horse on the same table, but lower the Difficulty by 1 for safe landing tests. Such paragliders cannot be concealed under clothes, but can be carried in a large duffel bag.

REMOTELY PILOTED VEHICLES

RPVs and UAVs (Unmanned Aerial Vehicles) have become major tools of espionage, military reconnaissance, and surveillance. They can be as complex as a Predator drone (500 kg payload, 150 kph cruising speed, 14 hour hover time on station, $4.03 million) or as simple as a really nice remote-control helicopter with an onboard camera (500 g payload, 200 m range, 10 minute flight time, $400). Ground RPVs vary similarly: a remote-controlled truck makes a fine bed for a camera, garlic tear-gas bomb, or anything else under about 5 kg. U.S. forces in Afghanistan and Iraq regularly used $300 toy trucks as C-4 delivery devices for EOD work, for example.

Mastering an RPV or UAV takes up a slot in Piloting; you can also use a Driving slot for remote-operated ground vehicles.

Rigging a normal vehicle to operate by remote control is a Difficulty 4 Mechanics test for most vehicles; for larger or more complex vehicles, Difficulty increases to 5; for large and complex vehicles, the Difficulty for remote wiring is 6. If the operator of the vehicle has a Driving/Piloting slot both for RPVs and for the vehicle being "driven" or "piloted," the Difficulty of the Driving or Piloting test is lowered by 1 as compared to tests using an RPV/UAV slot alone.

WINGSUIT

A wingsuit comprises three small ram-air airfoils under the arms and between the legs, to provide extra lift to a falling human body. It allows an agent to fly at a rate of 2.5 meters forward for every 1 meter that she falls, but requires an Athletics test to land without injury as from a fall at 50 kph. Assuming plenty of vertical falling room, a wingsuit can carry an agent over 20 km (the world record is just short of 30 km).

Wingsuits have Speed -1, Maneuver +1. Their speed falls between a dirt bike and a speedboat on the Vehicles table.

In the default **Night's Black Agents** world of well-rounded badasses, wingsuits combine with paragliders, BASE jumping chutes, etc. to take up a single Piloting slot.

In the real world, the skills are not that easily transferrable. Wingsuit is its own vehicle for Piloting purposes. A compromise solution is to increase all Difficulties for wingsuit ability tests (Athletics or Piloting) by 2.

VEHICLE-BASED EQUIPMENT

Installing equipment into a vehicle requires a test of Mechanics and some amount of time. Time to install drops by one day or by half (whichever is less) as the Difficulty of the installation test increases by 1.

> *Desmond wants to install the anti-blast sheeting in two days instead of three, so he increases the Difficulty of his Mechanics test to 5 instead of 4. To install the plates in half a day would increase his Difficulty to 7 (two days is Difficulty 5, one day is Difficulty 6, half that is Difficulty 7).*

NIGHT'S BLACK AGENTS – DOUBLE TAP

VEHICLE-BASED EQUIPMENT TABLE

ITEM	LOCATION	DIFFICULTY	TIME
anti-blast sheeting	underside of car	4	3 days
automated steel plating	windshield, rear windshield, door windows	5 (**6** with CCTV)	4 days
caltrop dispenser	rear bumper	4	1 day
disposable car skin	exterior of car	3 (lamination) 6 (electroplating)	2 hours 2 days
electroshock system	exterior of car	5	3 or 5 days (see text)
EMP cannon	front grille and engine compartment	5	3 days
fog dispenser	rear exhaust, front wheel well and bumper	4 (rear), 5 (front)	1 day
machine guns	headlights or front grille, tail lights or rear bumper	4 (front tracer), 6 (rear tracer with CCTV), 7 (targeting system)	2 days (tracer) 4 days (targeting system)
magnetic license plates	rear or front bumper	2	1 hour
nitrous oxide injector	engine	4 (single-port) 6 (multiple-port)	1 day 6 days
oil slick dispenser	rear wheel well and bumper	4	2 days
winch	trunk, bed of truck	4	2 days

The above table includes the item, the locations available for installation, the time needed, and the Difficulty of installing it. This does not include the Difficulty and time needed to build the more complex systems from scratch: installing machine guns implies having working machine guns to cut away and spot-weld to the car frame, for example. Simpler systems, such as oil slick dispensers, can clearly be built on the spot during the install: the Director will decide borderline cases depending on her game's pace and plausibility.

Note: The "base" car for these installations is assumed to be a relatively roomy sedan, van, or truck. Installing them into a smaller or more tightly engineered vehicle (such as a sports car, boat, aircraft, or military vehicle) increases the Difficulty.

⬤ Most of this gadgetry is purely cinematic, if technically possible. Icons indicate equipment that might be installed in a vehicle without disturbing the Dust mode.

⬤ ANTI-BLAST SHEETING

This 5-cm thick metal plate protects the cabin of the vehicle from explosives both external (land mines or IEDs driven over) and installed (bombs wired to the underside of the car). The sheeting prevents the blast from spreading upward into the cabin, as well as protects the car's innards (oil pan, gas tank, etc.) from possible rupture and inevitable explosion. Against such explosives only, it moves the car's occupants from effective Annihilation range to Debris range on the Explosion Damage table (*NBA*, p. 67). A successful Driving test (Difficulty equal to the explosive class +3) allows the vehicle to continue moving after the blast.

The sheeting also lowers the vehicle's Maneuver by -1.

AUTOMATED STEEL PLATING

Also called "dinosaur plating," these 2.5-cm thick steel plates rise up to cover the exposed glass surfaces in the car. The driver raises and lowers the plates with switches, like power windows. A car so armored cannot see to continue driving except at a substantial penalty (+2 to Difficulty, or +1 if the mechanic also installed a CCTV system inside the cabin). The plating provides armor -3 for the windows only, or for the doors when the system is down.

CALTROP DISPENSER

Metal shrapnel of various and jagged dimensions are ejected behind the car from a reservoir in the rear of the car. Pursuing cars must make a Driving test at Difficulty 6 or either slow down (their Driving spends restricted to 1 point for the next two rounds) or blow out their tires (*NBA*, p. 56). Cars that make the test *exactly* only blow out one tire.

In a thriller chase, pursuing cars that fail their Driving test lose 2 Lead.

DISPOSABLE CAR SKIN

Change the color of your car to aid your escapes. Entirely cosmetic, this paint job comes in two varieties — a laminate layer to be peeled off by hand (a Difficulty 5 Driving test while the car is moving) or an electroplated coating shed via electrical charge triggered from within the car. While the car wears the skin, the agents' Difficulties of Surveillance, Disguise, or other tests to evade hostile identification decrease by 1.

◉ Laminated skins are completely realistic, even if removing them during a car chase isn't.

ELECTROSHOCK SYSTEM

A system of relays routes a potent taser-like sting to anyone who makes contact with the surface of the car. The system is powered by supplementary batteries, most often stored in the car's trunk. It delivers a Moderate shock (***NBA***, p. 83). The system works on the car alarm circuit, and must be activated or deactivated remotely.

With two extra days' work, you can insulate the ignition and interior of the vehicle to allow normal operation with the electroshock system active. Agents can activate the sting while inside, or even while the car is in motion.

EMP CANNON

The size of a large motion picture camera, this weapon emits a single EMP pulse up to a range of 60 meters, perfect for disabling a single vehicular target, with a Shooting test (base Difficulty 5). It runs off a capacitor that fills the trunk, and must be recharged after 1-3 shots (roll after each shot). See *EMP Weapons*, p. 65.

FOG DISPENSER

Projects a cloud of thick, cohesive smoke either in front of or behind the vehicle, intended to obfuscate and aid in escape. It increases the Difficulty of opponents' Driving tests (to follow or pursue) and Shooting tests to hit the vehicle by 1.

In a thriller chase, pursuing cars that fail their next Driving test after the fog deploys lose 1 Lead.

MACHINE GUNS

Modified MP5s (or similar 9mm submachine guns) are trimmed down and housed within the chassis of the vehicle, water-cooled by a supplemental radiator and activated at the push of a button by the car's operator. Aiming is either by tracer fire or by a laser-optical range finder similar to the targeting system on helicopter gunships. Acquiring the latter is likely very difficult.

◉ MAGNETIC LICENSE PLATES

Escaping detection has never been easier now that a resourceful agent can slap on this new license plate. Combine this tech with 2-point Forgery or 1-point Mechanics and 1-point Driving spend and all that stands between an agent and a pesky border patrol that may ask too many questions is how fast they can push down the accelerator.

The Difficulty and time in the table refer to plates the driver can demagnetize and jettison by closing a contact on the dashboard.

◉ NITROUS OXIDE INJECTOR

This system is usually as simple as a tank of nitrous oxide (N2O or NOS) attached to the vehicle's fuel injector or manifold; the hyperoxygenated N2O increases the combustion temperature of the fuel, ideally translating into increased power. More complex systems attach to each intake port, with multiple cylinders of NOS controlled by solenoids and computerized flow valves.

Activating a single-port NOS injector gives you a 3-point Driving pool that must be spent within two rounds or be lost; a multiple-port NOS system gives you a 6-point Driving pool that must be spent during the chase.

A failed Driving test while a NOS system is active results in damage to the vehicle's engine: all Driving Difficulties immediately increase by 2 for that vehicle until it can be repaired. On any unmodified Driving roll of 1 for the rest of the chase, the vehicle either crashes or flames out.

OIL SLICK DISPENSER

This device sprays a pressurized jet of motor oil in a car-wide mist behind the car.

Pursuing cars must make a Driving test at Difficulty 5 (plus that vehicle's Maneuver) or spin out. Cars that make the test *exactly* slide badly; their Driving spend for the next round is restricted to 1 point.

In a thriller chase, pursuing cars that fail their Driving test lose 1 Lead.

◉ WINCH

This powered unit attaches to either the front or rear bumper of your vehicle and spools out 50 meters of cable, useful for dragging vampires out of holes and into sunlight or pulling your teammates up the side of a cliff they may have fallen down. A larger winch spool, mounted in the trunk, van interior, or truck bed, can hold up to 1,800 meters of cable. Winch motors are reversible: they can pay out line or reel it in.

Harpoon: A specialty head for a winch cable, a harpoon can be fired with a compressed-air (or gunpowder) charge or carried into a vampire den and hooked into a suspicious coffin. It is armor-piercing, doing +1 damage if wielded or thrown by hand using Weapons or +3 if fired with Shooting. (A full-sized whaling harpoon is a 2-meter long, 55-kilo hunk of steel fired by a 75mm cannon. In other words, unlikely to appear in operations outside Norway.)

For the driver to fire a winch-harpoon from inside the vehicle requires a Shooting or Driving test at a Difficulty 2 higher than normal, in addition to the penalties for attacking during chases (***NBA***, p. 56).

A small harpoon gun or similar installed in the back of a van or truck does not impose a targeting Difficulty penalty, but must be fired by hand using Shooting. The Director may still impose extra penalties for speed, range, or obstructions.

Harpooning another vehicle during a chase not only does damage, it also prevents the Lead from widening past 2 while the cable holds. (A harpoon can only hit another vehicle at Lead 5 or less; a hit immediately reduces the Lead to 2.) The driver of the harpooning car can also spend his own Driving pool points at 3 for 1 to affect the harpooned vehicle's Driving tests while the cable holds. This represents deliberately whipsawing the target car with the harpoon cable.

The metal harpoon cable has on average 3 Health (-1 armor), and will shear if cut, clawed, lasered, or otherwise wrecked.

NIGHT'S BLACK AGENTS – DOUBLE TAP

FIREARMS

Many *Night's Black Agents* playtesters requested a big list of guns. I was sympathetic to their request, but I just couldn't justify taking up a lot of space in the corebook with such a thing. Why not?

First and foremost, because with the advent of Wikipedia a big list of guns is just a mouse-click away. I mean, a *really* big list.

Even better than Wikipedia, for us anyhow, is the Internet Movie Firearms Database (http://www.imfdb.org/wiki/Main_Page).

Look up the movie, and bang, there's all the guns in it. What was that amazing grenade pistol Robert de Niro uses at the beginning of the ambush in *Ronin*? Why, it's a Heckler & Koch HK69A1 40mm Granatpistole. What does Sarah Connor use to take down the T2000? Just a little old Remington 870 12-gauge shotgun with a folding stock and a high-capacity magazine tube full of solid slugs. What's that machine pistol Kate Beckinsale shoots through the floor with in *Underworld*? A (very unlikely) fully automatic mod of the Beretta 92FS, with "compensators" to lengthen the barrel and counter the (imaginary) recoil.

Secondarily, damage modifiers and type of weapon (pistol, rifle, shotgun, SMG, assault rifle) aside, there is no rules-mechanical difference between guns in *Night's Black Agents*. A big weapons table would therefore contain almost no useful information, being merely a way to show off the fact that I know how to use the Internet Movie Firearms Database.

Compounding this lack of difference between different makes and models of guns, various makes and models of guns can be (and often are) rechambered in different calibers, redesigned to hold larger or smaller capacity magazines, and so on. James Bond's famous Walther PPK can be chambered in 7.65x17mm (.32 ACP), .22 Long Rifle, or 6.35x15mm SR (.25 ACP), all of which do +0 damage. Or in two different kinds of 9mm (Short, or .380 ACP, and Ultra, or PP-Super), both of which do +1 damage. It holds 7, 8, or 9 rounds (the PP in .22LR can hold 11). The same gun can also mount any number of tactical options from suppressors to laser sights depending on the user and the mission.

USERS AND MISSIONS

Which is where we could, almost, justify putting a big list of guns back in. Deciding, in a hurry, what the opposing force is armed with, or what's available on the black market in Bratislava, can be tricky for the less gun-happy Director. The weapons loadout listed for the various Opposing Forces pregens (**NBA**, pp. 66-67) provides the basic armament for the type of force (e.g., pistol and shotgun for the police; an assault rifle for a soldier) but the specific models are there primarily to illustrate the rules.

Hence, the *Firearms by User* table below. For each of the countries, and many of the organizations, listed on pp. 164-166 of the *Night's Black Agents* corebook, this table gives a first-order approximation of the weapons they field as standard issue. Standard issue is, however, not necessarily standard. Older weapons hang on; units involved in cross-training or special exercises with other armies may arm themselves differently. Border or interior troops may have slightly older weapons; elite troops slightly newer or better or imported models. You can always find an excuse to put a semiautomatic Glock 9mm pistol in someone's hand shooting at the agents: there are over 5 million Glocks in production, "standard issue" for some military or police force in over 50 countries.

And it can always get more complex. Special operations forces have access to, and use in the field, an even wider range of weapons. Delta Force and DEVGRU operators can and do literally arm themselves with any weapon in the world; Spetsnaz and other first-tier special forces likewise. Spies or covert operatives often use weapons associated with the host country or with a third party they intend to frame. Weapons selected for the table are thus "characteristic," not definitive.

> ### THE ARES SHRIKE 5.56 AMG
>
> I know I just said I didn't want to get into just listing a bunch of guns, but did you know there's a light machine gun that actually fits into a briefcase? The ARES Shrike belt-fed light machine gun uses the receiver, grip, magazine well, stock, and other lower body of an M4A1 carbine plus a belt-feeder, bipod, quick-change barrel, collimating sight, and baffle suppressor. It fires 5.56mm ammunition from either conventional M16 or M4 magazines or 200-round disintegrating belts. It still only does +0 damage, but thanks to that bipod, the cost of Autofire drops to 2 Shooting points for each extra instance of damage.
>
> A skilled shooter can have the Shrike out of its attaché case, assembled, and ready to fire in 20 seconds with a Difficulty 3 Shooting test.

The Colt M1911 .45 ACP, for example, is no longer standard U.S. military issue, but many (perhaps most) Delta operators much prefer it to the smaller, lighter (and double-action) Beretta M9 9mm official sidearm. U.S. Marine Corps Recon units still use it, rebranded as the M45A1. In the final analysis, the weapon is characteristic enough of American forces and American heroes in thrillers (such as, again, Robert de Niro in *Ronin*) that it deserves its nonregulation place in the table.

Where no damage modifier is listed, assume the weapon does standard damage for its type and caliber. A "carbine" is just a short-barreled assault rifle, usually configured for use in tight quarters such as jungle or urban warfare, or by vehicle mounted troops. A Personal Defense Weapon (PDW) is, essentially, a submachine gun (usually) firing armor-piercing rifle ammunition instead of the SMG's pistol ammunition.

The "special" column is especially not exclusive, representing weapons neat enough or characteristic enough to warrant a shout-out. For example, only

MATERIEL ■ FIREARMS : USERS AND MISSIONS

FIREARMS BY USER

UNIT OR AGENCY	PISTOL	ASSAULT RIFLE	SPECIAL
NIS (Bulgaria)	SIG Sauer Pro SP 2022 9mm	AR-M4 SF 5.56mm carbine	Blaser R93 Tactical .308 sniper rifle
People's Liberation Army (China)	QSZ-92 9mm or 5.8x21mm armor-piercing	QBZ-95-1 5.8x42mm	QCW-05 5.8mm suppressed SMG
GIGN (France)	Manurhin MR 73 .357 Magnum revolver	SIG SG 550 5.56mm	H&K 417 7.62mm Designated Marksman Rifle
2eme REP (French Foreign Legion paratroopers)	PAMAS-G1 9mm (licensed copy of Beretta 92G)	FN P90 5.7x28mm Personal Defense Weapon (+0 damage)	LGI Mle F1 51mm personal grenade launcher (Class 3 explosion)
Police Nationale (France)	SIG Sauer Pro SP 2022 9mm	SIG SG 550 5.56mm (RAID elite police only)	H&K MP5 9mm hollow-point SMG (RAID elite police only)
GSG 9 (Germany)	H&K USP 9mm	SIG SG 550 5.56mm	H&K MP7A1 4.6mm armor-piercing machine pistol (+0 damage)
SAS (Great Britain)	Browning Hi-Power 9mm	Colt Canada C7A2 5.56mm	H&K P11 underwater pistol (fires underwater at no penalty)
Special Branch (Great Britain)	Glock 17 9mm	H&K MP5 9mm hollow-point SMG (single shot only)	Benelli M3 dual-mode (pump or semiauto) 12g shotgun
Qods Force (Iran)	PC-9 ZOAF 9mm (Iranian clone of SIG Sauer P226)	KH2002 "Khaybar" 5.56mm	Nakhjir 7.62x54mm sniper rifle (Iranian clone of Dragunov SVD)
Sayeret Matkal (Israel)	SIG Sauer P226 9mm	Colt M4A1 5.56mm carbine	Uzi-Pro 9mm SMG (weighs 2.3kg, 30cm long)
Carabinieri (Italy)	Beretta 92F 9mm	Beretta AR70/90 5.56mm	Beretta 93R 9mm machine pistol (3-round burst or single shot only)
GROM (Poland)	FN Five-seveN 5.7x28mm armor-piercing	H&K HK416 5.56mm carbine	Barrett M107A1 .50 anti-materiel sniper rifle (armor-piercing)
Vulturii (1st Romanian Special Forces Bn)	Glock 17 9mm	H&K G36K 5.56mm carbine	H&K UMP 9mm SMG
Spetsnaz (Russian special forces)	Izmekh PB 9mm silenced	TsNIITochMash AS Val 9mm (+1 damage) suppressed	TsNIITochMash Vintorez "Thread-Cutter" VSS armor-piercing 9mm suppressed sniper rifle (can be broken down and fit in a briefcase)
OMON (Russian Interior Ministry militia)	GSh-18 9mm armor-piercing	AKS-74U 5.45mm carbine	Stechkin APB 9mm silenced machine pistol
Swedish Army	Pistol 88 9mm (licensed copy of Glock 17)	Bofors Ak 5C 5.56mm	Accuracy International Arctic Warfare Psg 90 7.62mm sniper rifle

[CONTINUED OVERLEAF]

FIREARMS BY USER, CONTINUED

UNIT OR AGENCY	PISTOL	ASSAULT RIFLE	SPECIAL
Çevik Kuvvet (Turkish National Police "Agile Force" anti-riot unit)	Yavuz 16 9mm (licensed copy of Beretta 92G)	H&K MP5 9mm hollow-point SMG	Akdal MKA 1919 12g shotgun
Ukrainian Army	Makarov PM 9mm	AK-74 5.45mm	RPG-29 "Vampir"
Delta Force (U.S.)	Colt M1911 .45 ACP	H&K HK416 5.56mm carbine	Milkor Mk 14 MGL-140 (six-shot 40mm grenade launcher)
DEVGRU (U.S.)	SIG Sauer P239 9mm	FN SCAR M17 7.62mm	H&K MP7A1 4.6mm armor-piercing machine pistol (+0 damage)
DSS (U.S.)	SIG Sauer P229 9mm	Colt M4A1 5.56mm carbine	Remington 870 pump-action 12g shotgun
Swiss Guard (Vatican)	Glock 19 9mm	SIG SG 550 5.56mm	Halberd (+1 damage)

one man on any squad in the French Foreign Legion 2nd Parachute Regiment carries the LGI Mle F1 51mm personal grenade launcher. But the fact that the Legion uses them at all as standard infantry weapons is noteworthy and evocative, and well worth listing here instead of yet another Designated Marksman Rifle or submachine gun.

GUN CHERRIES

This section can also add some difference back in in the form of *gun cherries.*

A gun cherry is a special feature of the weapon that provides a bonus of some kind when the user rolls an unmodified 6 on a Shooting test and hits a foe. (This also addresses another common playtest concern: players who rolled a 6 after spending a lot of points felt their good roll was "wasted.") More than one weapon can have the same gun cherry; no weapon should have more than one.

When you select your weapon, if your campaign uses gun cherries, you can assign it any *one* gun cherry. The "suitable for" line in the cherry listing is drawn either from a weapon's real-life performance characteristics or its military legend, but again — any weapon can be optimized for any sort of result given enough time and attention. The legendarily clunky, jam-prone WWII Sten gun, made of stamped metal by toy manufacturers, became the SAS' weapon of choice — *if* they got to keep the Stens they hand-modified between fights.

BFG
EFFECT: If a foe wishes to fire at you, he must first spend 1 Shooting point to nerve himself to the task. For each Intimidation point you spend on a single foe, that foe must spend 3 Shooting points to target you. This effect lasts until your next action.
SUITABLE FOR: Any gun chambered for Magnum ammunition, any gun over .45 caliber (11.7mm), Vintorez VSS 9mm sniper rifle, Remington 870 pump-action 12g shotgun, Milkor Mk 14 MGL, any anti-materiel rifle

HANDY
EFFECT: You may make an immediate Extra Attack at half Shooting cost as your weapon responds effortlessly to your aim.
SUITABLE FOR: FN Five-seveN pistol, any Glock, GSh-18 9mm pistol, SIG Sauer P239 9mm pistol, SIG Sauer Pro SP 2022 pistol, FN P90 PDW, FN SCAR M17 7.62mm assault rifle, any carbine, any PDW, H&K MP7A1 4.6mm machine pistol, Uzi-Pro 9mm SMG, Akdal MKA 1919 12g shotgun, Milkor Mk 14 MGL.

HIGH CYCLIC
EFFECT: The cost of each further instance of damage using Autofire (**NBA**, p. 71) is reduced to 2 additional Shooting points.
SUITABLE FOR: Colt Canada C7A2 5.56mm assault rifle, KH2002 "Khaybar" 5.56mm assault rifle, QBZ-95-1 assault rifle, AS Val 9mm assault rifle, any PDW, QCW-05 5.8mm SMG, Glock 18 9mm machine pistol, H&K MP7A1 4.6mm machine pistol, Uzi-Pro 9mm SMG

MOBILE
EFFECT: Multiple targets of your Extra Attacks *in the next round only* do not have their Hit Threshold increased.
SUITABLE FOR: SIG Sauer P239 9mm pistol, SIG Sauer Pro SP 2022 pistol, FN Five-seveN pistol, any Glock, FN SCAR M17 7.62mm assault rifle, KH2002 "Khaybar" 5.56mm assault

---

HAND-LOADING YOUR OWN GUN CHERRY

Assuming the Director lets you get away with it, feel free to design your own gun cherries to suit your own notion of firearm behavior. No cherry can have more than one effect; try to keep them in line with the options provided here.

When designing your own cherries, avoid "extra damage" as such. Extra damage, even on a 6, is an expensive bonus in the game economy: see, for instance, the Critical Hits and Special Weapons Training options (**NBA**, pp. 73 and 76). That said, note the Precision Accuracy cherry, which grants a damage bonus on the back end, as it were.

rifle, any carbine, any PDW, FN P90 PDW, Blaser R93 Tactical sniper rifle, H&K MP7A1 4.6mm machine pistol, H&K UMP 9mm SMG, Uzi-Pro 9mm SMG, Akdal MKA 1919 12g shotgun

PRECISION ACCURACY

EFFECT: If you spent any points on a Called Shot, refresh 2 Shooting points immediately.

SUITABLE FOR: H&K USP 9mm pistol, FN SCAR M17 7.62mm assault rifle, any sniper rifle or Designated Marksman Rifle, Akdal MKA 1919 12g shotgun

RUGGED RELIABILITY

EFFECT: The solid reliability of your weapon lets you concentrate on other matters; refresh either 1 Mechanics or 1 Preparedness point.

SUITABLE FOR: Colt .45 ACP pistol, any Glock, GSh-18 9mm pistol, Makarov PM 9mm pistol, Manurhin MR 73 .357 revolver, Bofors Ak 5C 5.56mm assault rifle, AS Val 9mm assault rifle, H&K G36K 5.56mm assault rifle, Dragunov SVD 7.62x54mm sniper rifle, Uzi-Pro 9mm SMG, Milkor Mk 14 MGL, RPGs; all Kalashnikovs and AK-clone weapons including AR-M4 SF 5.56mm carbine, AK-74 5.45mm assault rifle, AKS-74U 5.45mm carbine, AK-47 7.62mm assault rifle, etc.

SMOOTH ACTION

EFFECT: If you Jump In next round, you need only spend 1 point of Shooting to do so.

SUITABLE FOR: SIG Sauer P239 9mm pistol, M16A2 assault rifle, Colt Canada C7A2 5.56mm assault rifle, any carbine, any Glock, Uzi-Pro 9mm SMG, Akdal MKA 1919 12g shotgun

STOPPING POWER

EFFECT: The foe's action moves to the end of the ranking order in combat.

SUITABLE FOR: Colt .45 ACP semi-automatic pistol, QBZ-95-1 assault rifle chambered for 5.8x42mm, any gun chambered for Magnum ammunition, any shotgun firing slugs

ACCESSORIES AND AMMUNITION

There is literally no end to the "tacticool" stuff you can hang onto or fire out of a gun. Entire periodical series, reference manuals, trade shows, genres of fiction, and **GURPS** supplements exist to celebrate firearm gadgetry. Here are a few such things in a slightly more technothriller vein.

COLLIMATING SIGHT

This sight projects a red dot coinciding with the weapon's aim point onto a lens inside the scope (or sometimes, onto a small screen such as a visor's HUD). The dot, generated by a tritium illuminator or by a battery, is not visible outside the gun – this is not a laser sight (*NBA*, p. 103). A collimating sight can be (and often is) combined with a scope; it not only improves accuracy but situational awareness, as aiming is faster and can be done with both eyes open.

The Hit Threshold of a target inside your gun's normal range (Near for pistols, shotguns, and submachine guns; Long for rifles and assault rifles) decreases by 1 if you aim through a collimating sight. Like a laser sight, using a collimating sight lets you target a foe as if the level of darkness (*NBA*, p. 52) were one lighter: Dark becomes Night, and Night becomes normal. These sights cannot compensate for Pitch Black darkness, however.

The sight is not collimated for Extended Range attacks (*NBA*, p. 67) and provides no benefit for them. You cannot get the benefit of a collimated sight for Extra Attacks, Jump In, Reckless Attack, or any other maneuver that implies quick action at the expense of aiming.

COMPENSATOR

A compensator attaches to a firearm's muzzle, venting some firing gases upward and thus compensating for barrel climb and recoil. Using a compensator reduces the cost of Autofire, Extra Attacks, and other maneuvers involving multiple shots in a round by 1 Shooting point each.

It cannot be combined with a flash suppressor or silencer: it increases both muzzle flash and noise! Using a compensator is officially announcing that you don't care who finds you: Sense Trouble automatically succeeds, Infiltration fails.

CORNERSHOT

This almost meter-long mechanism has a 60° hinge in the middle. It mounts a video camera and a port for a sidearm on the muzzle end; a screen and an interlocked trigger remain on the butt end. The user inserts her pistol into the port and voila! The user can see, and shoot, around corners. The basic mechanism can accommodate most common Western-made 9mm pistols (Glock, SIG Sauer, Beretta 92, CZ); another model comes with an integral 40mm grenade launcher. Versions in design now will take NATO 5.56 assault rifles such as the M16. It takes a Difficulty 4 test of Mechanics (Difficulty 5 Shooting) to alter one CornerShot frame for a different make of pistol.

Although the trade name refers to the Israeli-American version of the device, China, Iran, Pakistan, and South Korea have demonstrated their own CornerShot equivalents optimized for their own preferred 9mm sidearms.

This attachment cancels the effects of the Handy and Mobile gun cherries.

SLEEVE HOLSTER

Made famous by Secret Service agent James West in the TV show *Wild, Wild West,* the sleeve holster was apparently invented by that show's prop designer Tim Smyth. (The WWII SOE "sleeve gun" was a one-shot silenced barrel-block Welrod gun with no grip.) A sliding rail holds a very small pistol kept up the inside of the user's forearm with a spring. The agent presses his elbow against his side, triggers the spring, and the gun slides down the rail into his waiting hand. (Unless the trigger, hammer, or sights catch on his sleeve, but that never happens to badass types like **Night's Black Agents** heroes.) In normal circumstances, the agent spends 2 Conceal or Shooting points to produce her "gun from nowhere." She automatically goes first in a gunfight — or gains surprise when the other side suddenly discovers they're in a gunfight. In a quick-draw contest against a worthy foe like a vampire-speed Renfield or a

U.S. Marshal, the agent gains a 2 point bonus on her first Shooting test only.

The gun for a sleeve holster is usually a .22, but West's famous Colt derringer was a .38 Special, and the most common derringer, the Remington 95, was .41 caliber. Loading a .41 derringer with a .410 shotgun shell is far from uncommon. James Bond's original gun, the Beretta M418 .25 ACP "pocket pistol," also makes an admirable sleeve gun choice.

Agents cannot buy, source, or otherwise scrounge up a sleeve holster; it must be custom built, *Taxi Driver* style, with a Difficulty 4 Mechanics test. (Whether the Director allows a sleeve holster to materialize with a Preparedness test is up to her.) With a Difficulty 2 Mechanics test, you can modify the sleeve holster to deliver a wooden stake, crucifix, minibar bottle of holy water, or other handy vampire surprise.

SPECIAL AMMUNITION

Sometimes traditional cartridges don't cut it. Sure they'll stop your average goon or make a mugger think twice about breaking down your door, but there exist creatures that can shake off bullets that way a good agent can shake off snowflakes. To that end, a resourceful agent makes use of non-standard ammunition.

BONE: Blessed bone (such as saints' relics) is another strong possibility for vampire killing rounds, although the supply is both limited and nigh-impossible to authenticate beforehand. Treat them as wooden bullets (**NBA**, p. 107).

BREACHING ROUNDS: Fired from a shotgun, these destroy hinges, lockplates, chains, and other obstacles to entry and then disintegrate without penetration or ricochets. Designed for law-enforcement forced entry, breaching rounds are made of sintered metal powder in a wax binder. With a magazine of "master keys" and a 1-point spend of Shooting, an agent (or other skilled shooter) can go through any door in one round except those with explicitly armored hinges and locks. Breaching rounds are most common in 12-gauge. Fired directly at a human target, they do -1 damage with no positive modifiers for range or shot spread.

CERAMIC: Most "ceramic" bullets are merely frangible rounds, intended to come apart when striking a surface harder than flesh (such as the cabin wall of an aircraft). Recently, German ammunition manufacturers have experimented with hollow bullets made with a ceramic shell and a disintegrating plastic nose. Unlike conventional hollow-point bullets (**NBA**, p. 104), they do no extra damage; in fact, damage drops by 1 point. Armor ratings increase by two: -1 armor becomes -3, for example. Why use them at all? Their potential payload of liquid cargo triples or quadruples. You can, for example, fit an entire clove of garlic inside a ceramic 9mm shell. The Director may rule that a "killing amount" of, e.g., holy water requires a ceramic Magnum round.

DISCARDING SABOT: Usually used in artillery rounds, a discarding sabot (usually a light alloy and nylon construct) protects the real round (traditionally a faster, denser, shaped round) from the firing process, then falls away in flight. DS rounds are a great way to fling blessed bones, silver flechettes, pieces of hawthorn, or other penetrative banes toward an undead target. In technothriller theory, a DS round could also encase holy water ice bullets, protecting them from melting during firing. So far, small arms DS ammunition only exists in 7.62mm calibers.

MATCH-GRADE: Propellant formulations, projectile weights, case alloys -- every aspect of the round changes its performance. Ammunition precisely calibrated for maximum accuracy and velocity is needed in shooting matches – hence, "match-grade" rounds. Commonly associated with snipers and usually hand-loaded (Difficulty 4 Shooting test hand-loads 20 rounds per hour), match-grade ammunition can only be used in one specific weapon. However, it lowers the Difficulty of a Called Shot by 1.

UV-EMITTER: The hard part of replicating the "liquid sunlight" rounds in *Underworld* is not the ultraviolet. A Japanese team has developed organic light-emitting materials, while ammonia and hypobromite in solution cause near-UV chemiluminescence; a 2-point Chemistry spend can surely tweak these formulae to produce a true UV-emitting binary. Alternately, LEDs measure only about 2 mm, meaning plenty of aluminum nitride UV LEDs could fit into a 9mm cartridge filled with a conductive gel transmitting the firing pin's impact as electrical energy to power them. No, the hard part is a transparent jacket to get the neat glowy effect. If you use transparent carbon fiber or some other doubletalk, treat UV-emitter bullets as tracers: your Hit Threshold drops by 1 against incoming fire for the next two rounds, but so does your target's. Ceramic bullets filled with UV-emitting liquid don't glow in flight, but release their glow onto or even inside the target! Regardless of the delivery system, UV bullets continue to glow (and potentially do damage to the undead) for 3-5 rounds after firing.

GRENADE LAUNCHERS

Pioneered during the Vietnam War, grenade launchers that attach to a rail underneath a rifle are standard issue in most major militaries. They have their own trigger and action separate from that of the rifle. Specialized grenade launchers remain in the arsenal, however: outmoded Vietnam-era launchers such as the shoulder-fired M79 "wombat gun" or "Thumper" are more readily available on the black market than modern underbarrel grenade launchers such as the M203.

Most modern grenade launchers fire 40x46mm grenades; some fire 37mm "civilian" grenades, and the now-abandoned M29 advanced assault rifle had an integral 20mm grenade launcher. Some grenades are "long" and don't fit all launchers. As with all conventional ammunition decisions, grenade minutiae are as relevant as you choose to make them in your game.

An underbarrel grenade launcher attachment cancels the effects of the Handy and Mobile gun cherries.

RIFLE GRENADES

The term "rifle grenades" is something of a misnomer, now that the majority of them aren't fired from the barrel of a rifle but from a dedicated launcher, but we use it to differentiate weapon-launched grenades from hand grenades. Rifle grenades have a maximum range of Long; Extended Range applies (**NBA**, p. 67). No rifle grenade works at Point-Blank range; improved modern fuses and technothriller convention allow them to work at Close range.

The most advanced grenades work integrally with the laser sight and computer-assisted launcher: such complex systems require a 2 higher Difficulty to source with Network and/or a 3-point Streetwise spend and excessive funds. They can be fired in any of four fuse modes set just before firing, and programmed by a computer chip inside the grenade:

AIRBURST: Using a laser designator, the user can select the exact range at which the grenade bursts. This usually negates Cover, as the grenade airbursts exactly behind and over the obstruction.

IMPACT: The grenade detonates on impact. Simple enough.

DELAYED IMPACT: The grenade explodes immediately *after* the first impact, making it ideal for firing through thin walls, light doors, drop ceilings, and so forth. This doesn't so much negate Cover as turn *everywhere* in a modern office building or tenement into Partial Cover.

WINDOW: The grenade detonates a standard 1.5 meters behind the impact point, a distance optimized for room-clearing shots through windows from outside.

In addition to, you know, fragmentation grenades (class 2 explosives, +6/+4 damage in damage/debris range), grenade launchers can fire all manner of special ammunition. Most of this ammo is very difficult to source (similar to the multi-mode grenades above), but relatively easy to cobble together with Mechanics (Difficulty 4). Another tempting option is to replace a grenade payload with a specialized anti-vampire bane: see *Grenades*, p. 65, for guidelines.

Some specialized grenades are low-velocity; this lowers the launcher's range.

ARMOR-PIERCING: The most advanced U.S. AP grenades can penetrate 76 mm of steel plate. Treat any amount of armor below a main battle tank or a Presidential limousine as negligible.

BATON: Normally a rubber anti-riot baton (+0 damage, no damage against armor, not usually fatal), this round can be replaced with a wooden stake lathed to fit (**NBA**, p. 107). Range is Near, not Long.

CAMERA: Fires a miniature digital camcorder on a parachute. The camera films and transmits imagery directly below it for up to 5 minutes; transmission range is 1.5 km.

FLASH-BANG: Just like in the corebook (**NBA**, p. 97), only fired from a grenade launcher.

GRAPNEL: U.S. Rangers have been messing around with rifle-grenade-propelled grapnels since D-Day. The M688/GLP is the latest version; it definitely works in technothrillers. See the climbing hoist (**NBA**, p. 98) for details.

HELLHOUND: A supercharged HE grenade developed in 2006 by MEI. Treat it as a class 3 explosive, with a fragmentation effect giving +6 damage in the debris range. Its metal core turns molten on detonation and gives it armor-piercing capabilities; it can shoot through a concrete wall, blow doors off their hinges, and ignore any vehicle armor lighter than -4. Replacing the metal core with silver is tricky, but might be worth it (see p. 65). Range is Near, not Long.

ILLUMINATION: Effects similar to a flare gun (**NBA**, p. 104). The M992 illuminates the area in only infrared, for use with night-vision optics.

NET: No, seriously. This round bursts and out comes a weighted 3m x 3m aramid-fiber net. Targets must make a Difficulty 9 Athletics test or be entangled for a number of rounds equal to their margin of failure on the test. Even if they succeed, all targets take +0 damage from the airburst shock. Entangled targets' Hit Threshold drops by 2, and they must spend 2 extra pool points for any physical action. This spend has no effect on the die result. (The Athletics test Difficulty to dodge a net that doesn't *explode out of a freaking grenade* is obviously much lower.) Range is Close, not Long.

SHOT: Turns the grenade launcher into an enormous shotgun: +4 damage at Close; +2 at Near; cannot be used at Long. Mentioned here primarily as a round that can be repurposed to hold silver links, holy bone fragments, pieces of ash-wood, or any other vampire-killing material.

SMOKE: Just what it says: colored or black smoke that lasts 4-6 rounds and covers an 8-meter radius. Completely blocks optical, IR, and laser sights; targets on either side are effectively concealed (+3 to Hit Threshold and to attempts to locate). Again, replacing the smoke charge with atomized garlic, holy water, silver nitrate, etc. is the real opportunity here for vampire hunters.

SILENT: Not the explosion, but the shot: the M463 "shoots itself" out of the barrel without smoke or flash. Range is Near, not Long.

TEAR GAS: Cloud of tear gas lasts 4-6 rounds and covers an 8-meter radius.

THERMOBARIC: This is why the U.S. military doesn't use flamethrowers any more. In addition to setting pretty much everything in the blast radius on fire, the M1060 thermobaric grenade collapses buildings and kills targets with its blast overpressure. Treat it as a class 3 explosive; all targets in its damage range also receive extensive exposure to fire; all targets in its debris range also receive partial exposure to fire if they fail the Athletics test. At the Director's discretion, the collapsing building may do yet more damage to those inside. Requires a Difficulty 7 Explosive Devices test and access to military explosives to hand-build.

THRILLER CONTESTS & MANHUNTS

This section adapts the Thriller Chase Rules (**NBA**, pp. 53-60) to other abilities besides Athletics, Driving, or Piloting, and to tension-building sequences other than pure chase scenes. Like thriller chases, thriller contests should be major set-pieces, not routine scenes during an operation. Not every hack is a thriller hack; not every stealthy insertion needs to take up half the game session. But when you want to change up the rhythm of the game, or insert some spotlight tension for a non-wetworker, think about putting in a thriller contest.

The last entry in this section, Manhunts, adapts the Extended Chase rules (**NBA**, pp. 90-91) and turns them around to face the players. How do the agents hunt a deadly foe without the resources of their old firm?

DIGITAL INTRUSION

These options model contests between a hacker and a system's programmed defenses or security professionals. Use this style of contest to pit data-hackers against a defended, encrypted mainframe or network while security-agent counter-hackers (or advanced automated programs) try to locate and thwart them.

Both hacker and defender use **Digital Intrusion** as their chase ability.

SPEED AND MANEUVER —

Digital Intrusion chases are almost always **normal chases** because the speed and ability ratings of the participants matter more than any pseudo-techno-maneuverability of their rigs.

Even as fast computers get smaller, big machines with redundant support elements and superior heat management often have the edge in raw speed. Rather than concoct a list of hardware specs for the occasional hacking sequence, use this simple rule: The bigger machine is faster unless the smaller machine has been tricked out (see box). If both machines have been tricked out, the advantages cancel each other out and you're back to the importance of size.

This is meant to describe the advantage (and purpose) of having big data centers. It gives the agents a target to reach physically and hijack for the purpose of outstripping a tricked-out digital-intrusion target. (E.g., "To get inside their system we'd need one of the data-processing machines the NSA keeps out in their Utah desert facilities!" "Then let's get one of those.") Many digital-intrusion sequences may not involve giant networked machines, of course, so a tricked-out laptop is often enough to outpace the portable, secret blackmail hardware of a low-level enemy agent.

Digital "maneuverability" isn't a factor in digital intrusion or, rather, it falls under the purview of the players to describe how their software is better or better employed when making rolls during the chase.

THE LEAD

In these contests, digital intruders hunt down vulnerabilities in computer systems that rush to protect themselves. Thus, in chase terms, the intruder is the pursuer and the system security is the runner. Lead represents how close the intruder is to exploiting a gap in the security or how close the security is to locking itself down. A Digital Intrusion contest is a chase the runner might not even realize is happening until the pursuer gains access or the runner decides to take full countermeasures.

Real digital intrusion can take hours that turn into days. Such contests are as doable using the rules as any rapid-fire minutes-long hacking contest. Frame and cut together the style of scene that's right for your mode of play, whether it's a ponderous test of cunning and endurance or a quick strike of powerful attack programs and gall. Describe each action as an hour or as a minute and the mechanics continue to do their part. You can even blend the pacing so that rolls made at a long Lead represent hours and rolls at near or shorter Leads represent minutes. As the intruders close in, every moment counts.

At the beginning Lead, no one has the advantage and the intruder's actions might seem like feeble pranks. Every roll in the contest matters, though, even if you want to describe how the intruders cleverly disguise their pursuit of weaknesses as something less sinister that security doesn't fully recognize at first.

When the Lead reaches 0, the intruders hounding the system get in and can investigate or manipulate the computers in question.

When the Lead reaches 10 (or the Director's modified goal describing a system that's more vulnerable or more secure than normal), the system's security goes into lockdown. Before a lockdown, security probably reacts to each roll in the contest with a certain degree of playfulness, obliviousness, or arrogance, thinking something like "I can handle this." It's when the Lead reaches either target number that things get finally settled.

THRILLER CONTEST RESULTS

What happens after the contest varies by computer system. The Director knows what clues are to be found within a hacked system (and what other mechanisms that system can manipulate) and the Director decides what enemy security does in response to a failed intrusion attempt.

A lockdown might mean the system becomes inaccessible from the outside (or from anywhere, in some cases) or that security operatives begin an investigation of the intruders. If the PCs are the digital intruders, they might now be the targets of a real-world manhunt or, if they had to get close to the target system to cut in, a flesh-and-blood thriller chase. Losing this contest means the intruders revealed *something* about their positioning or identity; that's the consequence for that kind of failure.

If the agents were manning the system under attack, they get to decide how to respond to an intrusion attempt that triggers their lockdown protocols. Again, it might mean a chase or an investigation, depending on how close the intruders are. If they want to carry out a manhunt of their own, see p. 87.

THRILLING ELEMENTS

Digital Intrusion is such an inward-facing contest, taking place inside minds and hard drives, that evoking the maximum of visceral thrills can be a challenge. The variety of locales is at once wide (because agents may be able to hack distant targets from laptops in any Internet-capable site) and narrow (because contests might focus more on secure digital-storage facilities than on backroom stacks of dirty servers). That the two sides of the chase may be miles apart, racing around in cyberspace rather than meatspace, can make things more challenging to describe.

TRICKED-OUT HARDWARE

Tricked-out hardware is functionally like a souped-up vehicle (**NBA**, p. 102): the tricked-out hardware is considered faster than other hardware of the same make. Tricking-out hardware requires a Difficulty 4 test of Mechanics and up to 24 hours of work to acquire and install necessary components. The Director can increase the Difficulty to 5 or the time up to 48 hours to represent tough markets or remote locations. (Use of Preparedness or Network might reduce the Difficulty or the timeframe.)

Machines get tricked out for specific jobs. Once one intrusion job is over, a computer needs to be tricked out again for the next job. This is meant to keep the players from holding on to a computer just because it's tricked out. The information stored in a computer should probably be a more compelling value than its hardware specs.

To give Digital Intrusion contests the kind of thrilling elements you'd find in a high-octane suspense film, try describing a montage combining what's happening at the keyboard and what's happening in the real world. Let the level of realism suit your players' tastes, remembering, too, that the game is a thriller about vampires, not a documentary about programmers. This is an area where you once again have great freedom from your ability to describe what vignettes in a montage *mean*, in a way that moving images and sounds alone cannot.

For example:

- Sweating hackers, out of water and soda, find themselves unable or unwilling to step away from their keyboards for even a moment.
- Lights flicker on and off as intruders tamper with power systems.
- LEDs on electronic lights blink from red to green to red as systems get overridden and then corrected by automated programs.
- The fans come on in a server room somewhere as the struggling systems start to overheat.

- Racks of computer hardware in a dark room come alive with red and yellow lights as firewalls come down.
- A late-night security guard notices Internet traffic spike in a report on his desktop monitor and he picks up the phone to call it in.
- A senior programmer's phone vibrates on a nightstand, over and over again, as warnings of suspicious activity get automatically texted to him.

A Digital Intrusion attempt might even occur in tandem with a vehicular chase as the hacker in the back of the van tries to finish the hacking job on a laptop while fellow agents drive and shoot at pursuing sedans.

SPECIAL THRILLER HACKING RULES

These parallel the special rules for Thriller Chases (*NBA*, pp. 56-60).

INVESTIGATIVE ABILITY USES

As described on p. 57 of *Night's Black Agents*, Investigative abilities (and General abilities used Investigatively) can influence the flow of a thriller contest, including Digital Intrusion. For example:

- **Accounting:** "I go after financial data that I don't need — slush monies, account records, that sort of thing — to see how they defend that sort of thing and get them on a goose chase." "That makes them reveal their spend first this round."
- **Architecture:** "They're running TX-990 generators, for sure, which are great hardware that ramps up to meet energy consumption — but they don't spike so well and can't be turned off without a security key, normally. Cutting power to the building will buy a few seconds as the generators ramp up and if we get in while they're coming on, they won't be able to easily cut power to keep us out of their systems." "Somebody near the site want to make a Difficulty 3 Mechanics test to cut out the power? That lowers their pool by the success margin of your test."
- **Bureaucracy:** "I know who's who and why; I start probing around the kind of files that'll get them in trouble with the bosses if they get cracked: personnel files and the like. Nobody wants to have to make that phone call." "They'll blow some points protecting that stuff, sure. Let's drop their chase pool by 2 points."
- **Bureaucracy:** "The circuits that cannot be cut are cut automatically in response to a digital intrusion incident. You asked for miracles, I give you Operations Protocol 9, sub-section E, paragraph two." "Awesome red-taping. They lose 1 point of Lead trying a workaround."
- **Cryptography:** "I spend some time breaking their encryption on the side and then feeding them totally valid passwords and credit-card data. Maybe they won't notice it's me." "That opens up a Swerve next round *or* this round if you spend Cryptography."
- **Data Recovery:** "I dig some files out of low-security areas and glean information out of them I can use to help winnow password possibilities and the like." "That should help you keep going; refresh 1 point of Digital Intrusion for the intruder, 3 if you spend a point of Data Recovery."
- **Human Terrain:** "I'm on the phone, doing some social engineering to keep calls going through to the security desk this whole time." "That'll distract them and keep them from trying a Sudden Escape until the Lead is 2 or less."
- **Law:** "Local ordinance demands that power get reduced in the event of an electrical fire on the same grid, so I've put a power tap on the edge of the neighboring property and fed the juice out to a dummy circuit box that can't handle the load. That ought to burn pretty good." "That's either a Mechanics or a Preparedness test, Difficulty 5 either way. If you guys make it, their Difficulty goes up by 1."
- **Traffic Analysis:** "I'm watching this all go down and figuring out which employees are on duty tonight, from the revealed duty rosters. Let's target their personal data in the system to keep them harried." "They'll definitely spend 2 points each round to protect that stuff, so I'll deduct that from their pool as long as you're there, reading the traffic for the intruder."

SWERVE

Swerves are viable maneuvers in a digital-intrusion sequence. As the pursuer changes up the attack pattern or the runner deploys the next-gen security software, or whatever other sudden change to the cyberscape is revealed, either can declare a Swerve.

Since computers don't have Maneuver ratings, anyone with 3 Digital Intrusion points to spend can declare a Swerve starting in the third round of the conflict. Lead changes are doubled as a result of a Swerve, as normal (*NBA*, p. 59).

Swerves depend on descriptions and riskiness, which can be hard to get across in a digital-intrusion chase. The changing Lead is usually its own risk, though, so keep in mind that the intruder/pursuer's risk usually involves getting detected or tracked while the defender/runner's risk involves leaving themselves open to intrusion.

The result of a Swerve might not be obvious to the participant who loses the contest. Swerving into a successful intrusion might leave the intruder inside the system with the defender thinking, "That was close! I'm glad that's over."

Here are some examples of digital Swerves:

- "While the virus does its thing, I start posting captured data on their own forums for all the world to see."
- "Let them chip away at the firewall. I start a system-wide trace of all addresses in contact with the system for the past 48 hours and look for patterns."
- "I broadcast the login data and keystrokes we're getting. See if I can't lure some random help in here to overload their system."

DIGITAL JUDO

PREREQ: Digital Intrusion 8+

Finesse and power are important when battling for control of a computer system but never forget that all warfare is based on deception. Get your opponent to waste time and effort protecting things that you're not after, then strike with hidden reserves at your true target. Do it with this rule to give cunning digital intruders an edge.

Once per digital intrusion contest, a hacker with a Digital Intrusion *rating* of 8 or more can spend Digital Intrusion pool points to force the opposition off balance. Each point spent requires security to roll one additional die for their Digital Intrusion test during the next round. Security must use the lowest of the dice rolled as their result.

Ivan spends 3 points of Digital Intrusion during a hacking contest. The Director, representing the Turkish air traffic control system, spends 2 points from the Turks' Digital Intrusion pool, but must roll four dice: 4, 5, 2, 1. The next round, the Turks' result is a 3 (2 spent + 1 on the lowest die).

SUDDEN ESCAPE

Sudden Escapes are the business of the runner in a chase, which means this option is enjoyed by the defending security in a digital-intrusion sequence. A Sudden Escape represents the desperate attempt to close down vital systems or access vectors in an attempt to keep the intruder out. This works the inverse of the way it works in a normal chase.

If the defender just wanted to end a digital-intrusion attempt outright, he or she could take their system completely offline or unplug the damn thing. That option doesn't become viable until the Lead is down to 3 or lower and the defender decides they'd rather lose functionality or operational capability than risk enemy intrusion. (Maybe getting the target to shut down their system was the point the whole time, though, and the Sudden Escape plays right into the intruder's hands…)

This Sudden Escape still involves a test to pull the boards, the cables, or the plug before the intruders can plant malware or viruses inside that'll do their dirty work when the system comes back online. The Difficulty for this test is always at least 1 higher than the previous Difficulty in the chase. Digital Intrusion or Mechanics are usually the relevant abilities, though Preparedness could reveal a pre-rigged kill switch for the system, too.

INFILTRATION

These following options model contests between infiltrators in physical space, avoiding physical security (like you might find in stealth-focused video games or heist movies). If stealthy intruders are slinking personally into a forbidden site, this is the contest for you. If agents under cover of everyday garb are trying to blend into a crowd, use the Surveillance contest options on p. 84.

An infiltration sequence is a chase between vigilant security (the pursuers, using **Sense Trouble** as their chase ability, usually) and one or more infiltrators (the runners, with **Infiltration** their chase ability). These thriller rules are apt for a level of suspicion and alertness between two extremes: oblivious security doesn't warrant a sequence like this while guards in active, immediate pursuit of a spotted or tracked infiltrator warrant a full-on "standard" Athletics-driven thriller chase. This model is for guards who suspect an intruder but have only leads — properly, the Lead — to go on to find that intruder. Some places are always on this level of alert.

Infiltration often comes down to a few agents on foot inside a building where they are unwelcome, but that's not an essential criterion. The conditions of the sequence reveal some of the variety possible:

An **open infiltration** describes an intruder on open ground, crossing a plain or desert or tundra to reach a target. Hiding spaces are few and tough to exploit but public traffic may provide cover for a disguise. This kind of sequence favors the guards roving around in jeeps or SUVs with searchlights and shotguns.

A **normal infiltration** is one with corridors or alleyways, sufficient hiding spaces for trained infiltrators, and a fairly stable environment where it may be difficult to judge who belongs and who doesn't. This kind of sequence favors fast, skilled infiltrators and includes most camps, bases, and buildings meant for comfortable or functional human movement, like office buildings, hotels, hospitals, etc.

A **cramped infiltration** is one with narrow access routes, hiding spaces that are small or confined or easy to search, and easily identified local traffic such that each guard knows each other guard. This kind of sequence pits the infiltrator's skill against the alertness of the guards, making it more about maneuverability and surprise than speed. Use this for tightly controlled areas with guards who expect to report or detain or shoot trespassers on sight.

A single infiltration sequence might cover all three conditions over multiple rounds as an intruder crosses a patch of icy ground, sneaks through a makeshift camp, and then infiltrates an enemy bunker. How long that takes depends on the Lead.

THE LEAD

In an infiltration sequence, the intruder tries to reach a specific target, like a computer or a file room or a hostage, in a patrolled or secure environment. The Lead describes how close the intruder is to the target *and* how close security is to the intruder, and it does both with one

Getting back out, from the target to freedom, may require either another sequence (possibly a thriller chase on foot) or the Director's call to end the scene. Running two thriller chase scenes back to back can drain tension (and will certainly drain ability pools); a full contest or even a player-facing contest against an Alertness Modifier reflecting the amount of ruckus stirred up on the way in may be the way to go. Again, let the story circumstances inform the decision; if the PCs were infiltrating a paramilitary airfield to secure a flight out, their escape flight might be an airplane chase or might go uncontested.

THRILLING ELEMENTS

Thrilling elements in an intrusion sequence include both obstacles to overcome (thereby showing how remarkable your character is) and details to use when describing hiding places and stealthy movement. A panning camera is as much a chance to demonstrate your ingenious or acrobatic dodging as it is a threat of detection.

STYLISHLY GARISH MANSION
- Giant vase, big enough to fit inside
- Banners blowing in the wind or AC
- Poorly trained dogs barking at nothing
- Security camera unplugged for a private tryst
- Pool with a layer of dirty leaves
- Lavish architecture with ample hand-holds
- Echoing great hall with marble tiles
- Art gallery brimming with invisible lasers
- Guest house out on the edge of the property
- Plastic sheeting in a wing of unfinished renovations

GRIMY INDUSTRIAL COMPLEX
- Wet floor with footprints from patrolling guards
- Crum/bling walls
- Rattling, rickety catwalk
- Giant, rusted ductwork
- Spinning fan, bigger than you are tall
- Flickering lights
- Stray cat
- Steam escaping an underground pipe

Lead track. The intruder is the runner, whose job it is not only to reach the target but to do so with time enough to get some job done (like hack the mainframe or free the hostage). Thus it's not enough to simply reach the goal — you must have the necessary Lead time on your pursuers.

The rules for beginning Lead and targets follow the standard thriller chase system, with the pursuers trying to capture the intruder at Lead 0 and the intruder trying to shake pursuit at Lead 10. Reduce the Lead goal to 6 or so to describe guards with no radio capability or a site with terrible sightlines and visibility. Raise the Lead goal to 14 or so if the site has electronic surveillance, RFID scanners, and other formidable security systems.

THRILLER CONTEST RESULTS

When the Lead becomes 0, things either escalate to combat or a chase contest (perhaps even a thriller chase), or the intruder is cornered and caught automatically. Directors, let the circumstances of the scene inspire your adjudication. Some agents may fight to the death rather than be captured. If they knew what was at stake going in, that may be the way that goes.

When the Lead reaches the goal (usually 10), the intruder can access the target with a few minutes to spare for investigation, interrogation, sabotage, or other antics. Unlike a foot chase, where the character is in the clear for the rest of the scene, an intruder in hostile territory might easily and accidentally draw further attention. Be wary.

- Plastic cleanroom setup in a dingy workspace
- Power-carrying cables snaking across wooden pallets

SPECIAL THRILLER SNEAKING RULES

These parallel the special rules for Thriller Chases (*NBA*, pp. 56-60).

INVESTIGATIVE ABILITY USES

Investigative abilities can influence the flow of an infiltration, whether they're used by the infiltrator directly or by agents in a support role. For example:

- **Architecture:** "That's one of the old standard Russian bunkers with the original venting, it should support a person's weight. The guards won't think of that as a possible short cut." "Good call; that lowers your Infiltration Difficulty by 2 for a round."
- **Electronic Surveillance:** "I've cut into the camera feeds from the roof and am feeding guidance down to her on the ground." "The opposition reveals its spend first for the next two rounds, or more if you spend."
- **Human Terrain:** "I spent last night reading up on the power dynamics of this group from my contact's deep-cover analysis. I figure I can help her figure out who to threaten on the ground to throw the group into disarray for a bit." "We'll call that a Swerve with a Difficulty two points easier for your side."
- **Intimidation:** "Can I get on their com channel and get them riled up, acting sloppy, by pushing their buttons?" "That'll get them to waste some energy and time if it works; spend and I'll lower their pool by 2 points."
- **Notice:** "Did you see that? The guard who just came out of the holding area left a wet footprint. Water's getting in there somehow. Is there another way in?" "There sure is and you can make a Sudden Escape to get in there at an earlier Lead, if you want."

A NOTE ABOUT DISGUISES

The Disguise ability offers a temporary assistance in these kinds of sequences but not a free pass. The trick is to have a great disguise that gets scrutinized for just a few moments, before anyone catches on. A security guard's outfit helps an intruder stroll past a grainy camera or wave to a distant guard but it's only a matter of time until someone realizes you don't work there. Points in Disguise are their own reward, but a generous Director might allow an ongoing +1 to Infiltration die rolls for a well-disguised sneaker until their cover is blown ("He's wearing a guard's uniform. I say again, the tango is dressed like one of us.").

The Difficulty for a Disguise test can be estimated based on the conditions of the sequence, though specific circumstances always trump these estimates:

- An **open infiltration** is Difficulty 3 or 4 when the disguise is only visible at a distance or lots of people are milling around.
- A **normal infiltration** is Difficulty 4 or 5, since a disguise might come under scrutiny for a few minutes at a checkpoint or via security cameras.
- A **cramped infiltration** calls for Difficulty 6 or 7 because everyone knows who belongs on site and an intruder is likely to be scrutinized in person.

More than anything, Disguise is a great ability for a Sudden Escape.

WATCHING THE WATCHERS
PREREQ: Surveillance 8+

Surveillance helps an intruder listen in on radio chatter, overhear a guard chewing gum from around the corner, or detect patterns in patrol routes. Thus the infiltrator knows when to move and to where. Once per infiltration sequence, a character with a Surveillance *rating* of 8 or more can earn a 3-point refresh of Infiltration *or* Surveillance by describing some detail or clue they glean out of the environment:

- "Every time that one guy with the haircut comes down here, he stops at that vending machine and eyeballs the honey-roasted peanuts. That's my cue to cut down the corridor."
- "I put a tiny radio in my ear and tune into the guard's channel for a few seconds to make sure they're all still investigating the hole I cut in the fence. Satisfied, I move into the IT building."
- "Seems pretty clear that Vladimir can't stand Reuben, so I wait until their patrols take them near each other. That way, if I screw up, they'll argue with each other about whose fault it is that I'm there before they coordinate."

If the detail is so evocative or so revealing that other players smile and nod, the Director may increase the award to a 4-point refresh.

Players, feel free to write out such details in advance and then see if they make sense to the chase in question.

SWERVE

Swerves are risky because they might give away the infiltrator's position. When a Swerve works, guards go looking in the wrong direction, defend the wrong position, or have a hole punched in their ranks. A Swerve might be to drop a grenade into the air shaft and let it explode three floors below, take out a guard and double back behind the security line, or spoof the alarm system to ring on another door.

What really matters is that the Swerve has a big result off a single roll and that you describe the risks and rewards to match.

ATTACKING GUARDS

One good Swerve is to attack a guard, either to take him out or to draw guards away from your true goal. E.g., "I drop from the ceiling, trying to knock him out in one swoop." Or: "I get my arms around him from the shadows and put him into a sleeper hold." This could be modeled as a special contest of Infiltration versus the guard's Hand-to-Hand, or a player-facing test of Infiltration against the guard's Alertness Modifier.

If the fight lasts two or more rounds, the guard has shouted, signaled, or been missed; the Lead drops by 1 for each extra round the fight lasts. If the sneaker kills or otherwise silences the guard in one round, the security team's chase pool drops by 4 and the chase continues.

Fortunately, guards are almost always mooks; the Director may apply the Player-Facing Combat rules (*NBA*, p. 64) to a Swerve. In these cases, Infiltration is always the "surprise" ability; if the attack fails, the Swerve also fails. An attack might also be just a very specific Infiltration challenge, or the player might decide to attack a guard for other reasons: to get his radio so she can listen in on the security channel, say.

A guard can go down to describe a Lead change in the infiltrator's favor. A guard can radio in cogent, precise descriptions of the infiltrator and her position to indicate a Lead change in the pursuer's favor.

RUN AND HIDE
PREREQ: Infiltration 8+

Depending on the conditions of the infiltration sequence, your maneuver rating can be vital. For any thriller foot chase or contest during or immediately resulting from your intrusion, you may substitute your Infiltration *rating* for Athletics to determine your Maneuver value on foot (*NBA*, p. 101) for that chase contest only.

SUDDEN ESCAPE

In an intrusion sequence, a Sudden Escape is actually an escape only when the Lead goal of the sequence stands for the escape for the infiltrator (like when the infiltrator is sneaking *out* of somewhere). When the goal is to get inside an area, to reach an item or a specific location, a Sudden Escape represents a final, brilliant, or daring push that confounds the pursuers and delivers the infiltrator unto the target.

This kind of action behaves like a Sudden Escape in every other way, though, by involving a test that might even short-circuit the abilities normally being tested. For example: Use Infiltration to hotwire the security overrides on the mainframe room's pressure door in mere seconds. Use Athletics to sprint, dive, and roll past cameras and lasers in a perfectly timed ballet. Use Surveillance to make sense of all the patrols' patterns at once and facilitate a simple, cool walk right through the rest of the compound and to the target. The risks remain high. Success means the infiltrator has reached her target. Failure likely ends in immediate detection and escalation to combat, chase, or capture.

SURVEILLANCE

The following options model contests between watchers and the watched, especially in a monitored public venue like Alexanderplatz or Waterloo Station. If someone's dressed like an ultramodern ninja to steal into a guarded fortress, use the Infiltration contest options. If everyone's trying to act casually and not disrupt the everyday throngs, this is the apt contest.

The watchers are the pursuers; the watched is the runner. **Surveillance** is the chase ability of both in the contest to corner, capture, or kill the runner without escalating things to an outright thriller chase on feet or wheels.

SPEED AND MANEUVER

First, let's understand what Speed and Maneuver ratings mean in this kind of thriller sequence:

Speed represents the fluidity of a character's movements *without raising suspicion*. If a crowd makes room for someone without anyone wanting to watch and see why, that's Speed. Uniformed police and obvious security agents may be able to cut through a crowd, but they are evidence that the sequence has come to a close and a chase, combat, or investigation is about to begin. What you're looking for is more subtle: a bin man at the train station or someone in a crew T-shirt at a musical venue might have greater Speed than background people. This means a Disguise test with a Difficulty of 4 or higher and *requires* suitable costuming, like a reflective jacket or the appropriate tee. Regular rules for disguises apply for actual social contact (*NBA*, p. 28).

The **Maneuver** rating, meanwhile, represents actual physical maneuvering, which is a function of both Athletics and Surveillance, on foot. A character with Surveillance 8+ *and* Athletics 8+ enjoys a Maneuver of +3, rather than +2, on foot (*NBA*, p. 101) because she knows when to be quick and when not to be quick to avoid giving herself away.

Note that this section assumes surveillance sequences will be played out on foot, but that's not a rule. Simply incorporate vehicles' Maneuver ratings for those sequences set on busy roadways and waterways.

When the sequence begins, the Director should determine conditions of the chase:

An **open surveillance sequence** covers the occasions where Speed comes into play, where one side is slower than the other. This is rare because moving at the ambient speed of the surrounding crowds is often important. Still, this might come up in a situation where the runners devise a way to move more quickly than the background folk without catching attention of their surveillance. Gaps in the surveillance contribute to this kind of sequence. Adjust the starting Lead by 1 in favor of the side with the higher Speed.

A **normal surveillance sequence** describes a situation with CCTVs and a few eyes on the ground but also plenty of background folk and distractions. This is the default condition, useful for most surveillance sequences in places like public plazas, sporting events, and festivals.

A **cramped surveillance sequence** covers situations with either teeming masses of people, staggeringly good surveillance coverage in the form of mobile units with cameras and CCTV support, or both.

Note that a surveillance sequence requires active surveillance, usually but not necessarily searching for a specific target (like a particular journalist or escapee) or a general category of target (like red-headed men). The passive surveillance that goes on in any watched site through the day-to-day application of CCTVs can simply describe a place's Alertness Modifier for non-thriller tests.

THE LEAD

A surveillance chase is still a chase. The goal of the runners is to escape without anyone realizing when and where they did. The goal of the pursuers is to catch the runners without the public realizing what exactly has happened.

Use the standard methods for setting the escape Lead and the beginning Lead. A good-sized crowd with ill-defined edges (like a street fair, maybe) might have a lower escape Lead, like 6, if it is being watched only by operatives on the ground or a few rooftop surveyors. A good-sized crowd with limited and monitored entrances and exits (like a stadium, for example) can raise the escape Lead to 14 or so, especially when security guards, cameras, helicopters, or the like are watching.

THRILLER CONTEST RESULTS

Reaching Lead 0 indicates that the watchers have caught the runners. This might trigger a fight, a foot chase, or a straightforward capture, depending on how the agents and the Director respond to the stimuli. For example, triggering a fight might result in the defeat of the pursuers and the restart of the surveillance chase at a low Lead, like 2 or 3. If caught, runners might, you know, run for real. (If so, their beginning Lead for a thriller chase is also low.) What outcomes are available depends on what's happening in the story and what decisions the characters make. Maybe there's nowhere to run, just yet.

Reaching the escape Lead of 10 (or other preset goal) gets the runners out of the surveillance area safely, leaving the pursuers confounded. If the PCs are the pursuers, the Director can go ahead and end the scene when the runners have escaped. Maybe she reveals this with a 0-point spend followed by no roll of the die. "You're confident," says the Director, "that they've slipped away."

THRILLING ELEMENTS

The thrilling element lists for a surveillance chase can seem pretty pedestrian since the whole idea is to blend into the background. Use these to inspire clever obfuscations of your character's actions or to describe the sorts of challenges you overcome along your way to freedom.

LIVELY STREET FESTIVAL
- A balloon vendor unknowingly provides cover
- A balloon pops
- A clown goes by on stilts
- A child throws a tantrum
- Applause erupts through the crowd
- A spot opens on a bench full of strangers
- Crowds gather around a street magician
- EMTs part the crowd

- A car alarm goes off by accident
- People dance and play in a fountain
- Random drunks start fighting

BUSTLING TRAIN TERMINAL

- The crowd murmurs and laments as the boards change
- A train-load of people come through in a wave
- Lovers reunite with hugs and applause
- Someone drops an iPad, breaking it
- Someone spills a beverage on someone else
- A loudmouth rants into a cellphone
- A busker startles the crowd with a loud bit of music
- Protesters come through, waving signs
- Kids sell cookies out of a wagon
- A soldier in uniform steps forward — but he's just a passenger

SURVEILLANCE RAISES

As a general rule, a Raise (**NBA**, p. 55) in a surveillance chase represents not an increase in danger, but an increase in confusion. The classic is "getting on then off a bus," or "heading into a crowded department store," but there are many more that will occur to the thriller fan. This increases the Difficulty for the chase for both parties if successful. Not only do the watchers (usually briefly) lose the runner, but the runner also has to spot his (usually new) watchers all over again.

In a surveillance chase, you can also make a Disguise test instead of a Surveillance test for a Raise. This is the "drop your red bag on the bus" or "shoplift a blue jacket" option. A successful Disguise test at the raised chase Difficulty means you've cleverly altered your look. You've either lost your pursuers (if you're the watched), or your quarry hasn't made you (if you're the watcher).

SPECIAL THRILLER TRAILING RULES

These parallel the special rules for Thriller Chases (**NBA**, pp. 56-60).

INVESTIGATIVE ABILITY USES

Investigative abilities can influence a surveillance chase even if the character using the Investigative ability isn't technically under surveillance or otherwise in the chase. Maybe the Investigative assist comes from someone on a nearby rooftop or helicopter, or someone in the crowd with expert skills but who isn't under direct surveillance (yet). For example:

- **Architecture:** "I've seen plans of this building from the op we ran here in 2007 and I remember how the utility corridors connect to the alley. Can I guide them through?" "Sure, let's call that a tactical advantage and give your side a lower Difficulty for a couple of rolls."
- **Electronic Surveillance:** "I used to do this kind of work. What's the standard equipment for this kind of operation? We should be able to spot them by the kinds of phones they use." "Nice. That'll increase their Difficulty by 1 for the next two tests."
- **Human Terrain:** "Local ordnance won't allow municipal cameras in a religious site. Is there a chapel on site?" "Sure. If you go in there, you can Swerve on any turn you want. They'll have to go investigate on foot."
- **Languages:** "Until they get a translator who speaks Basque into their command center, we can talk freely for a little while." "Let's give you a +1 Lead bonus if you win the roll this round, then."
- **Reassurance:** "I'm trying to keep him calm while we talk him through this sequence. 'You're doing great; not far now,' that sort of thing." "That helps. He can refresh three points of Surveillance for that if you're willing to make a spend."
- **Traffic Analysis:** "I'm curious if the CCTV coverage or movements of the mobile units tells me anything." "It does! They're giving up their search and are going to cover the exits, but they probably don't want that known yet. I'll reveal their spends first for the next two rounds."

ATTACKING WATCHERS

Like Infiltration contests, Surveillance contests have a human element. The runner may surprise one of her watchers in an isolated corridor or blind spot and choose to take him out quickly. (Watchers only catch the runner by surprise when the chase is over.) Use Player-Facing Combat (NBA, p. 64) to model this encounter, or run a single-round quick combat. If the fight lasts two or more rounds, the watcher has shouted, signaled, or been missed; the Lead drops by 1 for each extra round the fight lasts. If the runner kills or otherwise silences the watcher in one round, the watchers' chase pool drops by 4 and the chase continues.

OTHER GENERAL ABILITIES

General abilities like Conceal, Filch, and Infiltration (and their cherries) are great aids during a surveillance chase, too. Use Filch to pluck a knife from a café table, Conceal to hide it on your person, and Infiltration to unlock (and relock) the door to freedom, for example. These abilities do not require special maneuvers to describe and each comes with its own built-in benefits.

At the Director's discretion, a great description of one of these abilities can be used to grant 3 or 4 temporary points in Disguise or Surveillance. This counts as the once-per-chase refresh for the ability gaining temporary points but doesn't require 8+ points in the relevant ability, which can be helpful.

Also, see Blending Agent (p. 50), Quick Change (p. 51), and Watching the Watchers (p. 83) for more refreshing possibilities.

SWERVE

A Swerve in a surveillance chase is a big move that absolutely draws attention; the trick is to draw it on someone else. For example: tripping a passerby, swatting a hot beverage onto someone, or knocking over a rack of magazines might all attract attention but they're difficult to accomplish without being right there. Planting a phone and then calling it so it blares a ringtone somewhere else might work. Letting yourself get almost detected to buy everyone else a chance to grow their Lead with the surveillance is another option. Dropping a simulator into a potted palm to provide a distracting "gunshot," or using a delayed-action smoke canister to trigger a fire alarm are standards for a reason.

A successful Swerve is a distraction, getting the enemy to move the wrong way, look the wrong way, or act the wrong way.

A failed Swerve raises suspicion and keeps surveillance not only on the Swerver but on heightened alert overall.

SUDDEN ESCAPE

A Sudden Escape always involves risk. Maybe the cameras capture your face for a recognition database. Maybe a waiting sniper puts a bullet through you. A failed Sudden Escape can result in immediate detection (and its consequences) or an increase in the escape Lead's value by 2 or 3 points (for everyone in the area). It might even call for a total security lockdown of the area, ending the surveillance chase and triggering either a Difficulty 7 (at least) Disguise test for each agent to talk their way past the area's security guards or a straight-up foot chase starting at a very short Lead.

MANHUNTS

He must have escaped the blast; they never found his body. She wasn't there when the heat fell on her safe house and arrested everyone else. It killed your cohort and now it's on the run back to its home soil. Don't let them get away.

These sorts of manhunts worked very differently when you had a command center and satellite support and CCTV access through official channels. Now you hunt off your hunches and your instincts, chasing your quarry across borders by reading between the lines in the international news and, sometimes, by flushing them out.

You might be harried by the Heat on your trail but that won't stop you from hounding your quarry, too.

A manhunt is an extended chase carried out by the agents in pursuit of an NPC quarry. This system builds on the Extended Chase rules (*NBA*, p. 90-91), turning them around to face the players a bit more and testing them to see if they can catch their target before it does too much more damage. Players might conduct a manhunt even when their agents are in an extended chase as someone else's target. Such is life on the lam.

This system doesn't use Heat as something the players can put on their enemies because the players decide when they relax their investigation based on their interest and resources, not on the clock and maybe not on the evidence that convinces even the local jurisdiction. The players call their characters' shots. Still, Heat is an important part of this system, so check the Heat table (*NBA*, p. 88) to recall what sort of Heat and attention certain actions generate.

HOT LEAD

Hot Lead, however, is still a useful measurement for the actionable trail the agents have leading them to their quarry, so we still use Hot Lead to measure the distance between the agents and their target. Players want the quarry to spend and lose its Hot Lead; the quarry wants to slip past the agents' investigative net. When Hot Lead reaches 0, the agents have a chance to strike. When Hot Lead reaches 10, the trail is so cold or the target is so far underground that hunches and instinct aren't enough to close the gap.

The agents aren't the law, they aren't official operatives, they don't have official jurisdiction. No matter how good the evidence, they cannot guarantee the local authorities will act on their anonymous tip. They certainly can't trust the local authorities to have anti-vampire precautions in hand, and they probably can't trust the locals not to have Conspiracy ties or leaks. The agents have to act for themselves.

As a player-facing experience, a manhunt calls on the players to make the key choices. The Director doesn't simply play the harried foe, though. She still must sometimes phrase the foe's actions in the form of a scenario or a scene to play out, clues to uncover, actions to take. This system, in other words, is only part of the process; the quarry can turn up in an op near its last known position and take actions that change its Hot Lead as described on p. 88. What this system does is describe the *middle* of the extended chase — the rolls the agents make once per op to stay on the trail or flush out their foe.

STARTING HOT LEAD

The quarry's Hot Lead starts at 7, minus the highest Heat that brought the target to the agents' attention before it escaped. If the subject escaped after a grandiose, excessive car chase (Heat +3), then its starting Hot Lead is 4 (7 − 3 = 4).

CHANGING HOT LEAD

A quarry's Hot Lead doesn't go up and down quite like the agents' Hot Lead does. An NPC (or even a group of NPCs) can't hope to engage with the heroes in thriller sequences, combats, and so forth without risking death or capture. Such encounters are the agents' reward for driving the Hot Lead down to 0, after all.

Instead, it's on the players to push their quarry into actions that'll cause it to reveal itself. The agents are the pursuers. They are the ones with the net.

The quarry's goal is to get somewhere safe, somewhere that a more powerful force in the Conspyramid can protect it, and to do so without revealing much of the Conspyramid along the way (so that its nefarious accomplices don't slay it to protect themselves).

EARNING HOT LEAD

There are three main things a quarry can do to earn Hot Lead:

- **Crossing Borders:** Crossing a border increases Hot Lead by 1 for normal transit and by 2 if accomplished via smuggling, hiking, shipping, or other surprising means. As a rule of thumb, if the players can describe in three tries how their quarry got across the border, it's not surprising. Regular transit is never surprising because it leaves too much data for the agents to track, even if it does help increase Hot Lead.
- **Roosting:** When a superior on the Conspyramid takes in and protects a subject, that's "roosting." Roosting increases Hot Lead by an amount equal to the protector's Conspyramid Level minus 1. (So when someone at Level 4, the national level, takes the quarry in, that adds 3 to the Hot Lead.) This is risky, though, because it doesn't necessarily end the chase and it almost certainly leads the agents toward the protector. Roosting happens at the beginning of an op, before the Gambit roll, and often comes shortly before elimination (see p. 90).
- **Shaking the Net:** When the quarry takes action to survive or escape, it must attempt to traverse the net the agents put out to detect it. If the quarry is successful, it may slip through the net undetected. If not, it shakes the net as it passes through, giving the agents a trail to follow. This is the heart of the manhunt chase (see facing page).

MULTIPLE HOT LEADS

High-level, well-connected foes on the Conspyramid have the resources and lackeys necessary to attempt to vanish in multiple directions, leaving the agents chasing mists that turn out not to be vampires at all. This option manifests as multiple Hot Lead numbers to keep track of, which can be a pain if you have just a few players. Therefore, use this option only as a means of keeping several plays engaged, if necessary. The maximum number of Hot Lead trails a subject can have going at once is listed on the following table, but you probably don't want more than one trail per three players (or even three agents), either.

Decide in advance which Hot Lead trail (A or B or C) leads to the actual quarry. The others lead to lackeys from the lowest-surviving Conspyramid Level. The agents may get lucky and pursue just the true Hot Lead or they may attempt to pursue all leads, somehow, and not rest until the chase is done.

QUARRY'S CONSPYRAMID LEVEL	HOT LEAD TRAILS
1: Neighborhood	1
2: City	1
3: Provincial	1
4: National	2
5: Supranational	2
6: Core Leadership	3

PUTTING OUT THE NET

To track their foe without jurisdictional authority and the full resources of the law, the agents must gather intelligence, follow their hunches, and lure their quarry into making mistakes. Sharp wits, gut checks, and danger — that's what it takes.

Once per operation, the agents can put out the net that they'll monitor "in the background" for the duration of that mission. They're assumed to be operating locally, but what's local depends on how the agents get their intelligence and how the Director decides information travels. Getting Canadian news in the U.S. is easy but getting real-time police reports from other countries may be more difficult. Agents on a manhunt should expect to stay close to their quarry if they want the best chance of catching it. That means going where it goes, which can sometimes mean following it into a trap.

To do this, the agents set the Difficulty the quarry must achieve to traverse their net without alerting them. This is called the Gambit Difficulty. The Gambit Difficulty starts at 0 and goes up through the following actions to a maximum Difficulty of 7:

- **Investigative ability spends:** Any player can spend 1 or 2 points from any number of Investigative abilities to add that many points to the Gambit Difficulty. The precise ability doing the spending isn't of utmost importance, yet, though the player must describe to the Director how their spend helps them stay alert and on the trail. If the Director is unconvinced, the expenditure can be denied and the player can try again with another ability. The real cost here is that these points are not available to the agents during the "foreground" operation.

- **Network ability spends:** Up to 2 points can be spent by a Network contact to help spread the net. These points also add to the Gambit Difficulty. This is essentially an investigative use of the ability; the contact doesn't take any action except to observe and report until the player spends additional Network points to persuade the contact to take further action.
- **Make a Digital Intrusion or Infiltration test:** One agent per op can make a Digital Intrusion or Infiltration test to set up signal taps and relays on official channels to alert the agents if their quarry pops up on the grid in some secret capacity that might be protected by, say, Conspirators. The Difficulty of this test varies by the sophistication of the local governmental computers and failure may draw Heat onto the agents. If this roll is a success, the Gambit Difficulty increases by 1. Both a Digital Intrusion and an Infiltration test may be made per op.

All agents cooperate to add to the same Gambit Difficulty value or values.

Although the team needs to clean up this nest in Palermo, they don't want to stop their hunt for the vampiric necromancer Aleksandr Vikramsson. So they put out the net in the background of the Palermo op. Luc spends 1 point of Occult Studies: "I put the word out amongst the local streghe that a Black Prince has come among them — I'll hear what the rivals and wannabes find out." Desmond spends 1 point of Criminology to listen to the police scanner in the background. Jack pulls strings and gets Captain Corceri of the Italian Navy to put out a BOLO on Vikramsson's allies in the merchant marine, spending 2 points from Corceri's Network pool. Beatrice breaks into the cathedral with Infiltration (adds 1) to see if any unusual reports hit the archbishop's desk; Ivan hacks into the ROS computers with Digital Intrusion (adds 1) on much the same mission. The total Gambit Difficulty during the Palermo op is 6.

If they are pursuing multiple Hot Lead trails at once, each trail requires its own Gambit Difficulty. Agents may contribute to as many Gambit Difficulties as they can afford.

GAMBITS

The longer a quarry has been on the run, the greater the likelihood that it screws up somehow. At the beginning of the next op, or after a number of days equal to the quarry's level on the Conspyramid, the target feels the pressure and seeks out food, money, sex, blood, or something else it needs (or feels it needs).

In short, it tries a Gambit.

The Difficulty for the Gambit roll depends on the agents' expenditures to put out the net and monitor the area. Rather than spending points from its own pools, however, the subject takes actions that threaten to reveal its whereabouts or heading. The bonus to this roll is equal to the quarry's Conspyramid Level or the Heat that the quarry's actions would generate on the Heat table (whichever is higher). If the subject takes action that warrants Heat to earn a bonus to its roll, its Hot Lead decreases by the same amount. In other words, the cost in Hot Lead to add a bonus to the Gambit roll equals an action's Heat value. The maximum Hot Lead that can be spent on a roll is 4; anything more than that draws such Heat that the quarry is almost certainly revealed by local investigations anyway.

These actions may represent the quarry doing favors for allies in exchange for cover or succor or the quarry eliminating targets that could reveal it to the agents. More desperate subjects take more dangerous actions. Directors, use your judgment; while a subject on the run could take the most dangerous path to escape, lots of variety exists within the various levels of Heat gain. It's more likely the quarry hijacks a car and kidnaps someone (+3 Heat) to escape the local area than it is for the quarry to coordinate a prison escape for the same purpose.

Vikramsson has to beat a Difficulty of 6. He's a major enforcer for the Conspiracy, a Level 3 force all by himself, so he begins with +3 to the die. To beat that, he has to do something big: fortunately, the local 'Ndrangheta would love to have a vampire kill a pesky judge for them. After devouring the judge, Vikramsson has earned +4 Heat, and lost 4 Hot Lead, but he has a +4 bonus on his Gambit roll. If he had wanted to taunt the agents, he could have sent insect-demons to devour the judge on television, for a +5 to his roll and guaranteed success, but he didn't want to lose quite that much Hot Lead. And he was in the mood for Italian food.

If the quarry's roll is a success, the Hot Lead goes up by 2 for success, plus 1 or 2 if the quarry is able to cross a border as part of that action. Crossing such a border might allow the target to enter a territory where it can roost, as well. Note that these increases occur *after* the Hot Lead expenditure made on the Gambit roll. Sometimes a quarry may lose Hot Lead for the sake of getting closer to a roost.

If the quarry's roll is a failure, it gains no Hot Lead at all and must suffer the loss of Hot Lead it spent on the roll as news of its crime spreads. A quarry that doesn't attract Heat at all (rolling only on his Conspiracy level bonus) loses 1 Hot Lead anyway and is still potentially detectable by the agents.

The Director rolls a 5 for Vikramsson's Gambit: a big success. The 'Ndrangheta respect and fear him and happily smuggle him to Albania in their next human trafficking run. Vikramsson began the operation with Hot Lead 6 and spent 4 for his bonus; he gains 2 back for success, and adds 2 more because he not only crossed a border, he was smuggled into Dürres.

If the Director decrees that the quarry's action could reasonably be detected by one of the Investigative abilities spent by the agents to build the Gambit Difficulty, the agents automatically tie the crime to their quarry. The evidence that they get may not be admissible, of course, but it's enough for the agents' purposes. Otherwise, use the Manhunt table to determine what spend, if any, is necessary for an agent to tie an action to the quarry for the sake of their unofficial manhunt. ("See this report of a car chase in Bucharest? I *know* that's our monster. I just know it.")

LEVEL OF HEAT GAINED	MINIMUM SPEND TO TIE CRIME TO QUARRY
+1	2-point Investigative spend
+2	1-point Investigative spend
+3	Investigative ability use
+4	"I read the newspaper."
+5	Obviously linked headline blares on Sky News

Tying a crime to their quarry is especially useful when multiple Hot Leads are in play at once.

The agents had three possible leads to tie the judge's bloody murder to Vikramsson: the police scanner, Captain Corceri's watch list on ships, and the ROS files. They know he did it. Even if they didn't have those leads, an anti-Mafia judge missing most of his major organs and all of his blood (a +4 Heat atrocity) is pretty easy to spot as vampire handiwork.

The Director should reveal the current Hot Lead at the end of the op. In addition, the Director reveals the following details as circumstances warrant:

- **If the quarry crossed a border,** say this: "[The quarry] must have crossed out of the jurisdiction."
- **If the quarry's crimes are linked to it by the agents,** say this: "[The quarry] has left the area and turned up across the border in [the new area]." Directors, elaborate as you like on the details gleaned from the Investigative abilities.
- **If the quarry roosts,** the players can figure that out after the next Gambit by the increase in the Hot Lead.

ROOSTING AND ELIMINATION

The quarry roosts at the beginning of the next op if it is in an area (province, nation, etc.) controlled by superiors on the Conspyramid. If this doesn't push the Hot Lead to 10 or above, the quarry still feels hunted and makes a Gambit roll during that op to protect itself. Thus there is often one final Gambit roll that may lead the agents higher up the Conspyramid if their quarry makes a mistake and is caught in the vicinity of superiors. Being led toward a roost may help the agents track the Conspiracy to a potentially new location.

Vikramsson seeks sanctuary with the Conspiracy's node in Albania, a human trafficking gang/refugee NGO run by a slimy British expatriate obsessed with Byron. "Lady Augusta," as she styles herself, is on the Conspyramid at Level 4, so Vikramsson's Hot Lead climbs from 6 to 9 (Hot Lead 6 + Roost level 4 -1 = 9). Vikramsson is not quite home free. He has to make one last Gambit check to close off the loose end: kill the 'Ndrangheta cell that unloaded him here. Since he doesn't need to earn more Heat than his Conspiracy level, he just adds +3 to his Gambit die.

For this reason, the conspiracy may choose to eliminate a roosting or fleeing quarry — or its protector. Elimination raises the Hot Lead by a value equal to the Conspyramid level of the conspirator that does the eliminating (usually the level above the roosting subject or the protector, but it can be an even higher-level operative if helps secure the end of the manhunt). If this doesn't push the Hot Lead over 10, it still ends the manhunt since the quarry is off the board, but the dead quarry's Hot Lead decreases by 1 every 24 hours. When it finally reaches 0, the agents are able to home in on the body or the elimination scene or simply a trail cold enough to inspire the right conclusion: the quarry's gone for good.

DIRECTOR'S COMPANION

Risking life and limb is SOP for agents. They may be called to HALO jump onto a moving train, provide security for a yacht, intercept an armed convoy on a dusty desert road, or anything else a Director can provide as they develop the story of a Conspiracy and all the players therein.

It's that "anything else a Director can provide" that often turns out to be the roadblock. Directors have to juggle six layers of Conspiracy, a dozen dangerous nodes, a clutch of vampire monsters, and all the while decide what the well-dressed NPC is wearing in Copenhagen this year. Like contract killers, the Director's Companion is here to help out in deniable fashion.

It outlines a new set of tools for Directors, giving them more capabilities, more resources, and more options both for developing an ongoing narrative, and for creating a single-instance operation.

ELEMENTS

Versatility defines a good Director. And an arsenal of pre-generated NPCs, Cameos, makes that versatility seem second nature. Dropping in one of the Cameos below jump-starts the Director's crafting of a formal NPC.

A Cameo can save valuable time, and provide another hook the players can latch onto to better immerse themselves in the shadowy world of espionage and to deepen the Director's world.

Establishing Shots allow for a Director to insert a particular setting element into play, either to inspire a new operation, or to enhance an existing operation with shiny, camera-friendly set pieces.

CAMEOS

Cameos are instant NPCs suited to the spy thriller genre. Each writeup includes: important abilities, a physical description, a story hint in the text, and the preferred Interpersonal method to win their cooperation. Then come three things they can provide as an asset (for the vampires or for the agents), three clues they possess, and three handles for roleplaying them.

Remember: the Health ability values for NPCs (just like for player characters) are a factor of drama, not biology. Want Yuri to last a while? Health 6+. Want Yuri to drop fast? He's a Health 1 or 2 mook, or an "infodump kill." Change the ability ratings listed likewise.

ARMS DEALER
Athletics 4, Hand-to-Hand 4, Shooting 7

At the height of the Cold War **Yuri** moved fifty shipments a week through customs, and a hundred more no one knew about. Arms to Africa, South America, the Middle East – it didn't matter, the money flowed in and war was a possibility. Now though? It's all missiles and remote controls and the "art" of war is gone. And he's enjoying retirement, as you can tell from his silk guayabera, straw trilby, and white linen trousers. You couldn't afford what he'd charge to handle it personally. What, exactly do you need? (Explosive Devices and Shooting as Interpersonal skills, Negotiate)

AS ASSET: Access to firearms and explosives; able to bypass customs; access to cargo containers.

AS CLUE: Smuggled some unmarked containers of "artifacts" out of Saudi Arabia in the 70s; knows where the Russians are meeting down by the docks; knows which customs officials are on the take.

IN PLAY: Out-going, gregarious to the point of manic, you're always happy to see everyone ... and make a deal; everything is big, broad gestures and wide smiles, like everyone is an old friend or relative; your accent has all but vanished, thanks to too many trips to the States.

AUTO MECHANIC
Hand-to-Hand 3, Mechanics 8, Preparedness 2, Weapons 3

Oil-stained and always reeking of cigarette smoke, **Robbie** wears blue, constantly dirty coveralls. He denies that he's getting too old for the job, that his knees don't ache every morning and that the cough he's developing isn't getting worse. But there's no one better with a socket wrench, and he'll tell you all about it if you offer him a light. Somehow, some way, he's always got room at the shop for the car and always knows which part to replace without any of them fancy computers. A real gearhead and the last of the hard-smoking, hard-living man's men. (Mechanics or Driving used as an Interpersonal ability)

AS ASSET: Cars available at his shop; access to registration and repair databases; full supply of tools for Mechanics and Preparedness.

AS CLUE: Has modified cars to tint their windows for an "anonymous" client; is on friendly terms with the local mafia toughs; has been doing a lot of repairs on hearses lately.

IN PLAY: Make a face like you're always going to spit; constantly wring your hands; deliberately nod and cant your head.

BOOKIE
Filch 2, Gambling 6, Hand-to-Hand 5, Weapons 3
ALERTNESS MODIFIER: +1

Alexey doesn't care if you're betting on the big game or the outcome of fifty coin tosses; he's got your action. And if you win, sure he'll pay. But if you lose, you *will* pay, one way or another; all those thick rings on his hand aren't just for decoration. With one eye always on the phone or the game, he's got more than enough attention to pay to you, shifty. He's not above throwing down, but calm down, you're interrupting the game. (Gambling, Intimidation, Streetwise)

AS ASSET: Access to money laundering; leads on other people's gambling habits; knows a guy who knows a guy who can get you a handgun or two, no questions asked.

AS CLUE: Saw a guy like the one you described down at the track last week; has the address of that guy's girlfriend; got that phone number you wanted.

IN PLAY: Crack your knuckles when comfortable or when uncomfortable; never let them know you're a pent-up spring just waiting for a reason to strike; keep an eye on whatever game is going on at the time — it's more important.

BUILDING SUPERINTENDENT
Conceal 3, Infiltration 2, Mechanics 2

It's not that **Branko** is a bad man, he's just apathetic. Always wearing a stained sweat suit, unshaven, and reeking of Gitanes and cheap slivovitz, his building slowly falls apart around him. But he's been super in this building for a while, and he's seen the neighborhood change ... and not for the better. (Cop Talk, Intimidation, Negotiation)

AS ASSET: Has plans to his and several other apartment buildings in the neighborhood; can bypass a variety of non-electronic locks; keeps an apartment unrented for "emergencies."

AS CLUE: Just rented a pair of rooms to some very pale people; knows which moving company comes at night; gets his slivovitz from an Albanian informant.

IN PLAY: Look blearily between the players without focusing; ask them to repeat things; take apart an imaginary cigarette between your fingers; drink often.

BUREAUCRAT
Athletics 4 (gym membership)

Lara didn't expect this job when she graduated from college, but it's better than living at home with her mother. She epitomizes paper-pusher, working in a basement office that time forgot. Neat, thin, blonde, and pretty, she is officious and far too serious for her age. She still dresses for the job she wants: a little too much personality in the scarf and belt. (Bureaucracy, Flattery, Reassurance)

AS ASSET: Access to government forms and blanks for forgeries; friends in other departments who can do favors and bury reports; can wave people past security checkpoints in the government complex.

AS CLUE: Stamped some questionable documents for the Somalis three days ago on instructions from way upstairs; knows which security guard is a drunk; someone in the department receives weird phone calls weekly.

IN PLAY: There's a place for everything, and everything in its place; pick lint off your knees and lap; explain in a patient voice why that can't happen.

CAR THIEF
Athletics 8, Driving 4, Infiltration 4, Mechanics 4
ALERTNESS MODIFIER: +1,
STEALTH MODIFIER: +1

No car is an obstacle for you, **Marco**. You get paid in cash every night and every night is just the right amount of thrills and laughs. Sure you have to kick ten percent up to the manager when your shift is over, but that's a small price to pay for having this much fun and getting to dress this flash. (Intimidation, Streetwise, Driving as an Interpersonal ability)

AS ASSET: Access to cars and motorcycles; able to duplicate keys and alarm codes for cars; connections with chop shops and fences.

AS CLUE: Saw some mooks loading a truck with a coffin the other night; heard some Serbians talking about renting some construction equipment; knows where the Jamaicans are stashing their weapons.

IN PLAY: Relax, this is all a game; you look older than fifteen if you flex; keep that hat straight, nobody'll treat you right if you don't look cool.

CHOP SHOP MANAGER
Athletics 5, Driving 4,
Infiltration 5, Hand-to-Hand 4, Shooting 4, Weapons 4

There's not a car around he or his boys haven't boosted, gotten into or sold for scrap. **Stefano** has seen the imports before you have, and he knows exactly how many horses the new Italian model sports under the hood. Don't confuse him for a gangbanger though, he's a man of ambition — after all he "manages" a pack (maybe 6 -10, who knows really) of car "aficionados." That's why he wears a Hugo Boss suit. (Bureaucracy, Negotiation)

AS ASSET: Access to cars and motorcycles; access to car shipping manifests; access to the pier where the cars come in.

AS CLUE: Boosted a car the other night that had something in the trunk; sold some heavy trucks to some yakuza last night; dropped off an SUV to a cemetery early this morning.

IN PLAY: Confident and mature, every day is a chance to remind people that you're a businessman first and a car thief second; square your shoulders, make a fist; the bravado in your voice isn't all false.

COLD WAR VETERAN
Athletics 5, Driving 4, Hand-to-Hand 4, Shooting 4, Surveillance 8, Weapons 3
ALERTNESS MODIFIER: +1

To hear **Chad** tell it, he personally knocked down the Berlin Wall. Of course, Chad has to know you're the right kind of people before he tells it; operational security is still the name of the game, amirite? Three decades in Europe hasn't washed the Yale out of his accent, but he dresses Armani not Brooks Brothers. Money stuck to him somehow (along with about thirty extra pounds), and he's always happy to help it stick to friends. Or Americans. Or friends of Americans. Have another bourbon, why don't you? (Flattery, High Society, Tradecraft)

AS ASSET: Old friends in the Company and the Cousins who take his calls; a surprisingly non-bullshit take on the real power structure in Europe now; secret bank accounts and an obliging friend in Andorra who handles the cash.

AS CLUE: Knows which Stasi officials vanished completely in 1989; heard the real scoop on the coup in Bucharest; handled a handshake just the other week between an old MI6 colleague and a real up-and-comer in multinational pharmaceuticals.

IN PLAY: Call people "pal" and "friend"; smile too much; set your shoulders and upper arms expansively, you command here.

CONSPIRACY THEORIST
Digital Intrusion 2, Preparedness 2, Sense Trouble 3

Thierry might live in a basement apartment. He might be thought of as a loser. But no one knows the ins-and-outs of secret government labs and who-shot-who-when the way he does. He wears collared shirts and creased pants, both too tight. Pale, overweight, and a little gross in his habits, he's got his finger on the pulse of the shadow world … or does he? (Flattery, Reassurance, Tradecraft talk used to impress)

AS ASSET: Lifetime of research into conspiracies (2-point pool in any of Bureaucracy, Criminology, History, Research, or Traffic Analysis for purposes of mapping Conspyramid or tracing Conspiracy); online network of similarly obsessed weirdos all over the world; hoards old discarded government files.

AS CLUE: Believes he has found a war-criminal Serbian colonel who knows something; found a link on the Adversary Map that you haven't; believes he found the connection between smuggled guns and an art dealer downtown.

IN PLAY: Talk constantly; jerk your head around or thrust it forward urgently; wet your lips just before saying anything of value.

CUSTOMS AGENT
Athletics 4, Digital Intrusion 3, Infiltration 2
ALERTNESS MODIFIER: +1

Gianna is a thin, tanned woman who looks more like a tennis coach than a customs agent. She walks like she's always going into a stiff wind, and always makes a face like she's disbelieving a surprise party. She's crafty, thinks she's smarter than you, and always wants facts. Even out of uniform, she's in uniform. (Bureaucracy, Law)

AS ASSET: Access to shipping manifests; access to bonded warehouses, docks, and shipping containers; can bury paperwork.

AS CLUE: Knows where the Turkish cargo containers are; knows who the corrupt longshoremen and stevedores are; heard about a weird shipment coming in tonight at midnight.

IN PLAY: Move slightly hunched over; never crack a smile, this is serious work, damnit; keep your gestures small like your arms are tied to your chest.

DISGRACED DOCTOR
Athletics 6, Conceal 2, Medic 6

Rielle knew her days were numbered during med school. The Oxycontin addiction was getting out of hand, even for her standards, and she really didn't want to put out a shingle and spend fifty years wiping snotty noses and listening to old people complain about lumbago or gout. So she just never "applied herself" and after she graduated, she never went on interviews. Which is fine, interviews are for suckers. She dresses down; jeans and sweat shirts, just like residency. (Intimidation, Streetwise)

AS ASSET: Access to narcotics and tranquilizers; able to patch you up, no questions asked; can perform autopsies and determine causes of death.

AS CLUE: Saw a body leave a morgue *after* the autopsy; stitched up a few Serbians after a gun fight a week ago; prescribed some — okay, *a lot* -- of painkillers to a ranking Russian gangster.

IN PLAY: Nervous and high strung, you're forever waiting for the other shoe to drop; keep looking around the corner for the unpleasant surprise; sniffle, scratch, and tic your way through most conversations.

EX-CON FORGER
Athletics 8, Disguise 3, Forgery 4, Sense Trouble 4
ALERTNESS MODIFIER: +1

Tim is seven months out of prison after three years in lockdown for selling fake passports online. His track suit is new, as are his gold teeth. He swears he's clean, but you know better. No one that good can stay out of the game for long. He's skinnier than a crackhead, and prison made him strong and lean. And paranoid. (Reassurance, Streetwise)

AS ASSET: Access to forged documents and forging equipment; can help with cover identities; still wired in with the prisoner hierarchy.

AS CLUE: Sold a batch of passports to a Congolese death squad; forged customs documents to ferry a shipment of dirt into the U.K.; changed the timestamps on surveillance photos to get some Sicilians an alibi.

IN PLAY: Be nervous, high-strung, and jumpy; subconsciously "write" with a pen or scriber; avoid making big gestures as they can be threatening.

GYM RAT
Athletics 9, Hand-to-Hand 8, Medic 2, Sense Trouble 3, Weapons 5
ALERTNESS MODIFIER: +1

Still in great shape, **Willem** is toned and strong. It was just a misunderstanding that got him fired from that bodyguarding gig; another will come along if he keeps himself ready for it. He carries himself as though still on the job and that's usually enough of a deterrent for most folk. He's often found in a track suit or workout clothes lately, always on his way to or from the gym. (Flattery, Negotiation)

AS ASSET: Access to intimate client details; good knowledge of security protocols and plans; good man in a fight.

AS CLUE: Overheard two guys at the gym talk about a drug shipment; knows where the weak spot is in the local bank security system; stopped a strange mugging by the waterfront just before he got fired from his bodyguarding gig.

IN PLAY: Try not to be too menacing; flex often, drink water if you have any; mention how many reps you did in random conversations.

HACKER
Digital Intrusion 6, Disguise 3, Infiltration 2, Mechanics 4
ALERTNESS MODIFIER: +1 (non-visual only)

Isaiah wasn't always blind, but he also wasn't always a criminal. He dresses in all black; he can't coordinate colors, and doesn't want to look like a clown. When his eyesight went, he turned to hacking as a way to cover his medical costs. And his love of travel. And his dislike for insurance companies. (Negotiation, Reassurance)

AS ASSET: Can build and check wiretaps; keeps up-to-date accounts of latest intrusion gear; can help create false online identities.

AS CLUE: Was harassed by a Conspiracy enforcer; overheard a conversation he shouldn't have; has found a node on the dark net with a lot of weird traffic in and out.

IN PLAY: Pick a direction and look only there; keenly focus on what's around you; move your head with every sound; keep your voice even and flat.

HIGH-END ESCORT
Athletics 3, Filch 3, Weapons 2

Britney (née Bridget) does not care who knows what she does for a living. For a reasonably large fee, she provides men (and women) with companionship for the evening. What started off as a way to make money after uni bloomed into a career that has seen her on the arms of CEOs, footballers, and celebrities. Tall, brunette and exotic, she is used to having all eyes on her. A little red dress trumps a little black dress any time. (Cop Talk, High Society)

AS ASSET: Able to get into embassy functions; has access to clients' intimate details; access to cash quickly.

AS CLUE: Knows the security details for some respected Italians' security detail; talked to a Saudi prince about ancient artifacts last night; you would not believe the kind of weird shit this reclusive Romanian billionaire is into.

IN PLAY: Cool, polite, superficially interested; flick eyes up and down, find nothing particularly appealing; regularly check your nails and hair.

LOCAL LAW ENFORCEMENT
Athletics 4, Driving 4, Preparedness 2, Shooting 4, Surveillance 4, Weapons 4
ALERTNESS MODIFIER: +1

Not much gets past **Werner**. Sure, he's only a local cop, but he's savvy and he's a careful observer of things around him. His nondescript taupe-grey suit keeps him in the background until he wants to emerge. He's not out of his depth in a fight, and he's a pretty good defender of the law. (Cop Talk, Law)

AS ASSET: Access to police reports, cold cases, evidence lockers; can run background checks on people or vehicles; can put out a BOLO.

AS CLUE: Has an informant who's on the fringe of the Russian Mafiya; has seen an awful lot of hearses driving around lately; heard about the big Moroccan "deal" going down tonight.

IN PLAY: Move with a purpose; keep every answer short and direct; nod over your shoulder to see what could be coming up behind you.

LONGSHOREMAN
Athletics 9, Conceal 5, Hand-to-Hand 6, Mechanics 2, Weapons 2

Tanned by the weather, grizzled **Erik** wears a slick vinyl parka over dull clothes. He holds himself ready, a bit hunched over. His eyes size you up behind his cigarette smoke; he's done enough off-the-books deals and seen enough strange cargo come in to know you're not here by coincidence. He's had to cover for too many weaklings to have patience with them at his age; only if you seem tough will he pay attention, but not if you try to bully him (Athletics or Hand-to-Hand used as an Interpersonal ability).

AS ASSET: Access to cargo before inspection; access to ships; use of heavy cranes.

AS CLUE: Saw a coffin unloaded; knows who the mafiya stooge in the union is; knows which warehouse the Chechens use.

IN PLAY: Squint against the sunlight off the water; hunch your shoulders like you're about to pick up a heavy object; steal a quick look over the player's shoulder to see who's backing him up.

OCCULT BOOKSTORE OWNER
Conceal 2, Surveillance 2

Brendan's shop is small, tucked back down a side street next to a dry cleaner and an appliance repair shop. He likes it that way — he knows his usual customers and they don't mind the fact that he always looks like he's been asleep in the back. His cardigans are thirty years out of date, and he's got a bad comb-over, but there's no better researcher outside the University. (Flattery, Negotiation, Occult Studies used as Interpersonal ability)

- AS ASSET: Has access to rare and old books (2-point pool in any of Occult Studies, History, Vampirology); knows local (and online) occult and weirdo scene; shop sits near a ley line or place of power.
- AS CLUE: Knows who bought up that trove of 17th-century Dracula pamphlets that surfaced in Hanover; sold a series of old texts to a coven of witches last week; his is the only shop in his neighborhood not yet robbed in the dead of night.
- IN PLAY: Your hands ache from holding books all day; your eyesight is starting to wane, so peer nearsightedly; sigh, take off your glasses, and rub the sides of your nose.

PUBLIC DEFENDER
Athletics 4, Hand-to-Hand 2, Weapons 2 (mace)

Danielle is a hungry lawyer, determined to change the world, one case at a time. Her expensive shoes might look good, but they're murder on her feet. She's active, exhausted and more determined than a hungry dog with a bone. (Cop Talk, Law)

- AS ASSET: access to court dockets, prisoners, and courthouse rooms; on good terms with several judges; can get writs and stays.
- AS CLUE: Got a Belgian off on a charge of art fraud, but he disappeared soon after; knows who really killed Ivor Korbuyshev but can't prove it; attends a church where the priest was attacked during a baptism.
- IN PLAY: Your hair is in your face; square your shoulders; don't snap at people, no be patient, they can't help it, don't snap at people.

RETIRED COP TURNED ENFORCER
Hand-to-Hand 4, Sense Trouble 6, Shooting 4, Weapons 6
ALERTNESS MODIFIER: +1

Michel has lived a hard life. He walked a beat for twenty years and finally made detective. Then he took a bullet in the knee. Now thanks to three operations and his age, he's on the outside looking in, so why not do a little moonlighting as a legbreaker? It beats going to the gym. He dresses like a cop: cheap poly-blend suits. (Cop Talk, Negotiation, Streetwise)

- AS ASSET: Can call off the cops to buy you some time; can help you clean up a crime scene; knows the best way to avoid underworld entanglements.
- AS CLUE: Heard about the Russians on the police scanner this morning; remembers a cold case involving something stolen; knew a guy on the force who went toe-to-toe with a "monster" and lived.
- IN PLAY: Gruff, weathered and weary, you're always looking for the path of least resistance; sitting is a premium, lower yourself into the chair with a thud; look down your nose at people who just talk the talk.

RETIRED SECRETARY
Digital Intrusion 2, Sense Trouble 4, Preparedness 2

For years, **Elena** served her employer faithfully, working long hours doing administrative and secretarial tasks. Now she's retired, into her "golden years" someone told her, but she's still crack-whip sharp and smart and remembers far more than she lets on. She may look like someone's kind grandmother, but there's a twinkle to her eye that suggests she's got a few tricks up her sleeve. (Flattery, Negotiation)

- AS ASSET: Can dig back through old files to find information; has access to old rolodexes and schedules; knows how to handle red tape and bureaucracy.
- AS CLUE: Remembers a strange meeting your old employer took at the embassy; overheard the other secretaries gossiping once about a meeting with the Japanese; was once told to make a whole set of files "disappear" ... she didn't.
- IN PLAY: You're sweet as punch and twice as nice; every quaver in the voice comes with a twinkle in the eye; smile nearly constantly; call everyone "dearie."

SECOND-STORY MAN
Athletics 6, Conceal 3, Filch 4, Infiltration 4
STEALTH MODIFIER: +1

Narciso worked Monte Carlo as a dealer for years, until the robbery. He didn't plan it, mind you, but he wasn't exactly as innocent as he let on. He wears a clean suit and dark shirt, always. There's something calculating behind his eyes. He's observant and always one step ahead. (Reassurance, Negotiation)

- AS ASSET: Can provide codes for security systems; knows the best way to break into any vault or system; has access to B&E equipment.
- AS CLUE: Saw a coffin get loaded into a hotel freight elevator; overheard the Polish cleaning staff talking about avoiding the twelfth floor; knows the Corsicans just installed a J-Master 6000 security system.
- IN PLAY: Be smoother than good whiskey, you're no thug; play with the cuffs on your shirt as you talk; always make strong eye contact when you talk about Infiltration.

STREET THUG
Athletics 4, Driving 2, Shooting 4, Weapons 2

Jamal grew up on some hard streets. Escaped from foster care, he's always in secondhand clothes that are either too big or too small. When he got his first gun and robbed his first liquor store, he knew he found his calling. Now Jamal's an "entrepreneur" dabbling in boosting cars and drive-bys. (Flattery, Flirting, Intimidation, Streetwise)

- AS ASSET: Access to untraceable guns; access to safehouse; keeps a small circle of street informants.
- AS CLUE: Got chased off a corner by some tatted-up Russians; knows an old building with blacked-out windows

but no drugs; saw some ghul (like from grandfather's stories) leave a cemetery last night.
- IN PLAY: Trust no one, especially not an authority figure; touch your coat pocket or under your shirt for the gun you always keep there; be ready to run, because it can always be a trap.

TELEVISION REPORTER
Athletics 2, Driving 3, Surveillance 3

Tod covers local stories, going on remote after remote to the back end of the market. He hates it. He wants to be the lead anchor, and he's always looking for the big story to break. His teeth are bleached too white, his neckties are always a little too ugly, and he always sounds like he's "on camera." (Flattery, Flirting, Intimidation)

- AS ASSET: Access to news reports; access to television and recording equipment; growing list of sources for stories.
- AS CLUE: Researched a story two months ago about a rash of robberies at walk-in clinics; has notes about the rise of bloody crimes down by the docks; filmed hilarious "filler" story about drunks seeing bloody ghosts downtown.
- IN PLAY: Smile a lot, as if there's a lens flare off your front teeth; you're not easily impressed but you're willing to gladhand; assume everyone knows and loves you.

TRUCK DRIVER
Conceal 2, Driving 5, Weapons 2

Oguz is used to long hours and big stretches of alone time. Always in dusty jeans and a beat-up flat cap, he roams the motorways of Europe, working irregular hours delivering whatever's given to him, no questions asked. As a Turk, he knows the cops don't plan to help him any time soon; he returns the favor with interest. (Intimidation, Negotiation, Reassurance)

- AS ASSET: Can transport personnel and equipment without detection; knows off-the-path motels and safehouses; access to trucks and trailers.
- AS CLUE: Has hauled some strange containers out of the Balkans lately; knows which trucks the Triads use for smuggling; overheard a rumor about some "connected" Georgians muscling into the docks.
- IN PLAY: Spit often, and wipe your brow when you disbelieve what you hear; always look a little surprised; shrug and look away.

VAMPIRE-ENTHRALLED GOTH
Conceal 2, Filch 2, Notice 2

When **Kristina** met Her, the world seemed to stop. She was mesmerizing, and Kristina never stood a chance. From the first kiss to the first weekend in bed, to last week, Kristina has been little more than a meal and a cheap fling to the One who she knows so little about. But she wouldn't have it any other way. (Vampirology used as Interpersonal ability, Intimidation, really anything violent)

- AS ASSET: Has a direct line to a vampire; connections to club scene; doesn't look like a spy.
- AS CLUE: Knows habits and perhaps weaknesses of vampires; knows identity or can describe a vampire; overheard conversation with Renfield security about future deployments.
- IN PLAY: Shift in your seat to the beat you hear; twitch your leg back and forth; keep tone of voice over-serious to convince people that you're like for real.

NIGHT'S BLACK AGENTS – DOUBLE TAP

ESTABLISHING SHOTS

The Director can set scenes in these instant locations, run the thriller action montage right through them, or just sprinkle them into her subconscious. Each Establishing Shot includes a quick "stock footage" description, followed by the extras (and any Cameos) you might run into there, three clues, and any sensible rules effects. Then three elements of the location to use in a fight, and three elements of the location to use in a chase. (The type of Thriller Chase appears in parentheses: Open, Normal, Cramped.)

24-HOUR SEEDY DINER

"More coffee, hon?" You push your chipped porcelain mug towards the middle-aged waitress. It's 3 a.m. and she looks tired, her face lined and her eyes heavy. The nametag pinned to her apron reads "Elizaveta." The only other employee visible is an overweight fry cook muttering to himself back behind the counter, ranting self-obsessively about political conspiracies as he tosses another two burgers onto the grill. Say what you want, he makes delicious food. He drags on his cigarette, pulls fries out of the deep fat fryer, ducks into the walk-in fridge for some supplies, and reflexively spins his spatula in one hand before checking the rare, rare burgers.

The bench-style booths here are covered with torn and soiled vinyl. Metal chairs are scattered around each of the smaller tables. Old and faded photographs of long-time patrons are taped to the walls, lit up by the flickering neon from the sign outside. The diner isn't large; it's T-shaped, with stools at a long counter in front of the front door and a side dining room with more seating. There are bathrooms back there around to the side, but it's not recommended that you spend a lot of time in them. They have a certain distinct odor that may stick with you for a while. There's a pay phone back there too, and a utility closet containing a mop and a whole lot of bleach. No security cameras, though.

EXTRAS AND CAMEOS: Exhausted or exhilarated late-nighters, insane fry cook, sarcastic waitress; Longshoreman (on his way to work), Truck Driver, Vampire-Enthralled Goth.

CLUES: Secrets scrawled on napkins; a late-night private meeting over coffee; a distinct lack of mirrors.

RULES EFFECTS: There's something about an old diner that feels like home. All agents with lost Stability points gain 2 back, as if an ally had spent 1 point of Shrink.

IN A FIGHT: Pots of hot coffee, flung into faces; deep fat fryer; buckets of bleach.

IN A CHASE: Slide down the counter; leap through plate glass window into parking lot; many convenient vehicles for car-jacking. (Cramped)

BIG-BOX HARDWARE STORE

They're in almost every town in the nation. Flat and sprawling, carrying nearly any construction tool or device you could think of, along with quite a few that you've never heard of. The employees are usually retired craftsmen themselves, working under a high ceiling that allows space for a multitude of massive shelves.

EXTRAS AND CAMEOS: Newly returned combat veteran is a brand new employee-in-training, cheerful homeowners shop for kitchen cabinets, burned spy seeks tools to use with his Mechanics ability; Auto Mechanic, Local Law Enforcement (off duty), Longshoreman.

CLUES: Terrorists buy components for improvised weapons; blood-drained corpse secreted in a large pot in the Garden Center; window shades bought out by someone needing to block sunlight from every room in a house.

RULES EFFECTS: The Difficulty of Preparedness and Mechanics checks is lower by 1 while inside the store.

IN A FIGHT: Wooden fence pickets double as stakes; hatchets and hammers and chainsaws in abundance; nail-guns make impromptu weapons. (See *Tools as Weapons*, p. 44)

IN A CHASE: Drive a forklift through the aisles; thrown paint can briefly blind; climb shelves to hide. (Cramped)

CARNIVAL

The smell of fried food and cotton candy fills the air, and carnival barkers call out to you as you stride past their booths. It's a warm summer night and the carnival is packed to the edges. Children scream on half-sized roller coasters and teenagers pause in the shadows, exchanging hurried kisses while their parents hunt for them in exasperation. This carnival tours where the tourists don't, and wherever it goes children vanish in its wake. None are ever found.

EXTRAS AND CAMEOS: Screaming children, sleazy carnies, disguised clowns; Building Superintendent (as ride mechanic), Car Thief (as teen troublemaker/joyrider), Retired Secretary (with her grandnephews).

CLUES: A carnival booth's prize is more than it appears; disappearing teenagers mark this as a vampire's hunting ground; the mannequins in the haunted house ride (or wax museum show) are eerily realistic.

RULES EFFECTS: It's easy to hide in the crowd. If you have any points in Surveillance, gain a free 3-point pool refresh at any point in the scene.

IN A FIGHT: Off-duty cops struggle to draw their sidearms; whirling machinery makes short work of mooks; carnival booths with huge throwing darts provide impromptu weaponry.

IN A CHASE: Clamber up the Ferris wheel; lurk in ambush in the tunnel of love; disappear into the hall of mirrors. (Normal)

CASINO

The jangling crash of slot machines fills the air. You're surrounded by mass-market elegance, a vast honey trap designed to separate tourists from their money in a thousand little ways. Gorgeous couples saunter past towards the high-stakes tables, and tourists wearing Hawaiian shirts sit at slot machines and mechanically press the buttons to the sound of bells and chimes. Gossip in a dozen languages hangs as thick as the cigarette smoke.

- **EXTRAS AND CAMEOS:** Musclebound pit security, cheerful cocktail waitress, watchful dealer; Arms Dealer, Cold War Veteran, High-End Escort, Retired Cop turned Enforcer, Second-Story Man.
- **CLUES:** A personal marker signed by a person of interest; the best bodyguard (or hit man) in Montenegro is here; eye contact between a dealer, a guard, and a gambler indicates a grift in process.
- **RULES EFFECTS:** Omnipresent mirrors lower Surveillance Difficulties by 1. Omnipresent cameras raise Infiltration and Filch Difficulties by 1; also raise Heat of anything you pull here by +1. Agents with the Gambling ability can roll a die: on a 1, lose 2 points from Gambling; on a 2-5, gain 1 on even and lose 1 on odd; on a 6, refresh 3 points.
- **IN A FIGHT:** Spare gun as close as the nearest tuxedoed goon; handfuls of chips make a fine distraction; there's alcohol and fire everywhere, really.
- **IN A CHASE:** Steal the prominent "You could win this car!" sports car; run across the tables to make a stir and kick over piles of chips to tangle your wake; push through massive kitchens, cleverly connected to one another. (Normal)

CATACOMBS

Stone walls press in from all sides. The old metal gate led underneath the city, where the bones from seven graveyards were brought after reconstruction uprooted one cemetery after another. City renewal didn't allow time for niceties like keeping corpses in one piece. The reverent monks took pity on the scattered bones, and now catacombs lead from room to room, tunnel to tunnel, each a masterpiece of carefully stacked femurs and skulls and pelvis bones. This is morbid art, and tourists shuffle along beside you through the carefully marked tunnels, surreptitiously taking photos in the cold damp air and wishing they were someplace else. Tunnels that are marked as "off limits" fire the imagination. Are they unsafe? A staircase leads down into a flooded level, equally full of bones now inaccessible to anyone without diving apparatus and strong intestinal fortitude.

- **EXTRAS AND CAMEOS:** A vampire visiting the remains of old prey, disquieted tourists, a solitary priest, rebellious teenaged explorers; Bureaucrat (as officious tour guide), Occult Bookstore Owner, Vampire-Enthralled Goth.
- **CLUES:** Surreptitious graffiti leading to off-limits rooms; secret door behind a wall of skulls; fresh bones mixed in with the ancient.
- **RULES EFFECTS:** Forensic Pathology indicates the approximate age of a bone, revealing whether vampires are stashing inconvenient corpses in plain sight. Occult Studies indicates whether they're being stashed in a pattern.
- **IN A FIGHT:** Femurs used as clubs; gunshot or grenade triggers sudden collapses of floor or ceiling; undead rising from flooded tunnels.
- **IN A CHASE:** Closed iron grates block your path; duck into hidden rooms long forgotten by the catacombs' administrators; hide underneath a pile of thousands of bones in the sorting rooms. (Cramped)

CORNFIELD

The field must stretch for miles. The stalks of ripe corn grow from rich brown dirt and rise above your head. It's impossible to see anything beyond the row of corn that you're currently standing in. There's a farmhouse and barn nearby, but getting lost is as simple as walking for a few rows in a random direction and forgetting which way you came in. You can hear, though: the crop duster overhead, the buzzing of insects, your own labored breathing, and the crashing shouts of the assassins fanning out to find you.

Note that rye and wheat both grow below head height: outside North America, considerable maize crops grow in China, Brazil, India, Indonesia, France, and the Ukraine, among other places.

- **EXTRAS AND CAMEOS:** Local know-it-all, naive thug, kind-hearted stranger; Conspiracy Theorist (rural version, add Shooting 5 and shotgun), Disgraced Doctor (as off-the-books plant geneticist), Truck Driver.
- **CLUES:** Someone or something is buried out here; fertilizer contains unsavory chemicals; crop circles.
- **RULES EFFECTS:** It's easy to hide when you can't be seen; add 2 to visual Difficulties, and Infiltration tests to escape notice (except by air) have 1 lower Difficulty. If you have Outdoor Survival, get 1 free pool point to spend here.
- **IN A FIGHT:** Attack from hiding; deadly farm implements; confused farmers with shotguns.
- **IN A CHASE:** Hide between rows; catch a ride on a tractor; stay silent and escape. (Open)

DATA CENTER

This nerve center for the local high-speed Internet concern (or something of that sort) is a series of massive server banks, rows of network engineers solving problems behind workstations, and darkened control rooms where technicians monitor network traffic. Security guards the entrances and the hallways, but the data access it promises is tantalizing.

- **EXTRAS AND CAMEOS:** Brilliant and eccentric computer genius, harried middle managers, government agent arranging for a wiretap; Customs Agent, Hacker, Vampire-Enthralled Goth (at hated day job).
- **CLUES:** Racks of servers in a frigid room, with a single panel slightly out of place; security programs constantly sniffing out intrusion; a bribed technician working more independently than expected.
- **RULES EFFECTS:** Any hacking done here becomes much easier.

Difficulties for Digital Intrusion become 2 lower while in this facility, assuming you have an access code from an employee.
- **IN A FIGHT:** Monitors explode in sparks; Nerf gun distraction; lengths of cables can strangle or trip.
- **IN A CHASE:** Topple the monitor and the tower; monitor her flight with extensive electronic surveillance; run between a maze of server banks. (Normal)

GLASS SKYSCRAPER

It rises from the flat office park around it like a glass spear thrust up from the earth. Something this large has to be multi-purpose, and unsurprisingly it includes banks, restaurants, a high-end hotel, gyms, and endless offices. Sixteen high-speed elevators in four main elevator banks give access to every floor, assuming you can slide past the moderately bored officers at the security desk.

- **EXTRAS AND CAMEOS:** Office workers, cautious window washers, obsequious hotel receptionists; Building Superintendent (as janitor), Hacker, Retired Cop turned Enforcer (as security guard).
- **CLUES:** Penthouse hotel suites with blackened windows and no mirrors; office complexes with high-tech document safes; world-class rotating restaurant with a select menu that prominently features the blood of living prey.
- **RULES EFFECTS:** It's hard to guard this large a structure; Infiltration Target Numbers to enter and move about are 1 lower than normal. The outer glass can be climbed with suction gear at Difficulty 5, or without it at Difficulty 9.
- **IN A FIGHT:** Glass walls shatter, allowing inadvertent falls; helicopters or snipers outside the building can target enemies inside, particularly with rocket launchers; regularly placed fire extinguishers make good improvised weapons.
- **IN A CHASE:** Climb the side of a high-speed elevator shaft with deadly elevators shooting back and forth; jump and run down seemingly endless stairwells; evade the armed building security tasked with arresting all troublemakers nearby. (Normal)

GONDOLA

The small gondola dangles more than a hundred feet above the mountainside below, swaying in the wind as it passes support pylons on its way up the slope of the extinct volcano. From here you can see the popular tourist hotel at the summit; look down, and you can see cruise ships at anchor in the harbor below. Other cable cars are strung out along the cable like pearls on a necklace.

- **EXTRAS AND CAMEOS:** Outspoken tourist, mysterious contact, acrobatic gunman; Arms Dealer, Retired Secretary, Second-Story Man.
- **CLUES:** Secrets whispered amidst mid-air privacy; packages secreted beneath a specific car's seats; the site of an impossible assassination.
- **RULES EFFECTS:** The gondola's cable is sharp and frayed; Athletics rolls to slide down the cable have their Target number lowered by 1 if a belt or wire is used as the slide, and raised by 1 if the agent is trying to only use his hands. Targets hidden by a cable car's walls have Cover.
- **IN A FIGHT:** Gondolas can be used as sniping platforms, especially against enemies in other cars going the other way; dangle half out a car while struggling; throw foes to their death.
- **IN A CHASE:** Leap onto a support pylon; cling to the outside of a gondola; slide down a cable. (Cramped)

HIGH-SPEED TRAIN

The bustling, modern station is rapidly left behind as your streamlined bullet train pulls away. Only six carriages long, it is a marvel of gleaming steel and tapered aerodynamics that routinely travels over 350 kph. The government has conducted multiple campaigns to increase speed, and it shows; the verdant countryside shoots past you as you lounge in a comfortable, reclining seat. Somewhere on this train is the quarry you need to find; hopefully, she isn't clinging to the outside roof.

- **EXTRAS AND CAMEOS:** Introverted businessperson, eager backpackers, honeymooning couple; Cold War Veteran, Conspiracy Theorist, High-End Escort.
- **CLUES:** A fast escape without an airline's scrutiny; a private train carriage filled with coffins; a ticket that doesn't match the monogrammed Vuitton luggage.
- **RULES EFFECTS:** Explosives detonated on a high-speed train can be utterly lethal, and not just due to the confined nature and passenger density of the train cars. Any class 4 or higher explosion effectively damages everyone (debris range damage plus crash) on a rapidly moving train by causing it to derail.
- **IN A FIGHT:** Unusual luggage provides improvised weapons; screaming mook shields; tunnels plunge the train into momentary darkness.
- **IN A CHASE:** Watch out for the low-hanging bridge in that rooftop chase; disconnect a train car; long narrow cars limit your options for running. (Cramped)

MASQUERADE BALL

The ballroom of the manor house glitters with crystal and glass. The string orchestra plays on a small stage across from the bar and hors d'oeuvres, and a beautiful and elegantly masked crowd dances and mingles late into the night. The wait staff are in tuxedoes and domino masks, the guests are in (and out of) everything imaginable.

- **EXTRAS AND CAMEOS:** Debauched foreign royalty, debonair old world vampires, undercover investigative reporter; Bureaucrat (redirected an invitation for herself), Cold War Veteran, High-End Escort, Second-Story Man.
- **CLUES:** Masks and costumes that reveal as much as they hide; truths whispered behind fluttering fans by mistake to the wrong mask; darkened rooms that hide terrible secrets or deniable rendezvous.
- **RULES EFFECTS:** All agents, whether they have points in Disguise or not, gain 3 free pool points of Disguise for use while at the

party. Tests (Surveillance, Sense Trouble, etc.) to spot disguised foes are at 2 higher Difficulty.
- **IN A FIGHT:** Confused identity and slow knives; drugged wine or clubbed wine bottles; prop weapons that turn out to not be props.
- **IN A CHASE:** Stand still and hide in plain sight; climb to the rafters and chandeliers; sprint through the catering kitchen. (Normal)

MEGALOMANIACS SECRET LAIR

The mansion is perched at the western edge of the island of the Mediterranean tourist island, so ostentatious you wouldn't expect it would belong to anyone other than an eccentric multi-millionaire. Massive buildings look out onto an active surf and a sea of pristine blue. The main house catches the eye first: a great room large enough to hold a formal ball, a hotel-style kitchen, gorgeous bedrooms with private balconies overlooking the pool and front veranda. The architecture is 19th century designed to look 16th century, with dark wood and wrought iron setting off the numerous paintings of famous pirate ships from throughout history.

The guest houses are out back, as is the staff housing, security center and small power plant. Garages hold cars and trucks, SCUBA gear, enough food for weeks of isolation. Cameras and locked gates line the property, and employees carry plastic badges that get them through subtle security checkpoints.

The interesting rooms are hidden underground. A stone tower on the eastern cliff face may be designed to look like it was built hundreds of years ago, but the circular stairs in the tower drop farther than anyone could guess. They open up to laboratories and libraries and discreet prisons dozens of feet underground. Villainy happens here, hidden by sea breezes and the best security money can buy.

- **EXTRAS AND CAMEOS:** Evil and wealthy mastermind, lethal right-hand-man, bored and pleasure-seeking spouse; Arms Dealer, Cold War Veteran, High-End Escort (in a bikini by the pool).
- **CLUES:** A sloppy gate guard lets it slip that people who come in don't always leave by car; power consumption on the estate is far from normal; construction workers from the estate died mysteriously in their sleep weeks after the job finishes.
- **RULES EFFECTS:** Disguise and Infiltration Difficulties to infiltrate the estate are 1 higher than normal, due to the close-knit staff and focus on security. (Might be either a normal or cramped sneak; see p. 81.)
- **IN A FIGHT:** Guards have machine pistols and combat knives; laboratories are full of chemicals and half-human monstrosities; mastermind has a charismatic manner, winning smile, and no combat skill whatsoever.
- **IN A CHASE:** Notice a speedboat docked on the pier down the cliff path; leap off the cliff into the ocean; jump from the balcony into the pool. (Normal)

METH LAB

The windows to the house are boarded up, but there are definitely inhabitants; discarded bottles and stained coffee filters in the overflowing garbage smell like a mixture of cat urine and rotten eggs. The grass in the back yard is mostly dead. A "Beware of Dog" sign warns people away, but no barking can be heard.

The inside of the house is filthy, as are the meth-heads whose heads snap up as you come in the door. The chemical smell is worse here. Bottles, canisters, jugs, tubes, and burners line the main workroom, crowded onto small work tables. A large refrigerator is pushed against one wall, and a cooler full of small packets sits near the corner of the room. More than a dozen firearms lie around the house, placed near convenient hiding spots or within easy reach, and the addicts grab for them as soon as they hear you.

- **EXTRAS AND CAMEOS:** Strung-out meth addict, professional cartel representative, angry and brilliant chemistry teacher; Chop Shop "Manager" (as drug ring "manager"), Disgraced Doctor, Retired Cop turned Enforcer (to collect or to protect), Street Thug.
- **CLUES:** Weirdly alert guards; visitors at all hours of the night; non-standard additives slipped in by vampiric chemists.
- **RULES EFFECTS:** The lab is one errant cigarette away from exploding. Explosive Devices Difficulties are 2 *higher* here, and any explosion automatically becomes class 4.
- **IN A FIGHT:** Multiple loaded firearms; caustic chemicals thrown

in haste; panicked attempts to save the finished drugs. Oh, and a class 4 explosion.
- **IN A CHASE:** Tip over tables and spill dangerous chemicals; hide (don't breathe!) in rooms filled with hoarder-level piles of refuse; stay low, boarded windows stop sight lines outside of the house. (Cramped)

MORGUE

You wonder why morgues always seem to be in the basement. The elevator doors ding open to show you an empty gurney rolled up next to the wall, awaiting its next passenger. A sheet is folded neatly atop it. The smell of formaldehyde fills the air, and the air is chill. The tables in the autopsy room are currently unoccupied, standing vacant with medical equipment and scales nearby, but the drawers in the cold storage room are filled with unidentified corpses.

- **EXTRAS AND CAMEOS:** Creepy forensic scientist, corpse that's not as dead as you'd hoped, wise-cracking medical intern; Disgraced Doctor (perhaps not yet disgraced), Local Law Enforcement, Vampire-Enthralled Goth (at beloved day job).
- **CLUES:** Bite marks on a corpse's neck; a knocking coming from inside a closed drawer; a locked drawer in the autopsy file cabinet.
- **RULES EFFECTS:** Morgues are difficult places to fight the undead, even when you know to expect trouble. The Difficulty for all Sense Trouble tests is raised by 1 here.
- **IN A FIGHT:** Bone saw (+1); distracting spray of stored blood; sheets to bind and blind.
- **IN A CHASE:** Roll a gurney into pursuers or ride them past; hammer fruitlessly on the panel for the slow elevators; open oversized air ducts. (Normal)

MUSEUM

Statuary, paintings, and the wonders of antiquity surround you on every side. (Or, alternately, weird and garish splashes of color and insane constructions attract chattering wannabes and languid aesthetes alike.) You move along with other tourists, past bored museum guards and sophisticated alarm systems you could easily hack. The museum has high ceilings, a maze of large rooms filled with the detritus of history, and enough museum visitors to make action somewhat problematic.

- **EXTRAS AND CAMEOS:** Knowledgeable historian, pretentious art student, clump of foreign tourists; Ex-con Forger, Hacker, Occult Bookstore Owner, Second-Story Man.
- **CLUES:** Mysterious carved tablet recently put on display; obscure 17th century portrait that looks identical to a well-known billionaire; ancient weapon thick with legends.
- **RULES EFFECTS:** Spending a point of Art History allows the agent to befriend a museum administrator or art historian, giving them inside information about how the museum is run. Alarm systems range from Difficulty 2 to 6 against Infiltration tests, depending on the museum and the exhibit. Cinematic jewels or the main prize of the operation, of course, have multiple layers of security and a final, laser-filled Difficulty 8 chamber.
- **IN A FIGHT:** Ancient weapons and armor can still be used in combat; priceless statues too easily toppled; poles with velvet ropes still attached, used as crude bludgeons.
- **IN A CHASE:** Dive through interactive exhibits of video and holograms; lift disguises from the museum gift shop; slow and mingle with the crowd as a maze of room displays blend into one another. (Normal)

NIGHTCLUB

After you get through the metal detector, your eyes adjust. Multiple levels break up the enormous warehouse-like space. Sound is deafening, lights dazzling or dim. Two brilliantly lit big bars dominate the ends of the room, the middle is a dance floor broken geometrically by tables occupied by lounging douchebags and their parasitic girlfriends. VIP spaces up on the balcony and in a raised dais on one end provide architectural reinforcement of social status. The bathrooms are down the hallway; no, farther down than that.

- **EXTRAS AND CAMEOS:** Drug dealers and clientele, 24-hour party children of the rich and beautiful, dedicated fans of the sound; Car Thief (spending his take), Gym Rat or Retired Cop turned Enforcer (on the door), High-End Escort.
- **CLUES:** Traffickers talk while high or boasting; cold spots or missing mirror images; infrasound creates mesmeric trance in susceptible patrons
- **RULES EFFECTS:** People are here to be seduced; if you have Flirting, get 1 free pool point to spend here. Noise, motion, and darkness add 1 to visual and auditory Difficulties.
- **IN A FIGHT:** Bouncers and thugs have guns; bottles in the bar; cute hostages aplenty.
- **IN A CHASE:** Slide down the bar; foam drops down obstructing vision; jump off VIP area balcony onto dance floor. (Cramped)

OVERCROWDED TENEMENT BLOCK

You're in one of the most densely packed urban blocks in the world. More than 30,000 people are crammed into this 7-acre block, a labyrinth of fire hazards, tiny apartments, insufficient plumbing, makeshift storefronts, and organized crime. Somewhere in this unmappable series of buildings is the key to untangling out your conspiracy. Now you just have to find it.

Although this writeup is based on Hong Kong locales like Chungking Mansions and Kowloon Walled City, similar (though not quite so crowded) districts exist in Mumbai, Istanbul, Cairo, and many other megapoleis around the world.

- **EXTRAS AND CAMEOS:** Street children, suspicious elderly, tattooed young punks; Building Superintendent, Ex-Con Forger (rent is cheap and nobody talks), Street Thug.
- **CLUES:** Graffiti and gang signs; an under-aged guide who likes to gossip; the local community boss who must approve of outsiders.
- **RULES EFFECTS:** Everyone who matters knows someone here: agents with 1 or more point in Streetwise gain 1 extra point to spend while in the overcrowded block.

IN A FIGHT: Wrench a steam pipe away from the wall; dangling electrical cables invite electrocution; locals protect their own.

IN A CHASE: Burst through flimsy walls from one home to another; leap from one trash-crowded roof to another; squirm through crowded corridors and stairwells. (Cramped)

POLITICAL RALLY

The square is packed shoulder-to-shoulder with people. They chant slogans and hold hastily scrawled signs over their heads. A stage is set up at one end of the plaza, huge amplified speakers and a high-end microphone waiting for someone to take the stage. In the nearby park, protestors scream their objections, and the surging crowd around you screams back. Riot police around the edge of the square look uncomfortable, and stand nervously at the ready.

A woman takes the stage, and the cheering of the crowd rises to the heavens.

EXTRAS AND CAMEOS: Charismatic politician, riot police, racist hate-mongers; Gym Rat (as bodyguard), Local Law Enforcement, Television Reporter.

CLUES: Security detail doesn't appear on video; electronic subsonics incite the crowd to fear and violence; a protestor slips to the ground, mysteriously drained of blood.

RULES EFFECTS: Pick-pocketing becomes easy with this many people. Difficulties for Filch checks are lowered by 1.

IN A FIGHT: Rioting crowd around you adds +1 to Hand-to-Hand damage; riot police use non-lethal attacks such as pepper spray (model after tear gas; *NBA*, p. 81) to quell violence; smuggled-in beer bottles used as clubs (-1).

IN A CHASE: Intimidation spend to clear people from your path adds +2 to chase results for two rounds; Notice spend stops a quarry from losing himself in the surging crowd; run across the shoulders of the packed crowd, it could be the only way to quickly gain ground. (Cramped)

RAINFOREST

The air has wrapped you in a sauna-hot blanket of humidity. The sky overhead is a brilliant blue with bands of clouds, and the tropical sun bears down through the canopy in a dappled green pattern of shadow. Insects hum in the near-liquid air. Birds sing out, as do monkeys and less identifiable beasts of the jungle. The trees press in on every side, and if you lose the trail you will be inextricably lost.

EXTRAS AND CAMEOS: Local guide, traditional native shaman, jungle hunter; Arms Dealer (setting up a meet), Disgraced Doctor (with an NGO in the field), Longshoreman (as lumberjack).

Clues: A dart with curare; an unexpected patch of coca fields; riverside huts on tall stilts, windowless and thick enough to keep out the sun.

RULES EFFECTS: Strenuous activity during the midday heat requires a Difficulty 4 Health test, failure leaves you Hurt until the next day; omnipresent parasites and fungi reduce by 1 the Health restored by any Medic test. For every week in the jungle, non-natives and those without jungle warfare experience must make a 3-point Stability test against the oppressive isolation.

IN A FIGHT: Guides with machetes; poison frogs (use snake venom; *NBA*, p. 81) peeping from swampy pools; massive anthills contain stinging ants (-1 damage per round) for anyone foolish enough to blunder into them.

IN A CHASE: Thorny trees slash at skin if brushed past (-2 damage); quicksand glistens across the path (Difficulty 4 Sense Trouble to avoid or be trapped, start drowning after three rounds instead of five); listen to birds and pinpoint fleeing prey (Outdoor Survival spends count double for chases or TFFBs). (Open)

RED LIGHT STREET

In this part of town, people cruise slowly down the street with only two things on their mind. Drugs and prostitution are rife here, out in the open without even a show of enforcement by the heavily bribed cops. This street has its own enforcers, and they aren't the local police.

EXTRAS AND CAMEOS: Hooker with a heart of gold, dangerous pimp, corrupt vice cop; Bookie (as pimp), High-End Escort (before or after she hit the big time), Street Thug, Vampire-Enthralled Goth (on her way to a club, or not).

CLUES: A massage parlor's clients don't always exit; clients leave a red light apartment dazed and compliant; private parties for important underworld figures are easily arranged.

RULES EFFECTS: This is a street where people come and go and no one knows your name. Gain 2 free pool points to set up a safe house here (*NBA*, p. 112).

IN A FIGHT: Club-wielding enforcers pour forth from nearby stoops; women pull viciously sharp knives on a possible attacker; marital aids used as embarrassingly improvised weapons.

IN A CHASE: Unexpectedly interrupted patrons join a chase; accidentally (?) disrupt a poker game of local criminals; carjack a BMW from a cruising john. (Normal)

SKI RESORT

The popular mountain's snow-covered parking lot is crowded with cars and trucks. Wide doors lead into the fashionable lodge, ski boots clumping on scarred wooden floors, teenagers giggling and small kids running after their parents. The lodge has multiple levels linked by wide and low stairs, large gas fireplaces and a surprisingly sophisticated snack bar and restaurant. This resort is known for its singles population, and the lodge is peppered with dim and comfortable nooks where strangers can sit and talk to each other while maintaining the illusion of privacy.

The mountains loom up overhead, jagged and snowy, dominating sightlines. Carefully groomed, well-marked ski trails snake through the thick forest on the mountain slope. The line for lift tickets is long, but with seven ski lifts, chairlifts, and rope tows and even a gondola (see p. 100) for the summit trails, it's hardly surprising there are so many people.

- **EXTRAS AND CAMEOS:** Attractive ski instructors, precocious child, diligent ski patrol; Auto Mechanic (snowmobile and SUV mechanic), High-End Escort, Second-Story Man.
- **CLUES:** Ski chalets with improbably sophisticated alarm systems; secrets whispered on the ski lift; bodyguard teams sizing each other up – Conspiracy summit or Davos working group?
- **RULES EFFECTS:** Skiing and snowboarding use Athletics; snowmobiling requires a Driving slot. Give a contest advantage in skiing contests to any agent with arctic or mountain training (all special forces; all Canadian, Scandinavian, and Russian ex-military) or who spends a High Society pool point to flashback to Gstaad or Aspen.
- **IN A FIGHT:** Explosions trigger lethal avalanches; armed thugs on snowmobiles; convenient cliffs from which to deploy BASE jumping chutes (see p. 68).
- **IN A CHASE:** Make a massive ski jump; wipe out on inconvenient moguls; slip on melting snow on the lodge floors. (Open)

SLAUGHTERHOUSE

The smell hits you first. All the cold air keeps it down, but there's a certain coppery reek to spilled blood and raw flesh that even refrigeration doesn't cover. The herds are culled on the far side of the building, an unpleasant job for any but the most sadistic. Here in the refrigeration rooms, massive sides of beef hang silently on razor-sharp hooks.

- **EXTRAS AND CAMEOS:** Dead-eyed and undocumented immigrant worker herds beasts with an electric prod, murderous butcher with a cleaver and bloody apron, savvy restaurateur seeking the freshest cuts of meat; Customs Agent (as meat inspector), Longshoreman (as meat packer), Truck Driver (delivering undocumented workers or picking up meat).
- **CLUES:** More than dead cows hanging from hooks; unusual collection and storage of blood; hidden elevator leading to secret underground rooms.
- **RULES EFFECTS:** An animal stampede would disrupt the operation and draw all available personnel to solve the problem. If it can be somehow engineered, each agent gains a temporary pool of 3 Infiltration points to spend on entering or moving through the facility.
- **IN A FIGHT:** Electric prods (moderate shock; NBA, p. 79); buzz saws to mechanically separate meat (+1); ceiling hooks (+1).
- **IN A CHASE:** Hide behind swinging animal carcasses; look out for visible breath, it gives away locations in the cold; baffle the Renfield's keen sense of smell in the overwhelming odor of blood. (Normal)

STATE OR PROVINCIAL CAPITOL BUILDING

The corridors of power turn out to be tiled with polished marble and rich carpets. The main entrance has well-manned metal detectors, but service entrances may be less well guarded. Bored security stands around as lawmakers hurry past; tour guides herd packs of tourists past earnest young interns, politicians-in-training, and local reporters.

- **EXTRAS AND CAMEOS:** Corrupt politicians, tour guide, knowledgeable lobbyist; Bureaucrat, Public Defender, Television Reporter.
- **CLUES:** Fodder for bribery, blackmail, and brainwashing; hidden occult secrets in archived historical documents; the dome is known as a site for inexplicable suicides.
- **RULES EFFECTS:** This is where back-room deals are made; if you have Negotiation, gain 1 free pool point to spend here.
- **IN A FIGHT:** Well-armed police and anti-terrorism experts; politically-connected hostages aplenty; bored news media hunting for an interesting story.
- **IN A CHASE:** Force passage through the metal detector; history-steeped chamber echoes impossibly loud as you run through it; a multitude of poorly marked offices to duck into. (Normal)

STEEL FOUNDRY

The first things that hit you are the heat and the noise. It's loud in here even if you wear earplugs, and deafening if not. The cherry red glow of molten steel pouring out of blast furnaces dries the sweat on your face as soon as it forms. Huge vats and a welter of pipes rise up around you, and you can glimpse the control room upstairs through a large and filthy glass window on its front. The workers keep a sharp eye out for people who don't belong here; such folk are potential safety hazards.

- **EXTRAS AND CAMEOS:** Suspicious union organizer, indolent manager, whistle-blowing mole trying to keep her identity secret; Chop Shop "Manager" (as "union liaison"), Longshoreman (as steelworker), Truck Driver.
- **CLUES:** Stolen merchandise hidden somewhere in the foundry, and someone wants to protect it; human teeth in a pile of ash; steel baron's ancient secrets hidden in the plant he built.
- **RULES EFFECTS:** Mechanics can be used to spill, redirect, or operate the trough of molten steel and the blast furnaces that keep it molten.
- **IN A FIGHT:** Troughs of molten steel; fire hoses; heavy ingots, dropped from the floors above.
- **IN A CHASE:** Lose him in a confusing tangle of vats, machinery and pipes; shout warnings so plant workers try to stop the intruders; slam into locked fire doors. (Normal)

STREET FESTIVAL

Hundreds of people brush up against you as you force your way through crowded streets. The crowd is laughing, drunk, thrilled with the warm summer night and the delight of being young and beautiful. Your prey could be anywhere. Stores are open late tonight, muted neon competing with street lamps to light the surging crowd. Music surges from every bar, every open bandstand, from the mouths of the people around you. A massive puppet in search of a parade stumbles by, carried by three people late to an appointment.

The shoes of the second person, the one wholly inside of the papier-mâché puppet, are hand-made Russian loafers. Just like the shoes of your prey. Silently, you wheel around and follow.

EXTRAS AND CAMEOS: Young performance artist, beautiful tourist, drunken lout; Car Thief, Street Thug, Vampire-Enthralled Goth.

CLUES: Firecrackers cover the assassination in a back alley; knowledgeable street vendors with information to sell; vampires gather to easily thin the herd.

RULES EFFECTS: Spending a point of Urban Survival allows characters to easily navigate the surging crowds, moving in the direction that the drunken masses are not.

IN A FIGHT: Mook shields aplenty; huge dragon puppets actually breathe fire; packed crowds accidentally provide cover from Shooting attacks.

IN A CHASE: Local folk dancers grab the quarry for a brief dance; dodge into a crowded bar; topple a food cart. (Cramped)

URBAN TRAFFIC JAM

Smog hangs in sheets and exasperated drivers inch forward, bumper to bumper. It's still impossible to see what's holding up traffic, but that doesn't stop frustrated commuters from leaning on their horns to try and push traffic forward through sound alone. You'd have to be a spectacularly talented driver to chase someone through this tangle; it would be faster to get out of your car and just run.

EXTRAS AND CAMEOS: Road-rage-filled suburban parents, rich jerk in an ironically immobile sports car, vindictive cop; Arms Dealer (in the back of a limo), Car Thief, Truck Driver.

CLUES: Car sideswiped in your quarry's carelessness; a package idly tossed from one car into another; the reflective glint off a rifle scope from a bridge ahead.

RULES EFFECTS: In a thriller chase, the more maneuverable opponent adds an additional +1 to the difference between his Maneuver rating on the Vehicle Table and that of his opponents, raising the minimum bonus to +2.

IN A FIGHT: Start a chain-reaction crash; use vehicles as cover; open a door suddenly into a foe.

IN A CHASE: Abandon a car to flee on foot; weave a motorcycle through the tangle of cars; run across the tops of stalled cars. (Cramped in a car, Normal on foot)

MONSTERS

This section adds two more monstrous powers, and four more monsters from the world's store of vampiric and quasi-vampiric horrors. Modern Brazil, ancient Iraq, medieval Germany, and traditional Malaya staff our tour of terror.

It closes with another pre-built vampire, the nosferatu. The name comes from Bram Stoker's notes and seemingly nowhere else; the image comes from F. W. Murnau's film and from our archetypal nightmares of plague. This familiar fear lurks on the boundary between the supernatural and the unnatural, remaining uncanny as it does so.

BLOODWORKING

Some vampires can manipulate blood itself, either their own or that of someone else. This can be as simple as boiling a foe's blood in his veins (treat such an attack as a telekinetic blast attack; **NBA**, p. 132) or spraying her own blood as a blinding stream (see spit Venom; **NBA**, p. 138) or concealing fog (+2 to visual Difficulties, including Hit Thresholds). More baroque (and disgusting) vampires build poppets, weapons, or whole buildings out of blood, constructs kept in being by their will. A badly distracted vampire (one attacked with a Bane while at negative Health, for example) might involuntarily liquefy these projections; vampiric controls for such things might not extend across Blocks. A vampiric poppet has whatever stats seem right; use the homunculus or the animals on p. 154-155 of NBA as guidelines. It usually grants the vampire a clairvoyant connection (**NBA**, p. 128) to its "senses."

In general, a vampire must spend his Health to manipulate his own blood, the amount depending on the size of the manifestation (the Health of the poppet, for example), as well as spending the standard 2 points of Aberrance (3 points for blood-castles or the like). A bloodworking vampire might enter combat with two or three "blood bags," Renfields bulked up with victims' Health points to be turned into hovering, spinning blades or entangling webs.

CURSE

Depending on your chosen cosmology, this power might be supernatural or psionic. Whether it's the "evil eye" or an "entropy focus," the result is the same: bad luck for the vampire's target. Against NPCs, this power can do almost anything up to the full *Final Destination*-style Rube Goldberg death: change the cards in a deck, make a gun misfire or shoot allies, send a helicopter spiraling into power lines, or turn the edge of the roof slippery. Like Magic, it costs 2 Aberrance pool points per use. For 3 pool points, it affects all the NPCs in a scene, lasts for weeks or months (permanently cursing an agent's Network contact is really cruel), or has an enormous effect on the agents' whereabouts: the night watchman "accidentally" drops his cigarette and blows up the entire fuel dump, for example.

Against the agents, it has a more specific effect: for 2 Aberrance pool points, the vampire may change any one die roll made by a player to any other result (usually, but not always, a 1). This result counts as "unmodified" for the purpose of other rules effects. For 3 points, the vampire can make the effect "permanent" in the scene — jamming the gun (Shooting), breaking a leg (Athletics), etc.

The Luck of the Devil cherry (**NBA**, p. 30) supersedes this power; a Curse cannot change a Luck of the Devil die. Curses have no effect on MOS usage: a MOS automatically succeeds *without a roll*.

CHUPA

Beginning in the late 1960s, farmers and hunters in remote sections of northern Brazil reported "chupa lights" or "chupa-chupas" that somehow shone on them and sucked their blood. (*Chupa* means "suck" in Portuguese and Spanish; it's where the **chupacabra** or "goat sucker" gets its name. To make a chupacabra, add Drain and Vampiric Speed or Apportation to the dog stat block on p. 69 of **NBA**.) The chupa flap peaked in 1977-1982, and has since faded into the background noise of UFO incidents not easily explicable as alien saucers or government aircraft.

A standard chupa (although descriptions varied) is a beam or ball of red light that shoots at or illuminates the victim. Sometimes the light emanates from a point in the sky, which might be moving or stationary; other times it simply appears nearby. It may be silent, or emit a hum, purr, or whirring sound. Those struck by chupa light develop strange puncture marks on their bodies and severe, sometimes terminal, anemia. (Other reported symptoms include vomiting, leprosy, burns, and fatal blue spots.) Occasionally the chupa begins as a green light and becomes red while "feeding." The light winks out or zooms away after completing its meal.

Despite its UFOlogical context, the chupa does not have to be an alien vampire or a saucer's microwave-beam weapon. Medieval demons are conventionally "powers of the air" that need not take physical form. It might be the Brazilian equivalent of the murony (**NBA**, p. 152), one without a buried or living vampire nearby. The chupa's description matches some European fairy legends such as the **corpse-candle,** and its vampirism recalls the **feu-follet** of Cajun and hoodoo lore. Unlike the reported chupa, both these will-o-the-wisps have the ability to lure victims into following them; add the Mesmerism power Lure Into Following as a mental attack. They use Hand-to-Hand instead of Shooting to envelop victims in a glow.

For a chupa that beams its light at a victim, use Shooting; for one that appears on or floats onto a target, use Hand-to-Hand. Treat foes of the chupa as illuminated by its beam or glow; their Hit Threshold goes down by 1. Some

MONSTERS ■ CHUPA TO EKIMMU

survivors describe the chupa as crushing them in the night as they slept; if your chupa do that, model this power using the crush attack of the mara (*NBA*, p. 151).

GENERAL ABILITIES: Aberrance 5, Health 6, Shooting 11
HIT THRESHOLD: 3 (glowing)
ALERTNESS MODIFIER: +0
STEALTH MODIFIER: -1 (-2 if it makes a humming or purring sound)
DAMAGE MODIFIER: +0 (blood drain); +0 (crush attack)
ARMOR: physical weapons do no damage; *electricity does 1 point* (Immaterial)
FREE POWERS: Distortion, Drain, Infravision, *Plague, Remote Drain,* Unfeeling
OTHER POWERS: Apportation, *Infrasound,* Levitation
BANES: none
BLOCKS: *grounded knife blade jammed in the earth*
COMPULSIONS: none
DREADS: *electricity, lightning*
REQUIREMENTS: drink blood

EKIMMU

The ancient Mesopotamian cultures had a number of ghosts, specters, revenants, and demons that over the millennia changed names and roles. Beginning about 2500 B.C. the *Utukku Lemnutu*, a demonological text, describes "the seven demons" who "suck the veins" of humans and "ceaselessly devour blood." The vampirologist Montague Summers applied the Babylonian word *ekimmu* ("grasper") to those demons, a usage that continues despite its technical inaccuracy. The ekimmu was a spirit of an unburied (or improperly buried) man that wanders the earth (or the underworld) bringing bad luck, disease, or a supernatural curse to its victims. Most often, the ekimmu possesses or attaches itself to a living victim, but some ekimmu animate corpses.

This writeup describes the "post-Summers" vampiric Babylonian demon that possesses a man or corpse and carries a cloud of supernatural evil with it. It sucks the life out of mortals like a "swift wind." Unlike the bhuta or the murony, the ekimmu spends most of its time attached to or possessing a human or corpse, not least because (barring necromancy) it requires a human voice to interact with its Conspiracy colleagues. If it remains in the corpse too long, the skin shrinks over the bones and becomes pale or gray. Depict this corpse (often called or conflated with the *alu*) with the ghoul writeup (*NBA*, p. 150), adding ekimmu powers and blocks to suit. Without the Blood Phantoms or Curse powers, this writeup also works for other possessing spirits such as the **dybbuk.** For the dybbuk specifically, add a compulsion to eat candy, and garlic as a block. Like ekimmu, the dybbuk dreads red cloth; its exorcism is no longer Sumerian but rabbinical, of course.

In a non-supernatural vampire campaign, ekimmu might be incorporeal aliens, perhaps left behind at the "ancient astronaut" crash sites in Iraq. Or they might be a post-hypnotic program implanted by a secret mind control project, specific syndromes resulting from experimental injections or genetically modified spores, or any other mind-altering effect of black science.

Even more than usual, stats and powers vary widely for ekimmu. The value before the slash is the ekimmu's rating as a specter; the value after the slash is the amount it adds to its possessed victim's relevant score. Powers, banes, etc. apply in both forms unless specifically noted. Most of the dreads and blocks come from the *Utukku Lemnutu*, and were likely lists of possible anti-ekimmu materia rather than definitive counter-measures. Gold harms or confines ekimmu (if it does) because it is the sacred metal of Marduk, lord of the sun in late Babylonian myth.

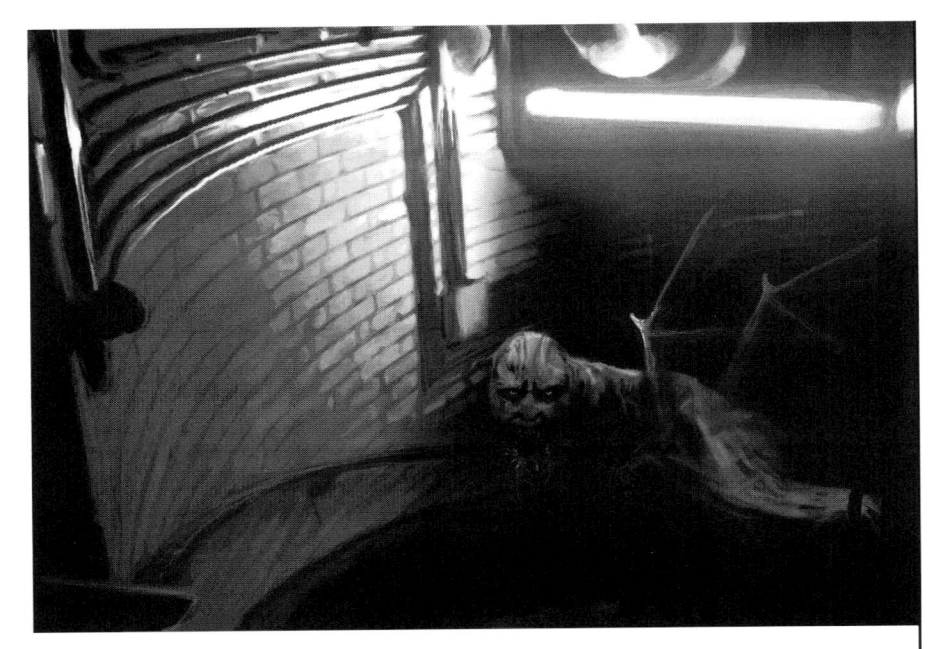

The ekimmu uses points taken from victims by its Drain and/or Psychic Vampirism to refresh its Health, up to double the ekimmu's rating.

BLOOD PHANTOMS: A wounded ekimmu bleeds in an atomized spray that takes the shape of a predatory bird or storm cloud. Similar to a bloodworking poppet, it attacks any un-possessed humans in the vicinity. Its Health is equivalent to the Health lost in the wound; its Aberrance and combat abilities are equal to the ekimmu's current pools. Its Hit Threshold is 4; it does +1 damage with its talon or tendril attack, adding its foe's lost Health to its own. It is Immaterial, and suffers the same banes, blocks, and dreads as the ekimmu.

ECLIPSE POWER: During a partial or annular eclipse (lunar or solar), ekimmu double their Aberrance and Health pool; during a total eclipse, they quadruple it.

GENERAL ABILITIES: Aberrance 10/+5, Hand-to-Hand 9/+4, Health 9/-2, Weapons 0/+4

HIT THRESHOLD: 6 (invisible specter)/+1

ALERTNESS MODIFIER: +0

STEALTH MODIFIER: +3 (invisible specter)/+0

DAMAGE MODIFIER: +1 (life drain as specter); -1 (savage bite)

ARMOR: physical weapons do no damage, fire does 1 point (Immaterial); possessed body takes half damage from all injuries

FREE POWERS: *Drain*, Psychic Vampirism (drain either Health or Stability), Unfeeling

OTHER POWERS: Blood Phantoms (embodied only), Curse, Levitation (specter only), *Magic*, Plague, Possession, *Telekinesis*

BANES: hawthorn, gold, Sumerian ritual of exorcism

BLOCKS: bitumen and gypsum, gold, hanged mouse, hawthorn, multicolored wool cord, Sumerian magic circle

COMPULSIONS: kill infants or children

DREADS: bright red clothing, drumming on copper, images of wrestlers, tamarisk

REQUIREMENTS: drink blood (embodied only)

HOMUNCULUS

The alchemist Paracelsus invented the homunculus, or "little human," in the 16th century, working from references by the 8th-century Arabic alchemist Geber. His formula for homunculus creation (in *De Natura Rerum* (1537)) begins with the alchemist ejaculating into a flask and ends with the requirement to feed the thing "wisely with the Arcanum of human blood" for forty weeks while it steeps in a dunghill or decomposing horse corpse. The result is a miniature man or woman, usually between 9 and 30 cm tall, with an appetite for human blood and the knowledge of alchemy literally baked into its brain.

Vampires with the Bloodworking power (see p. 106) can make homunculi out of their, or anybody's, blood. However they're made, if they're made with vampire blood (or sperm), homunculi might manifest other vampiric powers, along with vampiric banes, blocks, and so forth. On the supernatural end of things, you can use this template for **redcaps** or other small blood-drinking faerie (who traditionally have immense Strength and often Mimicry or Shapeshifting), or for witches' **familiars** (although adding Drain and Magic to a cat, rat, or other suitable animal can also work). The vampiric Lord William de Soulis (1285?-1321) of Hermitage Castle on the Scots border split the difference and had a redcap familiar. Homunculi don't require magic or the supernatural: they might be alien servitor beings (or even miniature robots or psychic projections), or the projects of some black bioweapons laboratory in Korea, Kamchatka, or Kansas.

If the Conspiracy needs instruction in alchemy, it might create homunculi for such purposes, but more likely uses them as infiltrators, planters of bugs, and poison-needle assassins. Without vampiric Strength, a homunculus can lift approximately 5 kg; they are not made for slugfests, but for subtlety. That said, the Conspiracy could arm its tiny minions. The Swiss MiniGun company manufactures the C1ST: a revolver 55 mm long, weighing 20g, and firing a 2.34mm (.09 caliber) round, which does -4 damage at Point Blank range. Special loads with titanium jackets and PETN instead of gunpowder could increase that damage to -2, and extend the range to Close. A similarly tiny rail gun could shoot a poisoned needle up to Close range (Near by spending 2 Shooting points for Extended Range; *NBA*, p. 67). For such mini-mooks, provide a Shooting ability pool.

Sorcerous homunculi and familiars can traditionally transmit visions and thoughts to their creator or summoner; this might also be true of alien pods or

MONSTERS ■ HOMUNCULUS TO PENANGGALAN

spore-creatures. Such homunculi make even better hidden scouts and sentries.

GENERAL ABILITIES: Aberrance 8, Hand-to-Hand 6, Health 7, Weapons 8
HIT THRESHOLD: 5 (small)
ALERTNESS MODIFIER: +1
STEALTH MODIFIER: +3 (small, very good at hiding)
DAMAGE MODIFIER: -2 (bite or kick or needle), toxin (from needle)
ARMOR: -2 vs. melee weapons; firearms and projectiles do half damage; crashes and falls do 1 point of damage (Rubbery; **NBA**, p. 126).
FREE POWERS: Drain, Unfeeling
OTHER POWERS: Clairvoyance, *Hive Mind*, Magic, Necromancy, Regeneration, Spider Climb, Strength (tests mandatory for feats of strength; **NBA**, p. 137), Summoning, Vampiric Speed, Venom.

BANES: acid, fire, *fatal damage done to homunculus deals its full Health in damage to its creator*
BLOCKS: *moving more than 1 km (or some other distance) from creator*, standard vampiric blocks for campaign (if made from vampire blood or semen)
COMPULSIONS: *obey creator*
DREADS: standard vampiric dreads for campaign (if made from vampire blood or semen); *cats*
REQUIREMENTS: *drink blood*

PENANGGALAN

This blood-drinking monster is called the penanggalan or penangglan in Malaysia, the kuyang in Borneo, the ma lai in Vietnam, and the krasue in Thailand. The Malay word *penanggal* means "detach," referring to the creature's habit of detaching its head from its body. The head floats around at night, dragging its internal organs behind it sparkling like a cloud of fireflies. Bile from its entrails leaves smoldering patches where it drips in the head's wake. The leyak of Bali is similar, but can also shapeshift into a tiger, a rat, a large bird, a ball of light (as the chupa or murony), or a motorcycle! The Filipino manananggal severs her whole upper torso and sprouts wings; the Japanese nukekubi can send her head off without her entrails to fly about on vampiric (or cannibalistic) hunts.

By day a beautiful woman, at night the penanggalan leaves her body behind and goes hunting. The penanggalan prefers the blood of infants and new mothers, but will drink any blood it can get if need be. Some stories say she floats in through the window; others say she roosts on the roof and sends her long tongue snaking down to suck blood. The thing may be able to use her entrails as tentacles to manipulate objects or pick locks. The versions of the legend that feature the penanggalan somehow oozing up through the floorboards or funneling itself through the keyhole contradict the most common block for the creature: thorns (usually of the jeruju plant) strung along every opening to catch the thing's dragging entrails. Such a trapped penanggalan may be vulnerable to machetes or other edged weapons, especially wielded against her soft lungs and stomach.

Once the creature has fed, she returns to her house and must soak her engorged organs in vinegar to shrink them. (Thus the odor of vinegar that a good Sense Trouble might pick up from a nearby penanggalan.) Only then can she fit back into her body and resume human form. The body is quite vulnerable; even turning it over might result in the penanggalan awakening with its head facing backward!

While most penanggalan are likely supernatural creatures or damned sorceresses, they might also be alien parasites nesting in human host bodies. Building a biotech mutant penanggalan strains credibility, although this could serve as the template for a **living disembodied head**, possibly the preserved cranium of a Nazi or Japanese war criminal. Change Flight to Levitation with Telekinesis, and remove Magic

NIGHT'S BLACK AGENTS — DOUBLE TAP

(Plague can be a biotoxin gland implant) and the intestine squeeze attack. If the living head has a cloned body to draw on, so much the better. Replace banes, compulsions, etc. with those suitable for biotech vampires in your campaign.

The listed abilities, powers, banes, and so forth only apply when the head and body are separate. Joined, the penanggalan becomes a normal woman; if killed, she rises again the next night. Burning the woman's body prevents her resurrection.

GENERAL ABILITIES: Aberrance 16, Hand-to-Hand 6, Health 9
HIT THRESHOLD: 4
ALERTNESS MODIFIER: +0
STEALTH MODIFIER: +2
DAMAGE MODIFIER: +0 (saw-like bite) or +0 (sucking tongue, extensible at Close range); +2 (intestine squeeze; plus bile as acid (**NBA**, p. 78)) or -2 (bile spatter, up to Close range, lasts 2 rounds)
ARMOR: none
FREE POWERS: Darkvision, Drain, Flight, Regeneration (full Health refresh when rejoined), *Remote Drain*, Unfeeling
OTHER POWERS: *Create Fog, Howl, Magic, Plague, Send to Sleep, Turn to Mist* (not against thorns)
BANES: bladed weapons, broken glass poured into the body cavity, sunlight, wooden stake
BLOCKS: *pineapples, salt, sticky rice, thorns* (becomes entangled if its foes succeeded at both a Conceal and Mechanics roll to trap it), *turmeric*
COMPULSIONS: kill children and pregnant women
DREADS: garlic, scissors, tamarind
REQUIREMENTS: drink blood, soak organs in vinegar after hunting

⊕ 🦠 NOSFERATU

One of the most recognizable vampire images, the fanged and taloned nosferatu resembles a pallid, humanoid rat. Its sunken cheeks, emaciated frame, chalky skin, red staring eyes, bloody fangs, and stiff fingers replicate the features of a tuberculosis sufferer. A spurious etymology traces the word "nosferatu" to the Greek *nosophoros*, or "plague carrier" — it more likely derives from a mistransliteration of the Romanian *necuratu*, or "the unclean one." In both cases, the word conveys the true power of the nosferatu: the power of disease to drain and kill the living.

This vampire similarly exists on the boundary layer between occult predation and biotech mutation. It might be an "elder species" driven into the shadows by torch-wielding Neanderthals, a demonic strain unleashed during the Great Balkan Plague of 1738, or an apex predator built by a forgotten Soviet bioweapons program or secret Nazi super-soldier project. Or, of course, the nosferatu might be a demon drawn to experiments in pain and degradation. Maybe even the Soviet surgeons who built the nosferatu don't know they've opened the human doorway to hell! This writeup preserves as best it can that sense of the uncanny and unknowable so central to horror.

None of its powers are clearly "impossible" — no flying, dissolving into mist, or transforming into a bat. But normal humans jacked up on PCP shrug off bullets and react with lightning speed, and creative gene-splicing might provide the equivalent of batlike hearing, chimpanzee strength, bloodhound smell, and even gecko hairs on palms and feet for clinging to walls.

Nosferatu do not circulate blood as such. Human blood, infused with certain hormones by the nosferatu's overclocked lymphatic system, becomes the fundamental fuel and oxygenator of all the body's organs and muscles, percolating between cells along a thin network of capillaries. That lymphatic cocktail feeds on complex viruses and bacteria very similar to those present in human decomposition: by sleeping in grave earth, the nosferatu restores expended energy faster. Those same microorganisms burgeon in the nosferatu's saliva and sweat, spreading disease by bite or contact. Many of the mutations in the nosferatu gene line piggyback on the sex drive; like the revenant vampire of the pre-Stoker Balkans, the nosferatu roils with lust. Thanks either to a chained mutation or demonic curse, the nosferatu's skin reddens and burns in sunlight, garlic makes its capillaries sieze up, and salt badly desiccates its muscle tissue.

Its Mesmerism might be advanced hypnotic or neurolinguistic training (either provided to super-soldiers or learned as part of its tribal lore), or simply powerful pheromone emissions to arouse and distract victims. Similar pheromone emissions attract rats — and nosferatu generally dwell in rat-infested buildings or graveyards.

Directors who want to play just a little bit closer to the realm of the plausible can require tests for feats of nosferatu Strength (*NBA*, p. 137), and possibly remove Spider Climb along with the requirement to sleep in graves. For not definitively demonic but slightly more supernatural nosferatu, add Apportation ("slasher movement"), Dominance, Heat Drain, Stifling Air, and Tunneling as other powers, and increase Regeneration to 2 Health per round. Whether demonic or designed, a nosferatu may well have a strong psychological aversion (treat as a dread, with the Difficulty of the Aberrance roll at -2) to mirrors or crosses to further muddy the issue.

GENERAL ABILITIES: Aberrance 13, Hand-to-Hand 13, Health 13
HIT THRESHOLD: 6 (cunning and superhuman reflexes)
ALERTNESS MODIFIER: +2
STEALTH MODIFIER: +1
DAMAGE MODIFIER: +2 (fangs), +2 (talons), -1 (acidic spit)
ARMOR: -2 (leathery hide); all weapons do half damage (rounded down) after armor; car crashes and falls do 1 point of damage (reduced blood flow)
FREE POWERS: Darkvision, Drain, Tracking by Smell (further +2 to Difficulty to evade), Unfeeling
OTHER POWERS: Cannot Drown, Extra Attacks (first extra attack is free, further attacks in a round cost 2 Aberrance or Hand-to-Hand points each), Infrasound, Mesmerism, Plague, Regeneration (full Health refresh each day), Spider Climb, Spit Venom (digestive acid), Strength, Summoning (rats), Vampiric Speed
BANES: beheading or otherwise completely severing spine, direct sunlight or ultraviolet light (does damage like weak acid, -2 to normal acid damage from exposure; nosferatu is Hurt if in direct sunlight), fire, garlic (strong allergy; treat exposure as tear gas), salt (treat as acid damage)
BLOCKS: direct sunlight
COMPULSIONS: attack sexually attractive target, kill and drain a fallen enemy
DREADS: direct sunlight, garlic
REQUIREMENTS: drink blood, sleep in grave earth

STORIES

At its heart (before getting staked, of course) a Conspiracy is a story, often one with dramatic and bitter twists, and more than the sum of its parts. It is the confluence of the relationships not only of Conspiracy elements to players, but also the Conspiracy elements amongst themselves.

While complicated story development techniques are not critical for building an intense story, always recognize the push-pull atmosphere at the heart of a thriller. The urgency of discovery, misdirection, and tension inherent in the question "Will this be found out?" drives the story forward.

Adding a Conspiracy at war with itself changes the "default" *Night's Black Agents* story in one way. What about subtraction? Taking away the other agents for one-on-one roleplaying amps up the isolation that lives at the heart of the genre. Finally, changing the background era throws the core story into relief, whether it's for one session or for a whole campaign.

PULLING THEM APART

What do vampires and organized crime have in common, besides murder, conspiracy, and Eastern Europe? When under pressure, they turn on each other. Criminal conspiracy breeds mistrust, while the nature of vampires is endless, unheeding consumption, like Saturn eating his children or Duncan's horses that "did turn and eat each other."

The heroes of vampire fiction often triumph by exploiting these betrayals and vendettas between creatures far more powerful than them. Alternatively, think of stories of vengeance against organized crime, like the Punisher, where the protagonists' progress is often intercut with the battles within the organization itself, V's actions against the Norsefire Party in *V for Vendetta*, or the self-immolation of Shakespearian villains.

MECHANISMS OF FACTION

To represent these kind of stories, as the agents move up the hierarchy of the Conspyramid, as well as prompting reactions against them from the vampires, they will also prompt stresses, suspicions, and conflicts within the Conspyramid itself. This is represented by the Suspyramid, detailed below, a veritable hurricane of suspicion and self-destruction.

FRAYED, STRESSED, AND BROKEN

As the Conspiracy turns on itself, the connections between groups crumble and snap, in a process known as fraying. Various reactions on the Suspyramid cause different connections to be frayed, but the Director may also directly fray connection as the result of agents' actions and operations designed to spread dissent, mistrust, and chaos within the Conspyramid.

When the connection between two nodes is **frayed,** the two groups aren't getting along. If the connection is horizontal (on the same level of the Conspyramid), they may see each other as competitors, or there may simply be personal tensions or ideological differences. If vertical, the higher-level node may see the lower one as overly ambitious or incompetent, while the lower-level node may see its superior as undeserving of its position, have moral qualms about working with them, or simply want their post. When agents exploit a frayed connection on the adversary map appropriately, they receive +3, rather than +2, to their pool (*NBA*, p. 113).

> **SUSPYRAMID?**
>
> Yes, I know "suspire" means "to sigh," and the word has no direct connection (aside from the common prefix) to "suspicion." But it sure sounds like it could, right? And besides, the allusion to sighs nicely plays off the Shakespearean conceit of the Suitors and Beloved that can drive the algorithm in the Suspyramid.
>
> This section's author, James Palmer, originally used the term "Vampyremid," alluding to the sparks of suspicion blowing up into the flames of civil war. The Conspyramid becomes a pyre, glowing with lovely funerary imagery. It's a beautiful term, but the trouble is that differentiating the Vampyremid from the Vampyramid is just a lost cause from the get-go. It's enough to make one sigh.

A frayed connection that's frayed again becomes **stressed.** When the relationship between two nodes is stressed, the two are openly quarrelling. If the connection is horizontal, they stop cooperating with each other on all but critical matters, refuse to share information, and complain bitterly to their superiors. If vertical, the higher-ranked party treats those below with open contempt, bossing them about and putting them at grave risk, while the lower-ranked either scheme to usurp their bosses, avoid contact where possible, or begin openly ignoring orders. When agents exploit a stressed connection on the adversary map appropriately, they receive +4, rather than +2, to their pool.

If a stressed connection is frayed, it is **broken.** When this occurs horizontally, either the two groups cut off all connection with each other, or they are at open odds. The second is more likely if they have no mutual superior, or if their ties with their superior are also frayed. Conflict can range from bureaucratic maneuvering to all-out warfare.

If a break occurs vertically, the reaction depends on the initiator. If the higher-level node is the instigator, they may simply move to destroy their inferior. They may also consume them, either literally, in the case of the most bloody-mouthed creatures, or metaphorically, by destroying their leadership and merging the remains of the node with themselves, or with another group. If all the node's connections are broken, they may instead be burnt, isolated from all contact with the Conspiracy in order to forestall investigation or prevent their problems from spreading.

If the lower-level node is the main actor, they may rebel, moving directly against their superior. This could be anything from a boardroom coup to a group of mafiosi ambushing their vampiric master with garlic and stakes. If the rebellion succeeds, the node may establish a frayed connection with a new superior, or may find itself burnt or consumed by far more powerful beings. If the rebellion fails, the group will almost certainly be destroyed.

Lower-level nodes may also switch allegiance, looking for a new, higher-level protector. This is especially likely if they already have a connection with such. In this case, fray any connection between the former superior and the new one. They may flip, attempting to leave the conspiracy entirely and striking a deal with either a rival organization or the authorities; this is especially likely for bottom-tier groups that have little inkling of the power of their masters. Finally, they may flee, breaking off all connections and running for cover, preferably in another country entirely.

Broken nodes give no bonus for using the mapped connection, but are likely to present numerous opportunities to cunning agents.

THE SUITORS AND THE BELOVED

One common dynamic, reproducible in almost any conspiracy, is the Suitors and the Beloved. The Suitors are two high-level members of the Conspyramid who compete for the favors (or influence) of another, the Beloved. The Beloved manipulates and exploits the Suitors for its own benefit; love (or more abstractly, loyalty), for the Beloved, barely enters into it. The Suitors may be a crime boss and a company president competing for the attention of a vampiric mistress, two ancient resurrected Egyptian princesses fighting over the Pharaoh they both served in life, or the anxious head of the secret police convinced his wife is sleeping with the head of another intelligence agency.

The Beloved is not necessarily on a higher level than the Suitors: in the Linea Dracula conspiracy (*NBA*, pp. 143-144), John Dracula and Vlad Tepes may be Suitors competing for the loyalty of lower-level vampires such as Radu the Bloody. Radu, meanwhile, is also the Beloved competed over by his subordinates Corvino and Kurusets in Marseilles (*NBA*, p. 176). It all depends on the Director's sense of theater, and on how complex she feels like making the intrigue. Remember, however, that players get confused by too many threads, and react to confusion by withdrawal. One big, sprawling rivalry is probably best for the Conspiracy at large, although lesser rivalries can inform specific cities or operations.

Picking a triad of Suitors and the Beloved is not necessary for the Suspyramid to function. That "story line" follows the right side of the Suspyramid up to its destruction, while the left side mirrors less romantic espionage and intrigue narratives.

THE SUSPYRAMID

The Suspyramid maps a dramatic algorithm for stories of disintegrating or factionalized conspiracies, which is to say, most of them. Like the Vampyramid (**NBA**, pp. 189-193), it is a guideline for drama, not an iron law of political science. If the Director has a better or more personalized idea, or one that sets up a glorious Yojimbo opportunity for the agents, she should go ahead and play that one. The Conspiracy can always enforce a brief truce or respite after such an operation; civil wars and faction fights don't follow timetables.

The Suspyramid is best suited for conspiracies where the nodes are relatively small-scale and personal. Directors in longer campaigns might use it to represent the conflicts within a group, like, say, the Armenian mafia in Odessa, one that is itself merely a node within the wider Conspyramid. But the possibility of "The CIA" and "The Russian Mafiya" turning viciously on each other or competing for the favor of "The Black Alchemists" also exists.

As the agents penetrate the Conspiracy, they uncover (or trigger, or cause) further dysfunction and factionalization within it. When the agents penetrate a level of the Conspiracy, choose a reaction from the corresponding tier of the Suspyramid. Note that these reactions are not necessarily caused by the agents' actions themselves, but represent existing tensions, hatreds, and fears. But the pressure of the agents' attacks and investigations exacerbates such fractures; the Director can easily aim the agents at promising vulnerabilities if she feels the Conspiracy's self-destruction requires an outside stimulus. The Director may even hold off on advancing the Suspyramid "story" until the agents take some action designed to force further stress and damage on the Conspiracy — the new Suspyramid reaction becomes a reward for a proactive, killer-instinct operation.

Some of the actions within the Suspyramid may not even directly affect the agents initially. Instead, the agents can get word of them through rumor, surveillance, interrogation, or documentation. Alternatively, an ambitious Director concentrating on personal intrigues within the Conspyramid may wish to run cut scenes, temporarily assigning the players the roles of the vampire lords and their minions themselves.

🜂 A real high-wire Director can run the Suspyramid on the agents' own patron organization: the CIA tears itself apart in political infighting and paralyzes the hunt for terrorist vampires, or rival cardinals' agendas roil the Vatican's secret undead-slaying order. If the players are open to it, the Suspyramid works amazingly well (perhaps too well) even on the small group level inside the party, with each agent being his or her own node. Each fray costs 1 Trust between the agents affected.

TIER ONE: INTRIGUE

INSULT: Members of one node insult another, whether unintentionally, such as by arriving late and unprepared to a critical meeting, covertly, like cracking a joke at someone else's expense that's deliberately passed on, or overtly, like calling attention to their failing in front of a mutual boss. Fray the connection between the two.

THE WENCH IS DEAD: Evidence of a past sin reemerges, or is remembered. Perhaps a dead girlfriend's body is found, marked money shows up, or a past affiliation with the police revealed. Fray any one connection.

DISRESPECT: A higher-ranking minion treats a lower-ranking one in a poor fashion, or a lower-ranking one fails to treat his superior with the respect he feels he deserves. Fray the connection between the two.

I COULD TAKE CARE OF YOU: A lower level node feels unhappy or unprotected by its superior, and so looks for new protection elsewhere. Stress the connection with the superior, but draw another connection to a node on the same tier as or one tier above the superior.

OTHER BUSINESS: One node becomes intensely involved in its own affairs, ignoring its work for the conspiracy in favor of drug-smuggling, hunting children, murder for hire, or other unpleasant pastimes. Fray one connection between the node and its superiors.

RIVALS: The competition between the Suitors intensifies. Fray any connection between the Suitors.

TIER TWO: STRIFE

CONFRONTATION: A meeting between two nodes becomes heated, though not physically violent. Tensions between the two worsen, and the strife spreads elsewhere. Fray the link between the two, and two additional links.

SECRET MURDER: A member of one node kills another in a private meeting, and then conceals the evidence of the slaying as best they can. Fray any two links from the node that suffered the death, depending on whom they suspect.

LEAK: One node deliberately passes on information to the agents, whether out of stirrings of conscience, or, more likely, in order to frustrate an operation by one of their rivals. Fray the link between that node and another.

YOU'RE WITH ME NOW: A node changes allegiance entirely, breaking any connection with their former superior and drawing a new connection, if one doesn't exist, to a higher-level node. The former master is likely to be extremely unhappy about this; fray one link anywhere between the former and current master.

FAVORITE: The Beloved picks one of the Suitors to favor, bestowing previously withheld powers, blessings, or attentions. The favored Suitor receives +2 to all pools, and the disfavored +2 to all Difficulties. (This is a general guideline intended to represent the increased assets and more robust connections of the newly favored node, and vice versa for the node out in the cold. The Director should take this status

SUSPYRAMID DIAGRAM

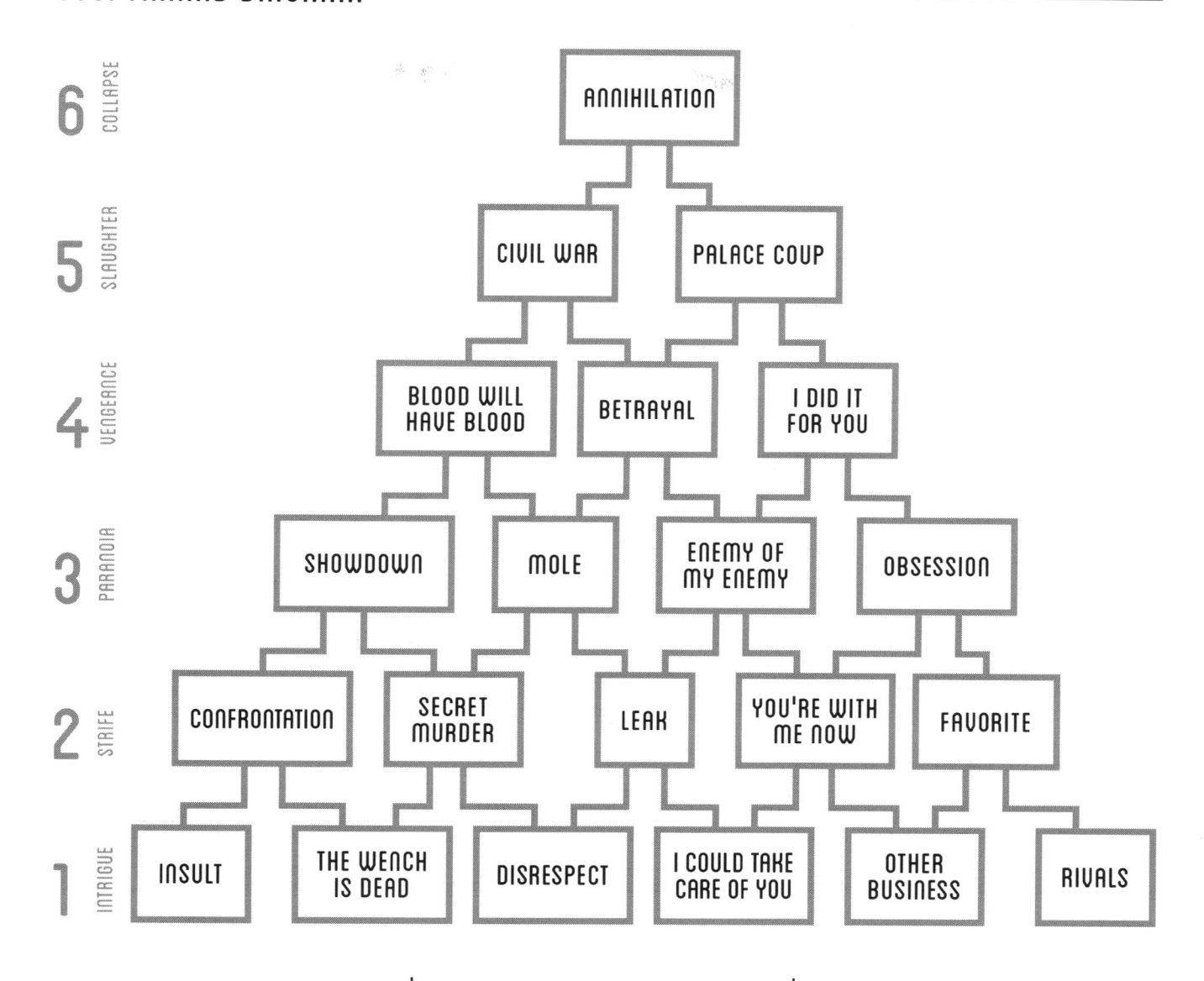

6 COLLAPSE — ANNIHILATION

5 SLAUGHTER — CIVIL WAR, PALACE COUP

4 VENGEANCE — BLOOD WILL HAVE BLOOD, BETRAYAL, I DID IT FOR YOU

3 PARANOIA — SHOWDOWN, MOLE, ENEMY OF MY ENEMY, OBSESSION

2 STRIFE — CONFRONTATION, SECRET MURDER, LEAK, YOU'RE WITH ME NOW, FAVORITE

1 INTRIGUE — INSULT, THE WENCH IS DEAD, DISRESPECT, I COULD TAKE CARE OF YOU, OTHER BUSINESS, RIVALS

into consideration, even if she alters or limits the specific additions.) Fray the links between the disfavored Suitor and two other nodes.

TIER THREE: PARANOIA

SHOWDOWN: A meeting between two nodes erupts into violence. The agents may well be watching events as they occur, may trigger the shootout intentionally, or may come upon the aftermath. Stress the link between the two nodes, and fray one additional link from each.

MOLE: The conspiracy becomes convinced, correctly or otherwise, that a mole exists within the organization. A witch-hunt begins for the suspected mole. Fray any six connections.

ENEMY OF MY ENEMY: One node provides information for the agents to fatally strike at another node, seeking to use this new force to do down their rivals. Stress the connection between the two nodes.

OBSESSION: One Suitor (or both) becomes obsessed with the other or with the Beloved, following and watching them (or employing their minions to do so) constantly. They receive +4 to the Difficulty of any roll that doesn't involve the other lover or the beloved, save for direct physical confrontations. (As above, the Director may alter this modifier to suit specific game conditions, but she should remember that the other node's operatives are almost certainly always on the scene.) Fray the connection between the two Suitors again.

TIER FOUR: VENGEANCE

BLOOD WILL HAVE BLOOD: In vengeance for earlier killings or slights, a prominent member of one node openly murders a member of another. The victim's colleagues, in turn, vow further vengeance, while his masters may try to keep the violence under wraps, perhaps by killing him themselves. Break the connection between the two nodes, and fray every other connection they have.

BETRAYAL: A node, out of vengeance, envy, or ambition, openly contacts the agents, offering them everything they know. Will the agents be betrayed in turn?

Stress every connection from the node.

I DID IT FOR YOU: One of the Suitors murders the other as a token for their beloved, but then dies themselves, either fatally wounded by the other Suitor or committing suicide after being spurned by the beloved. Think, for instance, Goneril poisoning Regan over Edmund, or Heyer murdering Harper, then being left to bleed to death, in V for Vendetta. In larger groups, this is a major hit or other deathblow to the rival node, followed by a mini-coup within the rogue node that paralyzes it and exposes its activities. Stress all the connections from the Suitors' nodes.

TIER FIVE: SLAUGHTER

CIVIL WAR: The conspiracy splits into two factions, now at open war against each other. The lords seek haven and direct their pawns against each other, preparing for grand battle. One side may actively offer to enlist the agents in their grand crusade against their rivals. Pick a side for each node, and break all connections between members of opposing sides.

PALACE COUP: An envious Level 5 node moves to seize power, attempting to eliminate the Level 6 lords of the conspiracy in one grand strike. The vampire lords themselves may be well aware of the coup, and use it as an opportunity to eliminate the underling. Whatever the outcome, fray every connection in the Conspyramid.

TIER SIX: COLLAPSE

ANNIHILATION: All bonds and alliances are destroyed. The conspiracy becomes a savage war of all against all. It might seem as if the agents' work is done, but if the war is left to play out, one vampire lord will emerge triumphant, bloated with the blood of his rivals. But a lord who might otherwise be unstoppable may also be fatally weakened at his moment of victory …

SOLITARY HEROES

The lone agent out in the cold is a classic setup for spy fiction. James Bond, Jason Bourne, and Tara Chace all have the world resting on their shoulders as they doggedly track down leads, infiltrate enemy compounds, and cut the right wire with seconds to spare. On the other side of the hill, a George Smiley or a Paul Christopher can trust no one as he pages through files alone in his flat. Tabletop gaming, however, is usually a social activity with a group. **Night's Black Agents** is built toward this group dynamic. For fans unwilling or unable to pull together multiple agents for a little night work, the game works just as well with a few slight modifications. Here are some notes for those Directors who want to set up a table of intrigue for two.

Solo games arise out of many different circumstances. Selling a new system to a group is challenging and only one player might be willing to take time off from beheading goblins to try something new. Solo games also often come about when a spouse or significant other wants to give gaming a try but feels self-conscious about doing it in front of other people. A smaller game has plenty of advantages. There's no need to sweat spotlight time because one player has the spotlight. The Director only has one member of the audience to engage which makes coming up with plots easier as the story unfolds.

When creating the agent, use the preferred point totals for a two-player game. Any Investigative ability the agent doesn't choose still has a nominal one-point rating. This rating represents other contacts who stay off-screen until the agent needs to use them. This represents the web of allies a lone agent has, both as active support and people who might owe him a favor. Core clues should not depend on any unselected ability; where possible, use a named contact as a possible lead. To turn the contact into a recurring character, let the agent spend Network to breathe life into the formerly faceless friend. For Network spent during a session, let it refresh normally afterward like any other General ability. The single agent has to cover more bases on her own, so large spends take a bigger toll. (On the other hand, solo Burn mode games will *really* feel like the source material if Network points still dwindle; one compromise is to start with non-Burn levels of Network that don't refresh.)

The Director should take a moment to study the ability selection of the agent. The character sheet is often a menu for the player. Someone who takes Flirting wants to seduce beautiful people. Someone with a high Infiltration expects to be able to sneak into most fortresses unobserved. Cherries are of particular note. Players pick big toys like that to use them and show off. The MOS is much the same. Directors who leave it in for solo play will have most episodes center around that clutch use. Directors who leave it out will force more varied solutions to the problems the Conspiracy presents.

If the abilities selected are a menu, the Sources of Stability are the wine list. The Director should involve at least one of them in every session. They don't have to be directly hit every time -- poor Maria shouldn't be kidnapped every time the vampires want to make a point -- but something in each session should remind the player why he picked it. If the Symbol is the American flag, take a moment to describe the baseball game playing silently on the TV behind the bartender. An agent who seeks Solace with a Sicilian firebrand might take a moment to watch a dark-haired beauty cross the street. There are plenty of times to hit the Sources directly for a hard choice, but moments like this keep the thriller machine humming in the background.

Communication between player and Director is the key to mutual satisfaction. This is a change to get in deep with backgrounds and themes from the beginning. Sometimes it takes a few sessions for a group to find its footing. Talking about what each side desires out of a game is a good idea. Both "spies" and "vampires" are a lot of ground to cover. The Director might want a big-budget Bond with high-collared Draculas and stake-launching Aston Martins. The player might want a gritty, shabby game where a lone, thankless bureaucrat uncovers ancient aliens in the halls of a forgotten CIA station. Talking about a game beforehand offers a better chance to discover a middle ground both sides will enjoy.

One of the most fun parts of being a Director is thinking up a conspiracy for the players to uncover piece by piece. With two contributors to the story, why only let one have the fun? Take turns filling out the slots on a Conspyramid. Bounce ideas about cool set pieces, neat villains, and staunch allies. There will still be plenty of mystery to discover through play. Some of those ideas will get used; some won't fit after the story plays out for a few sessions. Think of the process like assembling a trailer for your vampire spy thriller. Some of the scenes might be recognizable, but they become much cooler when they fit into the context of a narrative.

Daring Directors could take this one step further. Why not swap control of the agent between sessions, or between missions? Or have two solo agents — one American and one Russian would be the classic choice — both investigating the same Conspiracy. Alternating between Director and player keeps things fresh and keeps everyone guessing. This takes the game in more of a shared narrative direction. It may feel less like an RPG and more like a writing exercise. That doesn't make it any less valid. Two people telling the story together is the important thing. Sharing the power pushes both sides to be active in how it all turns out. Caring about the story and the agent equally makes things more thrilling.

The death of the agent need not be the end. In a group setting, carrying on to avenge a common foe is a classic motivation for the surviving agents. If the Conspiracy kills the agent, discuss which contact might take up the fight. The new main character might also be an old adversary, a rescued innocent, or even a member of the conspiracy disillusioned by the death of the old agent. For a real head turner, let the player get used to the new character and work the Conspyramid for a few sessions. Then bring the original agent back into the fold as a vampire working for the Conspiracy as new opposition. Spies fake their deaths all the time. Taking advantage of a setting where death is not the end is a natural fit.

VARIANT ERAS

After war and prostitution, espionage may be the third-oldest profession, closely combining as it does aspects of the first two. Vampires, of course, are immortal and eternal. Thus, Directors can set **Night's Black Agents** campaigns (or single "flashback" operations or episodes) in any period of history.

Key here is the idea that just as the setting for the story is variable, so too are the mechanics. Scale and tailor yours appropriately and you could easily hunt a brainwashed super-soldier through the middle of World War II, or bring a spy in from the cold during Ulysses S. Grant's first term in office.

The three eras in this section are all loci of spy thriller fiction and film, as well as being times when real-world espionage took unaccustomed center stage.

VICTORIAN ERA

This build assumes agents playing in the Great Game of the later Victorian era (c. 1880-1901). Many of the abilities on the GUMSHOE character sheet are somewhat anachronistic in the earlier Victorian period. Archaeology should probably be considered mere Antiquarianism until Layard publishes his excavation of Nineveh in 1848, or possibly until Schliemann pioneers the stratigraphic dig in 1871. Cop Talk really only comes into its own with the creation of modern police departments in Glasgow and Paris (1800), London (1829), and Boston (1838); before that, getting along with the town watch or prefects is Bureaucracy or uses other Interpersonal skills. Photography remains experimental Chemistry until Talbot's calotype process perfects the negative (circa 1840). See the specific ability writeups and changes below, also.

INVESTIGATIVE ABILITY CHANGES

The following two abilities are not yet available:

- Data Recovery
- Electronic Surveillance

Outdoor Survival no longer incorporates horsemanship, which falls under Riding (see below).

Add one new Technical ability:

TELEGRAPHY

Although precursor devices had existed since 1804, it was Samuel F.B. Morse's electrical telegraph of 1837 that rapidly revolutionized communication in the industrialized world. You can:

- use a telegraph sending key and apparatus to send and receive telegraphic signals
- decipher and encipher Morse and other major telegraphic codes

- perform minor repairs on telegraphic equipment, wires, etc.
- detect and recognize the "fist" of another telegrapher

Tapping a telegraph wire to intercept messages is an Investigative use of Mechanics.

SOCIAL CLASS

Interpersonal relations are defined by class during the Victorian era. To High Society (*NBA*, p. 21), this build adds three complementary abilities: Middle Class (including small landholders, clerks, and the urban bourgeoisie), Working Class (which includes the urban poor and immiserated farmers alike), and Below Stairs (for domestic servants). These new Social Class abilities cover the same sorts of skills and knowledges that High Society does, for their own class level. This grossly simplifies the actual arcana of Victorian class structures, but it's already inconvenient enough to model the resulting social and communication gaps.

Remember that many other Investigative abilities provide the equivalent of social-style Interpersonal connections to the various professions (Bureaucracy, Cop Talk, Diagnosis, Law, Streetwise, etc.).

At character creation, you receive 1 rating point in one of these four Social Class abilities for free. This represents the social class you were born into and brought up in. If you buy ratings in another social class than your native one, you must provide the Director with a plausible explanation: a High Society born agent with Working Class knowledge might simply be devoted to slumming it, while the reverse indicates a rogue and impersonator of the worst possible color.

🔥 💀 In Burn or Dust games, it costs 2 build points to buy 1 rating point in a different Social Class ability than your native class.

You must spend 1 point from the Interpersonal ability in question to use Bullshit Detector, Flattery, Flirting, Intimidation, Negotiation, or Reassurance at all on targets "outside" your native social class, even if you have a rating in more than one, unless you are successfully Disguised as a member of the class you are interacting with *and* you have the relevant Social Class ability.

The Difficulty of a Disguise test increases by 1 if the disguise also shifts a social class: e.g., for a working class agent to disguise himself as a butler in a gentleman's club. If it is intended to fool members of that social class, the Difficulty of the Disguise increases by 2: e.g., for a working class agent to disguise himself as a butler below stairs or in a tavern catering to those in service.

If the players don't want to build agents covering all social class bases, remember that you can use Network to build a trusted servant, working-class lackey, or aristocratic patron encountered during military service, at a Masonic meeting, or on one of those slumming excursions.

GENERAL ABILITY CHANGES

Digital Intrusion is not yet available.

DRIVING

Driving primarily refers to carriages, wagons, hansom cabs, and other horse-drawn vehicles, not motorcars. Outside major urban areas, automobiles are the playthings of the rich, and their controls are far from standardized. Driving a motorcar is a Mechanics test, and it requires a one-time 1-point spend of either Urban Survival or High Society to be able to do so at all.

Driving a railroad locomotive is also a Mechanics test; it requires a one-time 1-point spend of Working Class to have experience driving a train. With such experience, the Difficulty of the Mechanics test decreases by 2.

PILOTING

Piloting refers to boats, ships, and balloons. There are no heavier-than-air aircraft, and almost no gliders or dirigibles until 1900. The first rating point in Piloting is always refers to small boats (sailboats, rowboats, dories, etc.). Additional points can provide mastery of barges and tugs, sloops and schooners, steamships, clippers, balloons, etc.

RIDING

This new General ability deals with riding animals, primarily horses. You are a skilled rider of horses, able to keep your saddle and control your animal under the most adverse conditions. You can:

- evade or conduct pursuit
- avoid being thrown
- successfully ride across country or steeplechase
- keep your mount as fresh as possible while maximizing speed
- jump your mount over obstacles
- gentle or calm a mount
- manage your mount despite distractions such as monsters or gunplay
- feed and care for the animal
- maintain and adjust saddles, tack, bridles, etc.

Riding doubles as an Investigative ability when used to:

- estimate the age, breeding stock, sale value, or condition of a riding animal
- pick winners on the race course or spot nobbling
- interact with grooms, horsemen, and other equestrians as a professional equal

For every rating point in Riding, you may add another animal to your string. These might include: donkey, mule, camel, or elephant. In most campaigns, you likely won't need to bother, unless the Director is madly in love with Kipling or T.E. Lawrence.

WORLD WAR II

This build covers agents active during the 1930s and 1940s. The advent of concealed microphones and wire recording means Electronic Surveillance is available. The following changes from the corebook *Night's Black Agents* build apply:

- Data Recovery is not available. Recovering information from invisible ink or soaked paper is Tradecraft or Chemistry; aerial photo interpretation is part of Photography or driven by subject matter (fortifications are Military Science, ruins are Archaeology, buildings are Architecture, etc.)
- Add Radiotelegraphy as a Technical ability to represent the huge amount of radio traffic sent as Morse or other code signals. This ability covers Telegraphy as in the Victorian build above (see facing page), as well as the use of voice or keyed

radio equipment. Repairing or constructing radio equipment still falls under Mechanics; intercepting radio signals is Electronic Surveillance. Sending messages in adverse atmospheric conditions may require a spend; gathering core clues by radio never does.
- Digital Intrusion is not available; tapping telex, telephone, or telegraph cables is Electronic Surveillance and Mechanics.
- Add the General ability Riding as above. By this time, driving carriages or other horse-drawn vehicles falls under Riding, mostly to prevent skill bloat. A 1 point rating in Riding can represent great skill either in riding a horse or driving a buckboard or wagon.

For campaigns set during the active period of World War II (1937-1945 for East Asia, 1939-1945 for Europe, 1941-1945 for the U.S.), all agents receive 1 free rating point in each of Hand-to-Hand, Shooting, and Weapons, and 3 more General build points to distribute between those abilities as they desire. This represents the basic military training all active agents of the era underwent.

In Dust mode games, reduce the General build points budget accordingly, from 55 to 49 build points.

COLD WAR

This build primarily covers agents in the 1960s and 1970s. Agents in the 1950s transition from the World War II build to this one, and agents in the 1980s use the standard *Night's Black Agents* corebook build with hilariously clunky tech and skinny neckties.

INVESTIGATIVE ABILITY CHANGES

Data Recovery is renamed Data Retrieval. This ability now also includes getting information off of computer tapes, punch cards, etc. at all. Data Retrieval still includes air and satellite photo interpretation.

ERRATA: MARTINI, STRAIGHT UP

Agents during World War II and the depths of the Cold War are more likely to remain part of a larger organization, as covered in the "Martini, Straight Up" build (**NBA**, p. 195). This is an official erratum for that build. Apply it to any Martini, Straight Up campaign regardless of setting or time frame.

Unless you're playing in Mirror mode, you *can* put experience into Network. Like Bureaucracy, you cannot put experience into the Network ability if you gained Heat during the operation -- because the people you met "off the books" in this adventure won't respect your tradecraft if you made the papers.

As for Cover, in any mode the agency supplies that for most missions. The Director should provide a mission-specific Cover pool of (usually) 3 to 5 points per player, the Agency Cover pool. Agents can spend "normal" Cover points on Agency Cover tests, and vice versa. But anything the agents do using Agency Cover can be tracked by their agency.

In Mirror mode, any time an agent uses his Agency Cover pool, he gives his agency 1 Trust point.

Add Radiotelegraphy as in the World War II build above. Communications equipment isn't quite idiot-proof enough yet to be not even an ability, and radiotelegraphy is still prevalent enough that it's not just a minor filip on Electronic Surveillance or Mechanics as it becomes by the 1990s or so.

GENERAL ABILITY CHANGES

Digital Intrusion is not yet available: remote hacking of computer systems begins in the early 1980s as computer interlinkages grow. (Phone phreaking, the art of getting free phone calls and tracking unlisted numbers, falls under Mechanics and "social engineering" Reassurance.) Instead, add this new General ability:

COMPUTER USE

You can program, maintain, build, and repair computers, those big boxes with whirring tape spools on their front, slots for punch card input, and blinking lights throughout. You can program computers to control machines such as industrial robots or security alarms. You can program computers for specialized types of information analysis, but you still need to enter the data; programming a computer for traffic analysis, for example, requires taped or punched input data in specific formats. Data entry takes 1 minute per item (one personnel record, one surveillance report, etc.); programming can take hours or days depending on the difficulty or sophistication of the analysis to be performed. You can also deliberately mis-program computers to overlook data or to perform actions at the wrong time.

If digital intrusion is nevertheless possible, with a telex cable and remote terminal somehow slipped into the facility perhaps, this ability covers it.

Agents with Computer Use ratings of 8+ receive 1 free point in Data Retrieval.

AGING

If you wish, you might want to play a multi-generational campaign, in which young 1940s OSS operatives become cynical 1960s CIA men become venerable 1980s think-tank elder statesmen. You might want to play a flashback scene in the 1980s and then have those agents appear in a special episode of the modern campaign. For such temporally extended play, here are some aging rules. As always, they tend toward the cinematic: people age at wildly different rates in the real world, and in the movies a gray-haired geezer can still beat up a half-dozen young punks. The Director should feel free to alter them in any direction to suit her notion of cinematic reality or the campaign's theme.

Regardless of your agent's age at creation, she is assumed to be in top technothriller condition. These guidelines do not modify character creation. They kick in as decades pass for your agent off screen, during the "Twenty Years Later" intertitle. Helen Mirren in *Red* is a newly built agent; Helen Mirren in *The Debt* is an agent to whom these rules have been applied. These rules begin at whatever arbitrary point (40 years old? 50? 60?) the Director and player agree that "aging" begins.

For each five years past the beginning of aging:

- add 1 rating point to any Investigative ability
- add 2 rating points to Network
- add 1 rating point to Sense Trouble
- remove 3 rating points from any General ability or abilities except your MOS

Whenever (65 years old? 75? 80?) the Director and player agree the agent is officially "old" or "creaky" or "a fossil" who is "just coming back in for one last mission," the following rules also apply:

- you must spend on all Technical abilities
- your Athletics rating is capped at 7
- Difficulties for Digital Intrusion and (thanks to arthritis) for all fine manipulation tests (some tests of Filch, Infiltration, Mechanics, etc.) increase by 2.
- Difficulties increase by 1 for Disguise tests when attempting to disguise your age
- Difficulties for Surveillance tests decrease by 1 or by 2 for "static surveillance" — nobody looks at or even notices old people in most settings
- you gain a mental illness, if you did not already have one, when Shaken, not just when Shattered

Senile characters (most likely former player characters turned NPCs) always act as if Shaken: they cannot spend points from Investigative ability pools (except on Technical abilities, where a spend is mandatory but conveys no effect), and Difficulty numbers for all General ability tests increase by 1.

ADDENDA

NIGHT'S BLACK AGENTS — CHERRY SUMMARY SHEET 1

ATHLETICS	Hard to Hit (**NBA**, p. 27)	+1 to your Hit Threshold in combat
	Roll Through the Pain (p. 38)	Spend Health to succeed at failed Athletics tests
	Runner's Intuition (p. 38)	Spend 1 Athletics to judge opponent's Athletics rating level compared to yours
	8+ also allows Breakfall (**NBA**, p. 80), Like Smoke (p. 51), Parkour (**NBA**, p. 58), and Support Moves (**NBA**, p. 76) maneuvers.	
CONCEAL	Bug Stasher (p. 39)	Hide a bug against all but SIGINT-agency search or specialized equipment
	Perfect Holdout (**NBA**, p. 27)	Hide a small object on your person against all but X-ray or strip search
DIGITAL INTRUSION	Cracker's Crypto (**NBA**, p. 28)	1 free rating point in Cryptography
	Head of a PIN (p. 39)	Given any chance, if you see others input passwords you can guess them
	Mr. Clean (p. 39)	Your smartphones and other devices are untraceable
	8+ also allows Digital Judo (p. 81) and m4d sk1llz (p. 51) maneuvers.	
DISGUISE	Connected Cover (**NBA**, p. 28)	Can use Cover to create identity already known to an NPC
	Innocent Bystander (p. 40)	May spend Disguise pool points on Surveillance tests
	Just the Help (p. 40)	If in servants' or workman's uniform, lower Difficulties on Disguise tests by 1
	8+ also allows Alibi (p. 49) and Quick Change (p. 51).	
DRIVING	Defensive Driving (p. 40)	+1 to Hit Threshold and to Difficulty of ramming, etc. for you, passengers, and vehicle
	Grand Theft Auto (**NBA**, p. 29)	Spend 1 Driving point to steal any standard civilian or police vehicle you can drive
	8+ also allows Gear Devil (**NBA**, p. 56) and Signature Wheels (p. 52) maneuvers.	
EXPLOSIVE DEVICES	Bigger Bang (**NBA**, p. 29)	Spend 3 Explosive Devices points to add a die of damage to an explosive charge you set
	Maestro of Destruction (p. 41)	Your bombs cannot be disarmed without your aid, your wiring diagram, or this cherry
FILCH	A Lift in Time Saves Nine (p. 41)	May retroactively declare you lifted a small object during a previous scene
	No Slipups (**NBA**, p. 29)	May spend 2 points after failing a Filch test to increase the result by 1
GAMBLING	All In (p. 42)	Once per session, refresh any General pool at 0 by 3
	Everybody's Got a Tell (p. 42)	1 free rating point in Bullshit Detector
	Luck of the Devil (**NBA**, p. 30)	Roll one die at the beginning of the session; you may replace any one die result during that session with your roll
	8+ also allows Card Up the Sleeve (p. 50) maneuver.	
HAND-TO-HAND	Eye of the Tiger (**NBA**, p. 31)	Spend 1 Hand-to-Hand to judge opponent's Hand-to-Hand rating level compared to yours
	Haymaker (p. 43)	Roll two dice for damage; if you pick the higher, spend 1 point of Hand-to-Hand for each extra point of damage done
	8+ also allows Breakfall (**NBA**, p. 80), Extra Attacks (**NBA**, p. 74), Martial Arts (**NBA**, p. 75), Mook Shield (**NBA**, p. 76), and One-Two Punch (p. 53) maneuvers.	
INFILTRATION	Bono Cane (p. 43)	Spend 1 Infiltration to bypass guard dogs
	Escape Artist (p. 44)	Given enough time unobserved, you will get free of any restraint
	Open Sesame (**NBA**, p. 31)	Open or bypass any normal, commercial lock or alarm without a test
	8+ also allows Like Smoke (p. 51), Mark and Strike (p. 53), and Run and Hide (p. 84) maneuvers.	

NIGHT'S BLACK AGENTS — CHERRY SUMMARY SHEET 2

MECHANICS		
	Demolition Man (p. 44)	May spend Mechanics points on Explosive Devices tests to rig vehicles or machinery to explode
	Swiss Army Prep (**NBA**, p. 31)	May spend Mechanics points on Preparedness tests with jaunty narration
	Trapmaster (p. 44)	Spend 2 Mechanics to do two instances of damage with a non-explosive booby trap
	8+ also allows Grease Monkey (p. 51) maneuvers.	

MEDIC		
	⦿ Medical School of Hard Knocks (**NBA**, p. 31).	1 free rating point in Diagnosis
	On Your Feet (p. 45)	Give another agent a 1 for 1 bonus to her Consciousness roll by spending Medic points
	8+ also allows Verbal Trauma Unit (p. 52) maneuver.	

PILOTING		
	Grand Theft Aero or Aqua (**NBA**, p. 33)	Spend 1 Piloting point to steal any standard civilian or police vehicle you can operate; can create bogus flight plans or port documents
	⦿ Move Around the Cabin (p. 45)	While on a boat or aircraft, -1 to Difficulty of all Athletics feats, and to Hit Threshold of foes you attack with Hand-to-Hand or Weapons
	8+ also allows Gear Devil (**NBA**, p. 56) maneuver.	

PREPAREDNESS		
	Check Your Other Left Pocket (p. 45)	May spend Preparedness on behalf of other players
	⦿ Hoarder (p. 45)	Lower all Cache test (**NBA**, p. 94) Difficulties by 1
	In the Nick of Time (**NBA**, p. 33)	Retroactively plan for actions as needed; rolls still necessary
	8+ also allows Calculated Risk (p. 50) maneuver.	

SENSE TROUBLE		
	Combat Intuition (**NBA**, p. 34)	May use Sense Trouble rating instead of other ability rating to determine order of action in contest or combat
	⦿ Hawkeye (p. 46)	1 free rating point in Notice
	8+ also allows Danger Zone (p. 50) and Perfect Drop (p. 53) maneuvers	

SHOOTING		
	No cherries, but 8+ allows Extra Attacks (**NBA**, p. 74), Sniping (**NBA**, p. 76), Special Weapons Training (**NBA**, p. 76), Suppressive Fire (**NBA**, p. 77), and Technothriller Monologue (**NBA**, p. 77) maneuvers.	

SHRINK		
	Anger Management (p. 47)	May make a Shrink test to anger or enrage a subject known to you
	⦿ Talk it Out (**NBA**, p. 34)	1 free rating point in one of: Bullshit Detector, Flattery, Interrogation, or Reassurance
	Talking Cure (p. 47)	Mental illness cure tests are at -1 Difficulty; restore 3 Stability for 2 Shrink spent with psychological triage; refresh 2 Shrink or Stability for you and a subject after an emotional scene

SURVEILLANCE		
	Face in the Crowd (p. 47)	Losing your quarry doesn't blow your cover
	Tail Lights (p. 47)	May spend Driving on Surveillance tests while in a moving vehicle
	The Wire (**NBA**, p. 35)	1 free rating point in Electronic Surveillance
	8+ also allows Blending Agent (p. 50), For Your Eyes Only (p. 50), and Watching the Watchers (p. 83) maneuvers.	

WEAPONS		
	Quincey Morris' Bowie Knife (**NBA**, p. 35)	May throw balanced hand weapons within Near range at no penalty
	Riposte (p. 48)	After an attacker rolls a 1 and misses, you may do 1 point of damage per Weapons point you spend up to your weapon maximum
	8+ also allows Extra Attacks (**NBA**, p. 74), Martial Arts (**NBA**, p. 75), One-Two Punch (p. 53), and Special Weapons Training (**NBA**, p. 76) maneuvers.	

NEW THRILLER COMBAT OPTIONS

MARK AND STRIKE
- Requires Infiltration 8+ and successful surprise test
- May spend Infiltration points on first combat test
- May use this maneuver throughout Player-Facing Combat

ONE-TWO PUNCH
- Requires Hand-to-Hand 8+ or Weapons 8+ and two successful blows in a row to the same foe
- Spend 3 Athletics, narrate action
- +2 to damage, refresh 1 point of combat ability used for second blow

PERFECT DROP
- Requires Sense Trouble 8+ and Combat Intuition cherry
- Spend 3 Sense Trouble
- Consider Sense Trouble rating 3 higher for purposes of Combat Intuition once per session

THROWN CLEAR BY THE BLAST
- Spend 4 points of Athletics to move explosion effect on you up one row on Explosion Damage table
- Spend 6 points of Athletics to move explosion effect on you over one column on Explosion Damage table
- Can never move you completely out of blast radius; may be ineffective against class 5 or 6 explosions

GUN CHERRIES
- All require an unmodified Shooting die roll of 6 that hits the target
- One cherry per weapon

BFG
- Foe must spend 3 Shooting points to target you for every 1 Intimidation you spend
- If you spend 0 Intimidation, foe must spend 1 Shooting point to target you
- Lasts until your next action

HANDY
- May make immediate Extra Attack at half Shooting cost

HIGH CYCLIC
- Reduces cost of Autofire to 2 Shooting per extra damage die

MOBILE
- Multiple targets do not increase Hit Thresholds
- Lasts for next round only

PRECISION ACCURACY
- If you spent points on a Called Shot, refresh 2 Shooting

RUGGED RELIABILITY
- Refresh either 1 Mechanics or 1 Preparedness

SMOOTH ACTION
- Spend only 1 Shooting point to Jump In next round

STOPPING POWER
- Foe's action moves to end of ranking order in combat

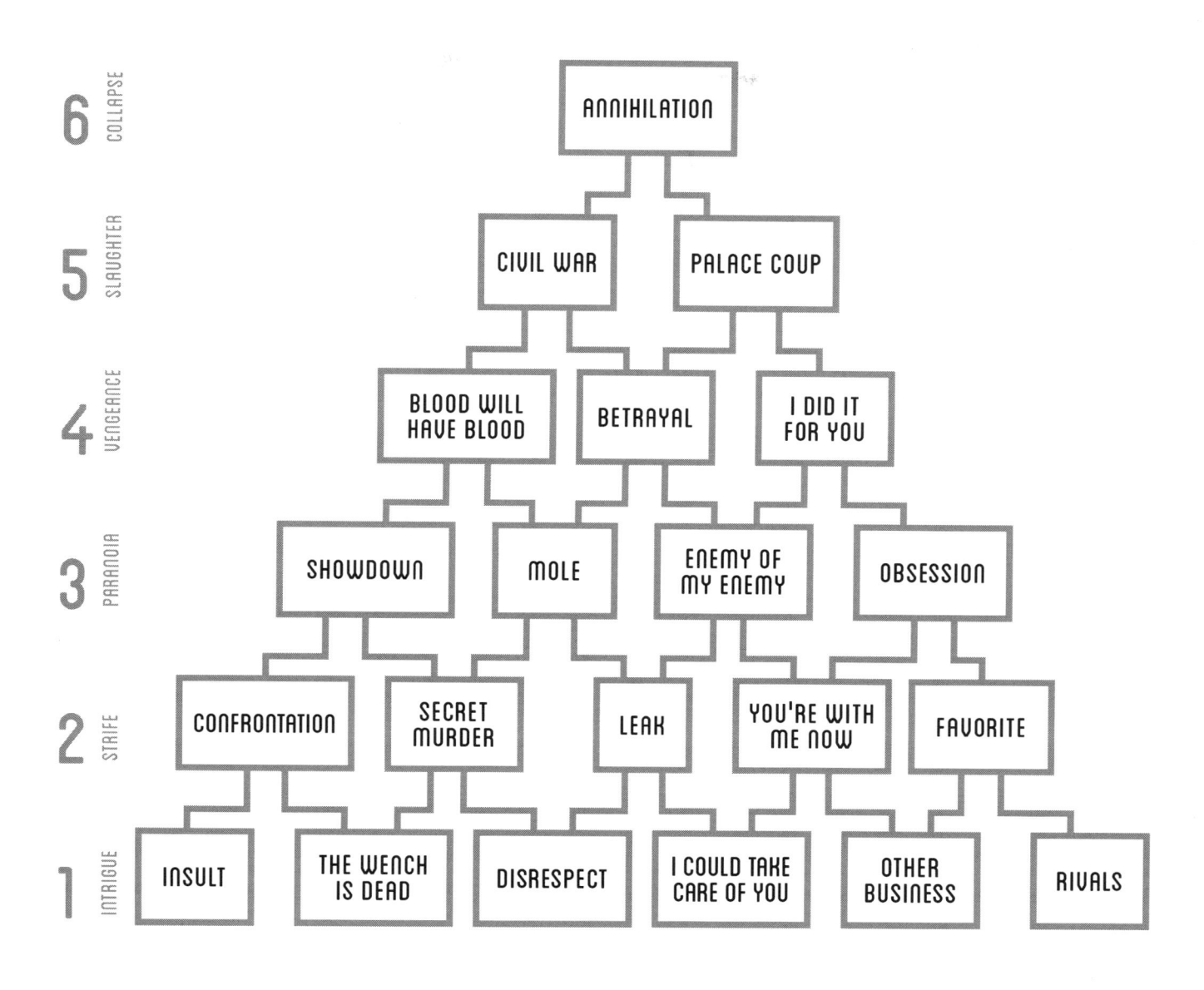

NIGHT'S BLACK AGENTS — SUSPYRAMID DIAGRAM

6 COLLAPSE: Annihilation

5 SLAUGHTER: Civil War | Palace Coup

4 VENGEANCE: Blood Will Have Blood | Betrayal | I Did It For You

3 PARANOIA: Showdown | Mole | Enemy of My Enemy | Obsession

2 STRIFE: Confrontation | Secret Murder | Leak | You're With Me Now | Favorite

1 INTRIGUE: Insult | The Wench Is Dead | Disrespect | I Could Take Care of You | Other Business | Rivals

NIGHT'S BLACK AGENTS — VAMPIRE POWERS SUMMARY SHEET 1

Power	Description	Reference
ADDICTIVE BITE	Treat bite as heroin (**NBA**, p. 81)	**NBA**, p. 128
ANAESTHETIC BITE	Bite might erase memory, knock out victim, act as truth serum, etc.; use Mental Attacks for bites to induce emotional state	**NBA**, p. 138
ANIMAL SENSES	Adds to Alertness Modifier or allows vampire to spend Aberrance on tests or contests of Infiltration and Surveillance; see Track by Smell	**NBA**, p. 128
APPORTATION	Appear within Near range at a location fulfilling a condition (coffin, blood, etc.); see also "Slasher Movement"	**NBA**, p. 132
ASTRAL PROJECTION	Send spirit out of body; equivalent to Clairvoyance in most cases	
BLOOD PHANTOMS	Lost Health fights on your side as phantom monster	p. 108
BLOOD WILL TELL	Wounds in vampire's vicinity never stop bleeding; lose 1 Health every 2 rounds	**NBA**, p. 129
BLOODWORKING	Construct objects, agents out of blood; manipulate blood of yourself or others	p. 106
BODY JUMPING	Move from body to body through spirit possession	**NBA**, p. 134
BONELESS FLEXIBILITY	Can fit through any space a large snake can fit through	**NBA**, p. 149
CLAIRVOYANCE	Can see at a distance; e.g., through eyes of familiars or victims	**NBA**, p. 128
CLOAK OF DARKNESS	Increase local Darkness by two levels	**NBA**, p. 130
CLOUD MEN'S MINDS	Convince witnesses they see nothing; Difficulty 6 Stability test to see	**NBA**, p. 130
CORPSE	Weapons do half damage; firearms do only 1 point of damage; shotguns firing shot do only 2 points of damage; Called Shots only effective on weak points (eyes, brain); crashes and falls do half minimum damage	**NBA**, p. 126
CREATE FOG	Call fog into being; +2 to visual Difficulties	
CURSE	Against NPCs, as Magic; against agents, change one die for 2 Aberrance, for 3 Aberrance effect is permanent	p. 106
DARKVISION	Take no penalties from Darkness	**NBA**, p. 128
DISTORTION	+1 or +2 to Hit Threshold	**NBA**, p. 135
DOMINANCE	Infected victims become servile; 7-point Stability test (Difficulty 8) to avoid Obsession with serving vampire; Difficulty 6 Stability test to act against master vampire	**NBA**, p. 129
DRAIN	Transfer victim's Health to vampire's Health pool; requires willing or helpless victim, or successful Hand-to-Hand bite attack; damage transfers, further attacks automatically succeed	**NBA**, p. 128
ECLIPSE POWER	Double Aberrance and Health pool during partial or annular eclipse; quadruple pools during total eclipse	**NBA**, p. 143
ENTER DREAMS	A Mental Attack; includes influencing, shaping, and reading dreams of victim	**NBA**, p. 132
FLUID	All physical wounds flow closed; fire, electricity, and acid do normal damage	**NBA**, p. 126
HEAT DRAIN	Prolonged touch (with or without Hand-to-Hand) does +0 damage to victim's Athletics; once drained to 0, takes damage from Health	**NBA**, p. 128
HIVE MIND	Gestalt consciousness with other vampires; for each extra hive mind in combat, one foe's Hit Threshold decreases by 1	**NBA**, p. 134
HOWL	Causes fear as Mental Attack or does damage as Telekinesis	**NBA**, p. 138
ILLUSORY SHAPE	Take shape chosen by you or plucked from foe's mind; as Mental Attack	**NBA**, p. 131
IMMATERIAL	Physical attacks do no damage; fire does 1 point of damage; may be disrupted or damaged by specialized attacks	**NBA**, p. 126

NIGHT'S BLACK AGENTS — VAMPIRE POWERS SUMMARY SHEET 2

Power	Description	Reference
INDESCRIBABLE	Cannot be perceived or remembered by human eyes or mind; applies automatically to anyone with Stability pool lower than vampire's Aberrance pool.	**NBA**, p. 130
INFECTION	Turn others into vampires	**NBA**, p. 129
INFRASOUND	Act as suicidal/depressive Mental Attack; triggers Borderline Personality Disorder and Depressive Disorder	**NBA**, p. 138
INFRAVISION	Take no penalties from Darkness to see warm or heated objects	**NBA**, p. 128
INVISIBILITY	+1 to +5 to Hit Threshold and to Difficulties to see	**NBA**, p. 129
LEVITATION	Hover in mid-air; move either at slow walking speed or flickering near-instantaneity	**NBA**, p. 133
MAGIC	Any effect; 2 Aberrance for minor or traditionally vampiric magics; 3 Aberrance for major or non-traditionally vampiric magics	**NBA**, p. 131
MEMORY HAZE	Vampire image disappears from mirrors, photographs, and memory	**NBA**, p. 129
MEMORY WIPE	As Mental Attack	**NBA**, p. 132
MENTAL ATTACK	Spend at least 2 Aberrance on roll; if total >4, victim must succeed in Stability test against total roll+spend	**NBA**, p. 131
MESMERISM	Resolve as Mental Attacks; includes Command, Deepen Slumber, Entrance, Send to Sleep, Sway Emotions	**NBA**, p. 131
MIMIC ABILITY	Mimic any ability seen; spend Aberrance on any General test	**NBA**, p. 136
MIMIC FORM	Take on victim's form	**NBA**, p. 136
MIMICRY	Imitate voices; Difficulty 4 Stability test to disbelieve	**NBA**, p. 138
MIND READING	As Mental Attack	**NBA**, p. 132
NECROMANCY	Speak with or gain information from the dead	**NBA**, p. 134
NO REFLECTION	Vampire casts no image in mirrors or reflective surfaces; may spend 2 Aberrance to deliberately cast image	**NBA**, p. 129
NO SHADOW	Vampire casts no shadow; may spend 2 Aberrance to deliberately cast shadow	**NBA**, p. 129
PACK ATTACK	Foe's Hit Threshold drops by 1 against third attacker in pack	**NBA**, p. 150
PHEROMONE CONTROL	Simulates some or all of Mesmerism	
PLAGUE	Spread disease with Hand-to-Hand attack; use anthrax (**NBA**, p. 81)	**NBA**, p. 129
POSSESSION	Control a person remotely or by spirit possession; as Mental Attack at +2 to resistance roll	**NBA**, p. 134
PSYCHIC VAMPIRISM	May drain Stability, Athletics, or Health; victim may not regain Stability or use Drive until the next operation	**NBA**, p. 128
REGENERATION	Refresh Health damage (exact rate and cycle varies; see **NBA**, p. 135)	**NBA**, p. 134
REMOTE DRAIN	Drain without physical contact	**NBA**, p. 128
RESURRECTION	Return to life after being killed	**NBA**, p. 142
RUBBERY	-2 armor vs. melee weapons; firearms and projectiles do half damage; Called Shots effective on eyes, head; crashes and falls do 1 point of damage	**NBA**, p. 126
SEND TO SLEEP	A Mental Attack, part of Mesmerism; against a roomful of foes, use Cloud Men's Minds rules (**NBA**, p. 130)	**NBA**, p. 132
SHADOW ATTACK	Remotely damage or Drain from a foe's shadow; -1 to enemy Hit Threshold except in Pitch Black	**NBA**, p. 153
"SLASHER MOVEMENT"	Can enter or escape a room undetectably if any possible entrance or exit is unlocked	**NBA**, p. 133

NIGHT'S BLACK AGENTS — VAMPIRE POWERS SUMMARY SHEET 3

Power	Description	Reference
SPIDER CLIMB	Climb sheer walls, walk on ceilings, etc.	**NBA**, p. 133
SPIT VENOM	Range is Close; venom may blind (+2 to all Difficulties), act as acid, etc.	**NBA**, p. 138
STEALTH	Spend Aberrance on feats of Stealth, or to raise Difficulty for agents' Sense Trouble or Surveillance tests	**NBA**, p. 137
STIFLING AIR	People within Close range start suffocating (**NBA**, p. 79)	**NBA**, p. 129
STONY	Immune to any weapon doing less than +1 damage normally; all other weapons do -2; -5 armor vs. crashes and falls	**NBA**, p. 126
STRANGLING GRASP	With successful Hand-to-Hand attack (Called Shot at +3 or spend 2 Aberrance), can grab and squeeze for +0; automatic squeeze damage +0 per round thereafter; foe must make two Athletics tests in a row to escape; Hit Threshold -2 against strangled foe; compare Grab (**NBA**, p. 149)	**NBA**, p. 151
STRENGTH	+1 or +2 to Hand-to-Hand damage, +1 more for 2 Aberrance; either any feat costs 2-3 Aberrance or feats require Aberrance tests using Difficulties from table	**NBA**, p. 137
SUMMONING	Summon allies, vermin, demons, etc.	**NBA**, p. 137
TELEKINESIS	Uses Weapons ability to throw items (damage by weapon type, plus 1 per 2 additional Aberrance spent); Shooting for telekinetic blasts (damage +0, plus 1 per 2 additional Aberrance spent); as Vampiric Strength for lifting, bending, etc.	**NBA**, p. 131
TEMPORAL DISTORTION	+1 to Hit Threshold; ignore laser sights; weird time effects; possible damage to computers or distortion of data	**NBA**, p. 129
TRACK BY SMELL	+2 to agents' Difficulties to evade	
TRACKING	Can follow any blood tasted or smelled over any distance; oceans and air travel interrupt the trail	**NBA**, p. 149
TUNNELING	Dig or ooze through soil with unnatural speed and stealth	**NBA**, p. 133
TURN INVISIBLE	+1 to +5 to Hit Threshold and to Difficulties to see	**NBA**, p. 131
TURN TO CREATURE	Take animal shape: rat, wolf, etc.	**NBA**, p. 136
TURN TO MIST	Become a mist or fog; Immaterial; +2 Stealth Modifier	**NBA**, p. 136
TURN TO MONSTROUS FORM	Take monstrous shape: camazotz, bhole, etc.	**NBA**, p. 136
ULTRASONICS	Shatter glass, harass guard dogs, communicate without being overheard	**NBA**, p. 138
UNFEELING	Never becomes Hurt by physical attacks, automatically makes Consciousness rolls; can still fight while Seriously Wounded	**NBA**, p. 126
VAMPIRIC SPEED	+1 or +2 to Hit Threshold; various speed stunts and maneuvers (**NBA**, p. 134)	**NBA**, p. 133
VENOM	Bite is poisonous; use snake venom (**NBA**, p. 81)	**NBA**, p. 138
VOICE	As Mesmerism	**NBA**, p. 138
WAVE OF MADNESS	Shooting attack against Hit Threshold of foe; damage +0 to Stability, increased by 1 per 2 additional Aberrance spent	**NBA**, p. 132
WINGS	Winged flight capability	**NBA**, p. 133
WORRYING BITE	If two bites succeed in a row, second bite does double damage; all bites thereafter automatically succeed; Hit Threshold -1 against foe clamped in your jaws	**NBA**, p. 150

INDEX

Symbols

1st Special Forces Operational Detachment-Delta (1 SFOD-D). *See* Army Compartmented Elements
3D Printers 67
21st (Artists) and 23rd Special Air Service Regiments of the Territorial Army. *See* Special Air Service (SAS)
22nd Special Air Service Regiment of the Regular Army. *See* Special Air Service (SAS)

A

Abilities
   General Abilities 36–48
   Investigative Abilities 8–36
   Psychic 26
Accounting (Academic) 8
ACE. *See* Army Compartmented Elements
Achievements 54
   Ad Hoc 56
Adaptive Tradecraft 56
Aggressive Driving Maneuvers 40
Aging 120
Alibi (Maneuver) 49, 122
All In (Cherry) 42, 122
Alpha Group (Russia) 24
Ambush 18
Ammunition 75
   Special 76
Amphetamine 28
Analysis
   Frequency 15
   Gastric 18
Anger Management (Cherry) 47, 123
Anti-Infrared Clothing 66
Anti-Surveillance Attire 66
Archaeology (Academic) 9
Architecture (Academic) 10
ARES Shrike 72
Arms Dealer (NPC) 92
Army Compartmented Elements 24
Art History (Academic) 11
Astronomy (Technical) 11
Athletics (General) 38, 51, 122
Atropine 29
Audio Jammer 63
Auto Mechanic (NPC) 92
Awareness. *See* Notice (Technical)

B

Banks, Underground 8
Battle Trance 23
Bennies. *See* Amphetamine
BFG (Gun Cherry) 74, 124
Bigger Bang (Cherry) 122

Binary Explosives 65
Biometrics 19
Black Market
   Currency Exchange 8
Blending Agent (Maneuver) 50, 123
Blood
   Bloodworking 106
   Diseases. *See* Hematology
Bloodworking 106
Bluejacking Software 68
Body Language 12
Bono Cane (Cherry) 43, 122
Bookie (NPC) 92
Bootlegger's Turn 40
Brass Knuckles 45
Breakfall (Maneuver) 122
British Police Jargon 13
Bug-Out Bag 34
Bug Stasher (Cherry) 39, 122
Building Superintendent (NPC) 93
Bulletproof Briefcase 59
Bullets. *See* Ammunition
Bullshit Detector (Interpersonal) 12
Bump and Run 32
Bureaucracy (Interpersonal) 12
Bureaucrat (NPC) 93
Burglar Alarm 45
Businesses. *See* Companies

C

C4 40
Calculated Risk (Maneuver) 50, 123
Caltrop Dispenser 70
Cameos 92
Cannabis 28
Capitol Building (Location) 104
Card Up The Sleeve (Maneuver) 50, 122
Car Hacking 67
Carnival (Location) 98
Cartagena Rules 60
Car Thief (NPC) 93
Casino (Location) 99
Casino Table Games 42
Catacomb 10, 99
Cellphone. *See* Mobile Phone
Check Your Other Left Pocket (Cherry) 45, 123
Chemistry (Technical) 13, 57
Cherries 122. *See also* Gun Cherries
Chop Shop Manager (NPC) 93
Chupa 106
Cipher 15
Classic Grift 30
Cocaine 28
Code 15
Coercion 23
Cohors Pedestris Helvetiorum a Sacra Custodia Pontificis. *See* Pontifical Swiss Guard
Cold War 119
Cold War Veteran (NPC) 94
Collimating Sight 75

Combat Applications Group. *See* Army Compartmented Elements
Combat Intuition (Cherry) 123
Combat Maneuvers 53
Common Tells 12
Communicate Despite Monitoring 58
Communications
   Gear 63–64
Communications contest 63
Companies
   Control Systems 21
   Core Values 21
   Legitimate 8
   Organizational Structure 21
   Power Structures 21
   Shell Companies 9
Compensator 75
Computers
   Data Recovery 15
   Failures 16
   Tricked-Out Hardware 79
Computer Use (General) 119
Conceal (General) 38, 57, 58, 122
Connected Cover (Cherry) 122
Conspiracy Theorist (NPC) 94
Context, Verbal 12
Cooper Color Code 45
Cop Talk (Interpersonal) 13
CornerShot 75
Cornfield (Location) 99
Cover Identity 45
Crack. *See* Cocaine
Cracker's Crypto (Cherry) 122
Criminal Slang 32
Criminology (Academic) 14
Crypt 10
Cryptography (Technical) 15, 58
Curse 106
Customs Agent (NPC) 94

D

Danger Zone (Maneuver) 50, 123
Data Center (Location) 99
Data Recovery (Technical) 15
Decomposition 19
Defensive Driving (Cherry) 40, 122
Delta Force. *See* Army Compartmented Elements
Demolition Man (Cherry) 44, 123
Determine when the Car Leaves 56
DEVGRU. *See* Special Warfare Development Group
Dexedrine 28
Diagnosis (Academic) 16, 57
Digital Intrusion 39, 51, 57, 81, 122
   Contests 78
Digital Judo (Maneuver) 50, 81, 122
Disgraced Doctor (NPC) 94
Disguise
   Gear 64
Disguise (General) 39, 49, 51, 57, 64, 83, 122
DMSO 29

INDEX

Document Forgery 19
Dracula. *See* Vlad III Dracula
Driving (General) 40, 52, 118, 122
Drugs 28
Dumpster Diving 34

E

Ecstasy 28
Ekimmu 107
Electronic Surveillance (Technical) 17, 57
EMMV Climbing Gloves 66
EMP Cannon 71
EMP Weapons 65
Equipment. *See* Gear
Errata: Martini, Straight Up 119
Escape Artist (Cherry) 44, 122
Espionage Jargon 33
Establishing Shots 98–105
Europe
   British Police Jargon 13
   EU citizenship 12
   European Firearms Pass 12
   Foreign Investor Passports 13
   Most Expensive Hotels 19
   Schengen Area 13
   Special Operations Forces 24
Everybody's Got A Tell (Cherry) 42, 122
Ex-Con Forger (NPC) 94
Explosive Devices (General) 40, 64–66, 122
Extra Attacks (Maneuver) 122, 123
Eye of the Tiger (Cherry) 122

F

Face in the Crowd (Cherry) 47, 123
Facial Masking Technology 64
Fake an Injury 57
Familiar Foe 52
Federal Security Service of the Russian Federation (FSB) 24
Fermi's Paradox 11
Filch (General) 41, 57, 58, 59, 122
Firearms 72–77
   By User 73–74
   European Laws 23
   European Pass 12
   Moving A Cache 24
First Aid Kit 44
Flattery (Interpersonal) 17, 58
Flirting (Interpersonal) 18
Fog Dispenser 71
Forensic Pathology (Technical) 18
Forgery (Technical) 19
For Your Eyes Only (Maneuver) 50, 123
Fourth Nail, The 9
Frequency Scanner 66

G

Gadgets. *See* Gear
Gambits 89
Gambling (General) 42, 50, 122
Gaslighting 23

Gear 63–71
   Tricked-Out Hardware 79
   Vehicle-Based 69–71
Gear Devil (Maneuver) 122, 123
Geiger Counter 13
General Abilities 36–48
Gestures, Emotional 12
Get in Without a Ticket 58
Glad Handing 15
Gondola (Location) 100
Good Cop, Bad Cop 22
Grail, The 9
Grand Theft Aero (Cherry) 123
Grand Theft Auto (Cherry) 122
Grease Monkey (Maneuver) 51, 123
Grenade Launchers 76
Grenades 65
Grenzschutzgruppe 9 (Border Police Group 9). *See* GSG 9
GROM 24
GSG 9 24
Gun Cherries 74–77, 124
Guns. *See* Firearms
Gym Rat (NPC) 95

H

Hacker (NPC) 95
Hand-to-Hand (General) 42, 53, 122. *See also* Martial Arts (Maneuver)
Handy (Gun Cherry) 74, 124
Hard to Hit (Cherry) 122
Hardware Store (Location) 98
Hawkeye (Cherry) 46, 123
Haymaker (Cherry) 43, 122
Head of a PIN (Cherry) 39, 122
Hematology 16. *See also* individual entries
Heroin 28
Hide Documents 58
High Cyclic (Gun Cherry) 74, 124
High-End Escort (NPC) 95
High-Performance Cars 17
High Society (Interpersonal) 19
High-Speed Train (Location) 100
High-Z Materials 13
History (Academic) 20
Hoarder (Cherry) 45, 123
Holy Grail, The. *See* Grail, The
Homunculus 108
Hotels, Most Expensive in Europe 19
Hot Lead 87, 88
Houses of the Dead 10. *See also* Individual Entries
Human Terrain (Academic) 21

I

Identity Theft 19, 34
Infiltration (General) 43, 51, 53, 58, 81–84, 122
   Contests 81
   Gear 66
Innocent Bystander (Cherry) 40, 122

Insects. *See also* Forensic Pathology (Technical)
Interrogation (Interpersonal) 22
In the Nick of Time (Cherry) 123
Intimidation (Interpersonal) 23
Investigative Abilities 8–36
Iranian Embassy Siege 25

J

Jack the Ripper 20
Jednostka Wojskowa 2305 (Military Unit 2305). *See* GROM
Jetpack 68
Just the Help (Cherry) 40, 122

K

Ketamine 28
KGB 24
Knife Grips 47–48

L

Land Mines 66
Laser 66
Law (Academic) 23
License Plates 71
A Lift in Time Saves Nine (Cherry) 41, 122
Like Smoke (Maneuver) 51, 122
Local Law Enforcement (NPC) 95
Locations 98–105
Longshoreman (NPC) 95
LSD (Drug) 28, 29
Luck of the Devil (Cherry) 122

M

m4d sk1llz (Maneuver) 51, 122
Machine Guns 71
Maestro of Destruction (Cherry) 41, 122
Make a Convenient Wall Safe 57
Manhunts 87
Marijuana. *See* Cannabis
Mark and Strike (Maneuver) 53, 122, 124
Martial Arts (Maneuver) 42–43, 122, 123
   Mixer 42
Martini, Straight Up 119
Masquerade Ball (Location) 100
Mastery 38
materiel 63
Mausoleum 10
Mechanics (General) 44, 51, 56, 57, 59, 123
   Gear 67
Medical School of Hard Knocks (Cherry) 123
Medic (General) 44, 52, 123
Megalomaniac's Secret Lair (Location) 101
Mescaline 29
Methamphetamine 28
Meth Lab (Location) 101
Microexpressions 12
Military 24
Military Base 25
Military Science (Academic) 24, 59
Mobile (Gun Cherry) 74, 124

Mobile Phone 17
   Cloning 17
Mole 12
Money Laundering 8
Monitor a Negotiation 57
Monsters 106–111
Montezuma's Revenge 13
Mook Shield (Maneuver) 122
Morgue (Location) 102
Moscow Rules 33
Move Around The Cabin (Cherry) 45, 123
Mr. Clean (Cherry) 39, 122
Museum (Location) 102

N

Nationality, Dual 12
Navy SEAL. See United States Navy SEAL
Negotiation (Interpersonal) 25
Nerve Agents 29
Networks
   Mobile Phone 17
Nightclub (Location) 102
Nitrous Oxide Injector 71
Non-Combat Maneuvers 49
Nosferatu 110–111
No Slipups (Cherry) 122
Notice (Technical) 26, 58
NPCs 92–97

O

Observation. See Notice (Technical)
Occult Bookstore Owner (NPC) 95
Occult Studies (Academic) 26
Oil Slick Dispenser 71
One-Two Punch (Maneuver) 53, 122, 123, 124
On Your Feet (Cherry) 45, 123
Open Sesame (Cherry) 122
Operation Feuerzauber 24
Operation Heavy Shadow 24
Operation Little Flower 24
Operation Neptune Spear 25
Operation Orchard 25
Order of the Dragon 20
Organizational Culture 21
Ossuary 10
Outdoor Survival (Technical) 28, 57
Overseas Accounts 8

P

Pandora's Box 9
Paraglider 68
Parkour (Maneuver) 38, 122
Passports
   Foreign Investor 13
   Forging 19
PCP 29
Penanggalan 109
Perfect Drop (Maneuver) 53, 123, 124
Perfect Holdout (Cherry) 122
Personal Inflatable Protection Sphere 68

Pharmacy (Technical) 28
Photography (Technical) 30
Pickpocket 41
Piloting (General) 45, 118, 123
Plane Crash 45
Plastic Explosives 40
Platelets. See Hematology
Police
   Interviews 22
   Jargon, British 13
Political Rally (Location) 103
Pontifical Swiss Guard 24
Post-Traumatic Stress Disorder 47
Precision Accuracy (Gun Cherry) 75, 124
Preparedness (General) 45, 50, 57, 59, 123
Pretend to Drink 59
Public Defender (NPC) 96
Pwn a Webcam 57

Q

Qat 28
Q Rule 63
Quick Change (Maneuver) 51, 122
Quincey Morris' Bowie Knife (Cherry) 123

R

Radiation 13
Radioactive Material 13
Radiotelegraphy (General) 118, 119
Rainforest (Location) 103
Reassurance (Interpersonal) 30, 59
Red Light Street (Location) 103
Refreshment. See also General Abilities, Investigative Abilities
   Achievements 54
Regeneration 127
Remotely Piloted Vehicles 69
Research (Academic) 31
Retired Cop (NPC) 96
Retired Secretary (NPC) 96
RFID Sniffer 66
Riding (General) 118
Rifle Grenades 77
Riposte (Cherry) 48, 123
Roll Through the Pain (Cherry) 38, 122
Roosting 90
Rudiger, Joshua 14
Rugged Reliability (Gun Cherry) 75, 124
Run and Hide (Maneuver) 51, 84, 122
Runner's Intuition (Cherry) 38, 122

S

Safe House 28, 35
Safety's On 51
Satanists 27
Sayeret Matkal 25
Scare Tactics 23
Schengen Area 13
Scrambler 63
SEAL. See United States Navy SEAL
SEAL Team Six. See Special Warfare Development Group
Séance 26
Second-Story Man (NPC) 96
Secret Archives 31
24-Hour Seedy Diner (Location) 98
See in Darkness 57
Semtex 19, 41
Sense Trouble (General) 45, 50, 53, 123
Shock and Awe 23
Shooting (General) 46, 123
Shredded Documents, Reconstructing 34
Shrink (General) 47, 123
Signature Wheels (Maneuver) 52, 122
Silencer 45
SIM Card Copier/Reader 68
Ski Resort (Location) 103
Skyscraper, Glass (Location) 100
Slang
   Cop Talk 13
   Criminal 32
   Vampspeak 35
Slaughterhouse (Location) 104
Sleeve Holster 75
Smooth Action (Gun Cherry) 75, 124
Sneaking Rules 83
Sniping (Maneuver) 123
Social Class 118
Special Air Service (SAS) 25
Special Ammunition 76
Special K. See Ketamine
Special Operations Forces 24–25
Special Warfare Development Group 25
Special Weapons Training (Maneuver) 123
Speed (Drug). See Amphetamine
Spends. See Under Each Investigative Heading
Spetsnaz 24
Spytech. See Gear
Standard Operating Procedures 60
Stars Are Right 12
Stash Spots 38
Steel Foundry (Location) 104
Stockholm Syndrome 47
Stopping Power (Gun Cherry) 75, 124
Stories, Developing 112
Street Drugs 28
Street Festival (Location) 104
Street Thug (NPC) 96
Streetwise (Interpersonal) 32
Support Moves (Maneuver) 122
Suppressive Fire (Maneuver) 123
Surveillance 47, 50, 83, 123
   Contests 84
   Gear 68
Survival Kit 28
Suspyramid 112, 114–116, 125
Swiss Army Prep (Cherry) 123
Swiss Guard. See Pontifical Swiss Guard

T

Tactical Fact Finding Benefit. See Under Each Investigative Ability
Tail Lights (Cherry) 47, 123

INDEX

Tainted Blood 16
Take Fingerprints in the Field 59
Talking Cure (Cherry) 47, 123
Talk it Out (Cherry) 123
Technology. See Gear
Technothriller Monologue (Maneuver) 123
Telegraphy 117
Television Reporter (NPC) 97
Tells 12
Temazepam 28
Tenement Block, Overcrowded (Location) 102
Thriller Combat Options 124
Thriller Contests 78
  Chase Rules 78
  Digital Intrusion 78–79
  Hacking Rules 80
  Infiltration 81
  Sneaking Rules 83
  Trailing Rules 86
Thriller Maneuvers 49
Thrown Clear by the Blast (Maneuver) 53, 124
Thunderbolt. See GROM
Time-Limited Message Discs 64
Time of Death 18
Tools as Weapons 44
Toxins 29
Tradecraft (Interpersonal) 33
Traffic Analysis (Technical) 34
Traffic Jam (Location) 105
Trapmaster (Cherry) 44, 123
Traps
  Setting 28
Tricked-Out Hardware 79
Tricks of the Trade 49
Truck Driver (NPC) 97

U

United States Navy SEAL 25
Unit, The. See Sayeret Matkal
Urban Survival (Technical) 34, 56

V

Vampire 21. See also Monsters
  Artifacts 9
  Murders 14
  Powers 126–127
  Subculture 35
  Vampspeak 35
Vampire-Enthralled Goth (NPC) 97
Vampirology (Academic) 35
Vampspeak 35
Variant Eras 117–119
Vehicle-Based Equipment 69–71
Vehicles 68
Verbal Trauma Unit (Maneuver) 52, 123
Victorian Era 117–118
Vitamin T. See Temazepam
Vlad III Dracula 20
Voice Synthesizer 64

W

Watching the Watchers (Maneuver) 53, 83, 123
Weapons 53, 123. See also Firearms, Shooting
Winch 71
Wingsuit 69
Wire, The (Cherry) 123
World War II 118–119
Write in Invisible Ink 58